Hugh James Rose

Untrodden Spain and her Black Country

Vol. II

Hugh James Rose

Untrodden Spain and her Black Country
Vol. II

ISBN/EAN: 9783337230302

Printed in Europe, USA, Canada, Australia, Japan

Cover: Foto ©Andreas Hilbeck / pixelio.de

More available books at **www.hansebooks.com**

UNTRODDEN SPAIN,

AND HER

BLACK COUNTRY;

BEING

SKETCHES OF THE LIFE AND CHARACTER
OF THE SPANIARD OF THE INTERIOR.

BY

HUGH JAMES ROSE,

M.A., of Oriel College, Oxford; Chaplain to the English, French, and German
Mining Companies of Linares; and late Acting Chaplain to
H.M. Forces at Dover Garrison.

IN TWO VOLUMES.
VOL. II.

SECOND EDITION.

London:
SAMUEL TINSLEY,
10, SOUTHAMPTON STREET, STRAND.
1875.

CONTENTS OF VOL. II.

CHAP.		PAGE
I.	Bandos and Ceremonies in Spain	1
II.	Spanish Scenery—Notes of a Winter's Walk in the Wilds of the Interior	18
III.	A Model Spanish Cemetery	30
IV.	Cordoba, and its Charities	40
V.	"El Pajaro," the Decoy-bird	55
VI.	Fairs and Festivals in Spanish Wilds	67
VII.	Robbers of the Sierra	83
VIII.	Social State of the Heart of Andalucia	93
IX.	A Spaniard's Estimate of English Politeness	108

SPANISH BLACK COUNTRY.

I.	Introductory	109
II.	Mines and Miners	119
III.	Underground	130
IV.	Miner's Medicines	146
V.	Surface-work at the Mines	158
VI.	Character and Social State of the Spanish Contrasted with that of the English Miner	170
VII.	Amusements of the Spanish Miner	187
VIII.	Cornish Miners in Spain: a Study of Character	199
IX.	El Carnaval in a Spanish Mining District	215
X.	La Semana Santa; or, Holy Week in a Spanish Mining District	229

CONTENTS.

CHAP.		PAGE
XI.	Good Friday at Baeza	245
XII.	Spanish Servants in a Mining District—Maria, Isidra	258
XIII.	A Study of a Manchegan Servant—Isabel	272
XIV.	The Spanish Miners' United Prayer Meeting	285
XV.	Literature of the Spanish Miner	288
XVI.	A Sunday's Walk among the Spanish Miners	304
XVII.	Life and Character of German and Spanish Miners Contrasted	314

ENGLISH CEMETERIES IN SPAIN.

I.	Cadiz	324
II.	Cordoba	335
III.	Sevilla	343
IV.	Linares	349
	The Author's Adios	354

UNTRODDEN SPAIN,

AND HER

BLACK COUNTRY.

CHAPTER I.

BANDOS AND CEREMONIES IN SPAIN.

ALTHOUGH, taken *per se*, they are rather dry reading, yet a certain amount of interest attaches to the form taken by proclamations, official documents, ceremonial letters, and the like, differing in different countries. I therefore present a short sketch of some of those with which the traveller in Spain will become conversant.

First of all in importance comes the "Bando de guerra," or proclamation of martial law in a province. The surroundings and accompaniments of the proclamation of martial law are much as follows, and, having twice been resident in a town while martial law has been proclaimed, I may vouch for the accuracy of the picture drawn. There are certain towns in the interior which always enjoy an unenviable notoriety for being the head-quarters of disaffection, whenever disaffection—as in ill-governed Spain is far from uncommon—comes to a head. With one of these towns I was for some time familiar; it was a notorious rendezvous for the Intransigentes, and, indeed, some of the governing powers of the town were supposed —though, I think, unfairly—to have a sneaking sympathy with those unhappy and misguided men.

One day, during last summer, the Intransigentes made a quiet entry into one of these towns. Save for whispers here and there, and the "run" upon the numerous shops where revolvers and cartridges are sold, and the numbers of armed men in the streets, one would hardly have known that the existing Government was being assailed, in many a secret gathering, with fierce invective, and being diligently plotted against.

Into the town marched a detachment of "Civil Guards": a few arrests were made, every one was disarmed, and every disaffected house entered, and the proclamation was that no *old* licences to carry firearms should be valid, and that no new ones should be issued for three months. These proclamations are printed, and pasted up at the post-offices and courts of law; they are also served on the leading employers of labour, at their office or counting-house.

It should be noted that, with that courtesy towards the "extrangeros," or foreigners, resident in Spain, which has characterized the various Republican Governments of this country, these proclamations are not applied to *them* in their full force.

A short time ago a body of the Municipal Guards went from house to house to levy "horse-impost." The horse-impost is not often had recourse to, but during the late troubles had necessarily been resorted to. It is this: every one, if called upon, must give up his horse for the use of the Government in carrying on the war. He receives, in lieu of his horse, a Government "bill," accrediting him to be paid the full value of the animal when matters (las cosas de España) become "mas tranquillas," and the coffers of our country better filled. The Municipales came to my house, official register in hand, and proposed to enter my stable. I said, "Come in, by all means, señores; my stable would hardly hold a borrico (donkey), much less a horse."—"We need not enter your stable, señor,—doubtless, it is a very good one,—we see you are an extrangero. Adios."

In a later change of Government the bando was that of war—*i.e.*, martial law was proclaimed. This, then, was the run of events. Arms were brought into the town; notoriously disaffected persons walked about openly; the town authorities were powerless. A telegram was sent to Madrid, and at the small hours of the night we heard bangs as of thunder all down the silent streets and over the sleeping township. Looking out of the window, under the cold, pale light of the moon, and steely, cold grey winter sky, studded with its myriad stars, were to be seen in the street little knots of soldiers, in their long, heavy great-coats, some with comforters round their necks, some with their sleeping mantas thrown across their shoulders. This was the entry of the troops from Madrid; they were knocking up the half-frightened inhabitants for "billets" for the night.

Never did the people of our township sleep so soundly as they did that night! There were passing few "light sleepers," I ween, or the knockings had never gone on so long. But no one need fear offering a "billet" to a Spanish infantry man. He never—gentle, merry, chubby-faced lad as he is—comes home tipsy, like an English militia-man; never uses violent

or abusive language; wanders about the streets with
a semi-important, semi-amused, and *nonchalant* air,
his rifle in one hand, and his flat cake of bread in the
other; or sits on the door-step of his "billet," cleaning
his rifle (which seems almost bigger than himself) or
mending the strings of his sandals.

Well may he value these latter, for, though he
carries boots for wet weather, experience will prove,
even to an English pedestrian, that it is a wise
economy that allows the Spanish soldier to "march at
ease" in his low, loose, string-tied sandals, of canvas
or esparto-grass. The scorching sun and scorching
road, on a summer's day, with the perspiration, constantly blister the feet and make them swell, and the
boot can hardly be put on; if you attempt to walk in
it, you walk with pain; the heat "draws" (to use a
technical term, but one for which I know of no
equivalent) the leather; and when you draw off the
boot, you often find, after a hard day's walking, the
stocking saturated with blood!

Next morning, at sunrise, the "bando" was delivered at every house of public resort, and a copy of
it pasted up in every street, a translation of which
shall be subjoined. Once more arms were taken
away—once more soldiers with fixed bayonets, and
officers with clanking swords, paraded the streets—
once more shops were half-closed, and the shutters of
private houses, in the lower stories, were "up!"

Going out for my morning's stroll, all was quiet as
ever, save the above-mentioned appearances, but few
persons were about. I heard a dropping shot or two,
and followed the sound. It was a quarrel between
the "new" and the "old" staff of night-watchmen.
The old set, with the change of Government, had

received their dismissal, but received it unpaid, as is too often the case with the poor Spanish official. A quarrel arose, revolvers were drawn, and a shot or two fired.

Next day, "the old order ceased, giving place to the new"; and, instead of "Viva la Republica Democratica Federal," the stilly night and the wakeful head heard, "Ave Maria purisima," the old-established prelude to the hour! But "Hail, Mary, purest of women," *does* blend better with the dews of night than the political party-cry, "Long live the Democratic Federal Republic!"

Presently, two officers, in full uniform, followed by a straggling train (not marching in any rank or file) of guards of all sorts, and regulars, passed down the street where I stood, with the usual elastic, springy step of the untiring Spanish soldiery. They were evidently, as a ragged urchin in the market remarked, "bent on mischief." "Visitas, malo," said a Spanish gentleman to me, turning away with a shrug of his shoulders—"visitas," visits, being a term constantly used—a euphemism, in fact—to denote a visit for the purpose of seizing arms or treasonable papers. A few hisses rose from the crowd as the train passed through the market. I followed them to a suburb of the town, and, looking at a tiny paper they held in hand, the officers in pairs, the men standing in a semicircle outside, quietly, without ceremony, entered house after house to search for arms, and seize the papers of those supposed to be disaffected. They were unsuccessful. A day or two afterwards, however, the Civil Guards made a further search, and, knocking down a partition, made booty of fifty rifles and bayonets, with which they marched triumphantly through the streets.

Many arrests were made; many of the disaffected fled; recruits were taken from the young men of the town; the officials of the town were deposed, and fresh blood took their place. But, although English newspapers are so fond of conveying a dreadful idea to their readers by that very vague term (as applied to las cosas de España), such and such a town is "in a state of siege,"—which often does not, and cannot, as I have proved, imply more than what has been related above,—yet we all go on pursuing our daily round of work, and I have very often felt more secure living in a town when reported to have been "in a state of siege" than at other times; for the "state of siege" of the English press does not necessarily mean "bloodshed and blockade," but merely means, "in such a town martial law has been proclaimed." I value the English press, and the noble work it does for my country—work that could not be done by any other influence—highly indeed, but the term "in a state of siege" might far oftener with truth be rendered, "under martial law."

Here, then, is the bando militar. I give the original, as it may interest some to compare it with its fellow proclamation in England:—

CAPITANIA GENERAL DE ——,

Numero 1000.

BANDO.

En cumplimiento de lo mandado por el Gobierno supremo de la Nación Ordeno y mando.

Articulo 1º. Quedan declaradas en estado de Guerra las cuatro Provincias del distrito militar de ——.

Articulo 2º. Se establecen consejos de Guerra ordinarios en cada una de las Capitales de —— ——.

Articulo 3º. Se prohibe el uso de toda clase de armas, sin prévia autorizacion legal para ellas; los contraventores serán reducidos á prision, y sujetos al fallo de la Ley.

Articulo 4°. Los que, de cualquier modo, alteren el orden público provocando á la rebelion, de palabia ó par escrito, y los que resistrésen á las órdenes de mi autoridad, con armas ó sin ellas, seran juzgados militarmente.

Articulo 5°. Las autoridades judiciales y civiles continuarán en el ejercicio de sus funciones, reservándome el conocimiento, de cuanto se refiera ó tenga conexion con el orden publico, y limitándose, en cuanto á este, á las facultades que mi autoridad les delegue.

(Date and Signature of Captain-General.)

An educated English reader will see at a glance the drift of this bando. It is sent out by the military Captain-General, or Governor, of so many provinces to all the towns under his authority, but, of course, only in those disaffected are its decrees actively put in force, as above described; and it provides (1) that the said provinces are to consider themselves under martial law; (2) that in each of the capital cities of those provinces courts-martial are established; (3) that those found in possession of arms, without a special licence, will be imprisoned, &c.; (4) that any one disturbing the public peace, by word or writing, with arms or without them, will be dealt with by court-martial; (5) that the law courts, &c., will still exercise their special functions, subject to, &c.

It will naturally be asked, with what equanimity does the Spaniard bear these arbitrary measures? He certainly cannot be said to accept them, for they are forced upon him by the right of might in too many instances.

Some of the townships bear these sudden changes of government with sullen distrust and indignation, that smoulders, and only bides its time to break out into a flame. Some acquiesce in it all, even with lightheartedness and carelessness; for though every Spaniard who can read and write is a politician, and has his partisan wine-shop, and his political argument over his ration de vino there, yet the throb of the pulse, religious or political, does not reach beyond the towns, and does not trouble the vine-dresser, or the olive-guard, or the leather-clad cazador (sportsman), or gitano, who combines the chase with guardianship of olives, and walks, Moorish gun on shoulder,—often have I seen his picturesque figure,—striding into the disturbed town, surrounded by his dogs, as careless and unconcerned as though nothing were happening, though the streets are thronged with soldiers, and arrests are being made at every corner. Some, again, do not bear the yoke at all, but rise in arms at the first sound of a change, and of the strong arm of a strong Government coming down upon them, and a fierce battle with the soldiery marks the progress of the new Government. Alas! poor fellows! they have some cause to view with apprehension a Government that installs itself by the sword. Said a Spanish gentleman to me but the other day, sadly enough, "Yes, it might be needful, the *coup-d'état*, but, for me, I prefer reason to the sword."

With the high passions, the love of seeing power centred in small bodies of men who know something of those they are to rule, and have common sympathies, common hopes and aims with them,—the pride of having a share in directing the things of Spain, —above all, with the bitter recollection of the undue severities of past Governments rankling in his mind, with the great absence of education and enlightenment of a great proportion of the population of this country,—it is hard to know exactly for what sort of

Government they are fitted, and what sort they would like. They are so divided among themselves, that in one town will be found a regular clique of Moderate Republicans, another of Cantonales, and a third of Carlistas, or, at least, Monarchists.

And, as regards the undue severities and highhandedness of past Governments, well may the Spaniard feel bitterly when such messages as the following have been sent to Provincial Governors by men in office:—"Do not telegraph a rising unless you can, at the same time, telegraph that you have shot half the rioters;" and when, literally, redress for injuries has been ofttimes sought in vain of those in whose power it was to grant it, and in whom the doing so would have been merely an act of justice. It is impossible to wonder at the state of feeling among those of the lower orders in Spain who think, and read, and feel.

"A little knowledge is a dangerous thing,
Drink deep, or taste not the Pierian spring,"

sings one who knew much of human nature; and, perhaps, even the artisan of Spain, who reads, writes, and thinks, hardly knows enough to know what is for his good. Still, the less a man knows, the more he thinks he knows; as he who has climbed but half-way up the mountain bounds his view by its seemingly near summit, and never dreams of the blue ranges beyond, which make his more earnest or adventurous companion pause in wonder and shrink within himself; and so the Spaniard, with his little knowledge, often thinks that las cosas de España are within his own ken, and wearies and harasses himself in vain.

But the Spanish character, like the Spanish clime,

has a tendency soon to recover itself from every storm or day of darkening clouds. If the storms of the Spanish political horizon be frequent and sharp, they are surely followed by a speedy sunlight.

All night long, and through the wintry day ofttimes, the tropic rains fall heavily here, as though they would never be stayed; but the sunlight of another morn floods hill and dale, as though it would not be refused, and the dark clouds, as if by magic, have been rolled away to other climes, and you would think the bright, clear, blue, sunny sky had always reigned supreme; and the song and dance are begun, and the chairs are placed in the streets for the merry out-door workers, and the sandalled or bare foot may tread almost unsoiled the dusty road. And, as his climate, so is his character. Last night may have heard the tramp of armed men along his moonlit street; the morning may see the bando pasted up on the walls of his township; houses may be entered by force, and their occupants led off to prison between dark-browed files of civil guards; aye, and even the morning sun may have seen, as it saw in one city within my ken, a grey, dew-covered heap of dead, lying stiff and cold where the stalls of the fruit-venders should stand; but all that, as the Spaniard himself says of sorrow, "has gone when it has gone," and with the light-hearted, volatile Andaluz, when it is over, it is forgotten as a dream, and dismissed as a disagreeable dream, not to be thought upon again. The clouds have passed away, the sun has broken out, and the light guitar tinkles in the streets, and the wild Andalucian ditty is sung, and the mules are yoked, and a shrug of the shoulders, and a meaning, half-pitying glance, are his only comment on the troubles of yesterday—

are his only epitaph over the grave of many a violent and misguided, but withal nobler companion.

Well, perhaps, for the Andaluz, that it is so! Of the "bando militar" no more need be said.

We pass on from the bando to minor matters of public documents, ceremonies, and the like.

There are two matters of daily occurrence in which Spain, with all her defects, seems to me to be more clever than her sister England. First, in regard to telegraphic messages. In England, having despatched a message, you have no acknowledgment, or had not, that you have done so; and, therefore, if a message did not reach, you could gain no redress, as you would have no means of proving that you had sent it. In Spain, however, the case is different. At the time of sending your message, you receive a sort of receipt or acknowledgment, and, as the day, hour, and destination are written upon it, you can obtain redress if your message be delayed or miscarry. Here is a copy of the "telegraph talon":—

Telegrama para Madrid.
Núm. 697, Palabras 18.
Dia 12, mes. 9, hor. 8: de 1873.
Pagó en sellos valor 8 rs. vn.

The talon system is also very well carried out, on the same principle, with regard to goods sent by rail. The consigner states the particulars of the parcels he is sending, and receives a talon, which he sends by post to the consignee. Unless this talon is produced at the time of claiming the goods, the authorities at the station refuse steadfastly to give them up.

The "Funeral Notices," occupying, as they do, a prominent place in the columns of the provincial newspapers, next claim a few lines. They are of three distinct kinds. First, the ordinary printed summons to attend the funeral of a friend, which is sent to you by post, inserted in the provincial papers, and laid upon the table of your casino or club. It merely advises you of the time of the funeral, and asks your attendance.

And these appeals are always heartily responded to, both among the poor and rich. To perform this last courteous act to the dead is a *point d'honneur*. The wealthy man pushes aside his cup of coffee, wraps his capa round him, and follows to the grave. His humbler brother quits his work, losing the half-day's pay, (in Spain, men do not grub and slave for money, as in money-loving England; they can afford time and loss for these little amenities of social life!) and joins his humble throng. Here is a specimen of the ordinary kind in use among the better classes:—

✠

LA SEÑORA DOÑA ISIDORA ——,
viuda de D. Juan y Garcia, ha fallecido el dia 9 del corriente á las 6 y 40 de la mañana.
R. I. P.
Sus desconsolados hijos D. Carlos, doña Maria de las Gracias, doña Tomasa y doña Isabel; su hermano, hermana politica, sobrinos y demas parientes, suplican á sus amigos que por olvido no hayan recibido esquela de invitacion, se sirvan encomendarla á Dios y asistir á la misa de cuerpo presente, que en sufragio de su alma tendrá lugar mañana 10 á las once de su mañana, el la iglesia parroquial de San Juan, y acto continuo á la conduccion del cadáver al cementerio de la Sacramental de San Ginés; en lo que recibirán favor.
En duelo se despide en el cementerio.—Se suplica el coche.

In this, as will appear at a glance, the bereaved family solicit the attendance of friends at the mortuary mass, and to follow the body to the grave.

The next kind of funeral notice advertises the death, asks the friends of the family to commend the soul to God by their prayers, and gives notice that the prayers in a certain church, at a certain day and hour, will be offered specially for the eternal rest of the soul of him who has been taken from them.

I give these notices in detail, because they seem to me to contain the germs of much that is very beautiful in the Spanish religious ordinances. The funeral in England is put into a corner, and confined to a few friends and relations. In Spain, a tradesman even will put his notice into the papers, and not only the friends, but even those who were bound to the dead by no closer link than their oneness in political ideas will join in the long procession of sable-cloaked followers.

I subjoin here this second form of funeral notice:—

✠

EL ILLMO. SEÑOR DE JUAN DE ——,
ha fallecido en Arenas a las doce y media del dia 4 de febrero de 1874.
R. I. P.

Sus hijos D. Wilfredo y Don Carlos, su hija politica, los sobrinos, parientes y testamentarios, suplican á sus amigos se sirvan encomendarlo á Dios.

Todas las misas que se celebren en la iglesia parroquial de San Sebastian el dia 10 á las diez de la mañana, por los señores sacerdotes adscritos á la misma, seran aplicadas por el eterno descanso del alma de dicho señor.

The mention of the third recalls to my mind many striking associations. It is called the "Anniversary Notice," and is inserted in the provincial newspapers, and sent to the various houses of the friends and relations of the dead, for whose soul prayers are to be offered on the anniversary of his death or funeral. He who once, at morn, has knelt and wandered in the magnificent cathedral of Seville; has feasted his eyes

on the paintings, only seen in their full beauty, among
their fit surroundings, by the dim religious light of
the hundred windows; has gazed at the 'Dorothea,'
the 'San Antonio,' and, more beautiful still, the
'Angel de la Guarda' of Murillo; has stood, with
rapt gaze, before the marvellous 'Virgin and Child'
of Alonzo Cano—two countenances so full of expressive
sweetness that they haunt your path and bed when
once seen; has stood before that picture, so life-like
in form and feature that even Murillo stood transfixed
to the spot as he gazed upon it, the 'Descent from the
Cross,' by Campaña; and, with the spell of this atmosphere of the past still upon him, has passed into the
mortuary chapel of the cathedral, where nearly every
day is offered a mass for the soul of some inhabitant
of that teeming city on the anniversary of his or her
death,—will never read even the bare "Anniversary
Notice" without a thrill. The dimly-lit, indeed,
nearly dark chapel, the sable forms of the cloaked
or hooded sons or daughters of Sevilla, the silent
prayer of the kneeling priests, and the dim and few
wax candles alight, the beautiful altar-piece, all these
leave an impression of reverence and awe upon a man's
mind not easily to be effaced.

It is in these striking displays that the Roman
Church excels; in her externals she enchains and
fascinates the heart. Her appeal is to the eye and
ear more than to the reason; the senses she holds her
own. It is with an unceasing stimulus that she plies
her sons and daughters; and if, in the Roman Church,
too much stress is laid on the adornment and the beauty
of the music, there are many religious bodies, surely, who
pay far too little attention to these things; others who

"Dum fugiunt .... vitia in contraria currunt."

Has any Church of Christ yet found and kept to the "golden mean"? Has not each one, in its day, missed the mark? Is not the old saying, "Many men have many minds," ignored or forgotten by most of the Churches of our day? "Four bare walls and a pure heart" is considered by some the acme of pure Divine worship, and, for some, the four bare walls may be sufficient. But for many, surely some appeal to the senses through grand architecture, through solemn or pathetic music, through exotic flowers, is a needful of Divine worship; and are not these handmaids given by God as helps to His worship, and, therefore, not to be despised? How many a fresh spring breaks forth in the world-worn heart at the singing of a well-known and once well-loved hymn! Let a poor emigrant lad's words declare it. Writing from the "bush," in a remote part of Australia, he said,—"The greatest pleasure and blessing I have had here—it made the tears start—was when I rode to a place of worship one Sunday, and found, as I entered, that the congregation were singing one of our old church tunes at home!" How many a simple peasant has thought, for the first time, of his prayers ascending, when, in the dim religious light of his parroquia, he has seen its symbol incense steaming heavenwards! In how many hearts has the voice of a spring-bird, or the sight and scent of a country flower, awaked holy thoughts of childhood, and of simpler, holier days! Did not "the first daisy" throw a strange spell over exiled hearts but a few years ago? I confess I can never enter a church abroad without a certain sobering of feelings, a calming and elevating of the mind, which the bare walls of the Puritan would never inspire.

Here is the "Anniversary Notice" in use in Spain:—

☨
Quinto aniversario.

Todas las misas que se celebren el domingo 15 del corriente en la iglesia de religiosas Trinitarias, seran aplicadas por el eterno descanso de
LA SEÑORITA DOÑA AÑA DE GARCIA Y DE TEANO.
En sufragio de su alma estará S. D. M. de manifiesto.
Sus inconsolables padres ruegan á sus amigos se sirvan encomendarla á Dios.

A Spanish funeral has been described at length in a previous chapter, and, therefore, I dismiss that matter.

The Spanish baptism of children differs little from that of the English Church save in these respects. A little salt is put by the priest on the upper lip of the child, probably as an emblem that, through baptism, the soul will be preserved, and not suffered to decay and waste or lose its savour; a cross is also made with the holy water on the top of the head.

The christenings in the interior generally take place on a week-day, about three or four o'clock in the afternoon. The little procession, the women each with some white article of dress, among the poorest generally a handkerchief like snow over the head, with the babe, march in pairs to the church, and then returning home, have a little "family gathering," when congratulations are offered, the baby inspected, and every person, as he leaves the house, becomes

$\mu\alpha\nu\tau\iota\varsigma\ \dot{\epsilon}\sigma\theta\lambda\omega\nu\ \dot{\alpha}\gamma\omega\nu\omega\nu$

for the little Christian.

As regards weddings, a few words may, perhaps, be said elsewhere. But two points connected with the subject shall be mentioned. Those to be married must confess to the priest on the eve of the ceremony.

It should also be remembered that, as a rule, should an Englishman be about to marry a Spanish lady, the Church requires that he should be re-baptized.

A civil ceremony is often performed, at the wedding of the well-to-do, after the religious ceremony. The religious ceremony with those classes is performed in the bride's house; after that is concluded, a "marriage before the judge," or civil marriage, takes place in the same room. This I have touched upon elsewhere.

CHAPTER II.

SPANISH SCENERY—NOTES OF A WINTER'S WALK IN THE WILDS OF THE INTERIOR.

It has been beautifully said, by one whose faithful and simple delineations of home scenery will live as long as the English language is spoken—the poet Cowper,—

"God made the country, and man made the town."

Words surely they are which have a significance far deeper and wider than would, at first sight, appear.

It would seem to me, that the scenery of the place in which he lives has, or may have, a great effect upon the mind and heart of a man; and it is impossible, or well-nigh impossible, to doubt that scenery has a vast effect upon national character.

The peasant of the Lincolnshire fens, with his few aspirations, his quiet, almost sluggish, and certainly unexcitable nature, shares in the characteristics of his peculiar clime, with its clouded skies, its rich green flats, and its stagnant, reedy dykes. The Swiss mountaineer, adventurous, fearless, and affectionate, seems to me to draw his inspiration from the spreading lakes and ice-glittering peaks of his romantic land; and is not the Hollander, in his land of flats and slow-flowing dykes, rightly called the "phlegmatic" Dutchman—slow, as his rivers; as his climate, cold?

And certainly the sailor draws his character from

the sea, his constant companion, in all its changeful moods.

It has often struck me that a most interesting essay might be written, although to write it would take years of research, on " the influence of climate and scenery on national and individual character, especially as regards religious temperament." True, the ethnologist will tell us that special features of character attach to different races, and of this there can be no doubt; but whence came these various features or characteristics?

Have not climate and scenery a great deal to do with it? Would not the Hollander in time become the merry, vivacious Andaluz were he transplanted to the orange-groves and sunny skies of Seville? and even the song, and dance, and ever-tinkling guitar, and flimsy cigarette of the Andaluz be exchanged for the phlegm, and repose, and quiet, and substantial meerschaum of the Hollander, were he transplanted (how little he would relish the change!) to the flats of Rotterdam? Would any one deny that he feels, in his own case, the effect of climate and scenery on his own heart and mind?

Here is an old fisherman's philosophy, in whose tiny boat the writer has spent many a rough hour off the circle of the Bognor rocks, and the long, low-lying coast of Selsea Bill:—" I shouldn't like to live in-shore. No; a crust with the sea is better than roast-beef without it. I never feel as if I could do a dirty action when I'm looking at the sea."

Not only, then, to cease from speculations and theories, because I thoroughly love every different phase of scenery for its own sake, but because I ever find a real benefit, a real blessing, to accrue to my mind and heart from the contemplation of it, have I made it a rule, wherever my lot has been cast in life, to visit and drink in the spirit of the scenery of the surrounding country. I look upon scenery as upon music—as a real gift of God, as a religious influence, calculated, if rightly used, to purify, and ennoble, and exalt, and bless the heart and mind.

Not vainly was it said, by the old Scottish Covenanters, so grandly and naturally portrayed in 'Old Mortality,' that the wild crag and the dusky heath were "helpers to prayer." Never does the soul feel so alone, so brought face to face with its God, as in a lone, desolate landscape, or in a wild night at sea. Once I experienced the truth of this last assertion, when, having gone out for a night's fishing off the Shoreham coast, in a small lugger, we were becalmed in a heavy, dripping sea-fog, and the whole night nothing could be seen, save our own faces, as we lit a match; nothing heard, save the wailing fog-horn of some benighted vessel passing down Channel. It was a weird, strange, lonely, solemn time, and a scene well calculated to make one serious and thoughtful. We carried no lights, and so might have been run down at any moment.

Nowhere is scenery more varied than in the heart of Andalusia. True, there is no wild sea-coast, full of romantic and soul-ennobling associations; no

"League-long roller, thundering on the shore;"

but the scenery is wild, barren, varied, and oftentimes magnificent in the extreme.

Come for some walks with me in the Spanish interior. One of the wildest and most romantic walks is that from a mining town, by name Linares, to the old Roman bridge of Badallano, some seven miles thence, "as the crow flies," close to the station of Linares.

All Spanish scenery is wild—wild and far-stretching even in the most cultivated districts. There are no hedges, as in England; no green, enclosed fields of grass; and the fields, or rather slopes, wide-stretching slopes of corn, are marked out by conical blocks of stone, set up some distance apart from each other, called the "boundary-stones," which form a rough but effective line to mark off the property of one person from that of another. Possibly, in the words, "Cursed be he that removeth his neighbour's landmark," reference is made to this sort of boundary-line.

I started with a friend, on a bright, sunny afternoon in January, for the bridge. The first glimpse of truly Spanish scenery was when we entered upon the wide, rude track, called by courtesy, "the road to Linares Station."

Behind you, as you enter the first valley, lies the grey, stone-built town of Linares, and all around are undulating slopes, each enclosed in a crumbling and broken stone wall, and planted with dusky rows of olives. These are the olive-groves of Spain, and, the soil being of rich red earth, they are very productive. They have, however, little beauty, save by night, when the moon shines clear and bright, and gives a certain wild charm, a beauty of their own, to these dusky groves of stunted trees. In each grove stands the little stone-built cottage of the olive-dresser, or, as he is here called, the guard of the olives. It is a square, stone cottage, flat-roofed, with hardly a window to let in the light, certainly no glass. Within are two dark rooms, pitched with common round stones, and without one trace of comfort or of neatness.

And here comes the guard, a wild-looking Andaluz, as light-hearted, as careless, and as uncouth in dress and tongue as the peasant of the interior always is. He is dressed in a rough suit of untanned leather; with him he bears the insignia of his office, the old Moorish or Spanish gun, and the belt across his breast, with brass plate inscribed with his master's name.

"All those olives," said my companion, pointing to one plantation, "have just changed hands; they were lost, in a single night, at the gaming-table."

In a quarter of an hour we were walking along a wild, barren ravine, very narrow and very rocky; hill after hill, with nothing but stunted, prickly herbs, rose on either side. At our feet trickled a little stream, along whose side, and out of whose waters, grew the green oleanders, green as ever, but bearing their red pods, now bursting open with the woolly seed, which is partly like thistle-down, partly like the seed of the cotton-plant. Rocky gulley kept on opening upon the road, now dry and dusty, but which had but lately been a foaming torrent, pouring down to one of the many sluggish tributaries of the Guadalquivir.

A few flocks of goats were browsing about the hill-sides, some with their bleating kids nestling in the prickly, dry, aromatic herbage at their feet. Most of these goats are of a dull red colour; some few are white or dark brown, and, with their tinkling bells, and the wolf-like dogs that guard them, form a somewhat picturesque group. These were the only signs of life on the wild, wind-swept hills, save the countless flocks of frailecillos, plovers, called by the common people "avefrias," that flew away in dusky clouds from slope to slope, rising far out of gun-shot, and settling so far off that the ear could hardly hear their plaintive, wild call-note.

There was, perhaps, no great beauty in this valley; and yet, as Charles Kingsley has said of the fens of Lincolnshire, in his exquisitely true and faithful delineation of them, these wild, uncultivated, undulating valleys have a beauty of their own. They partake somewhat of the nature of the Sussex Downs, in their grey sweep, with their coombes and deans, as you ride from Brighton to Plumpton; but their beauty is wilder, and the idea they give you of perfect freedom is greater.

Again, the blue sky of the Sussex Downs is flecked with passing cloudlets: the trim village, the snug farm-house, and the well-hedged fields of corn, smile at their feet, all telling of security and labour; while never cloudlet flecks the sky of Spain, nor is there seen any enclosure, or farm-house, or smiling village here.

One valley opens into another as we pass through a most romantic ravine. On our left, sheer down, lies a deep narrow valley, with two "huertas," or market-gardens, each with its picturesque square stone cottage. In these irrigated gardens are one or two orange-trees, laden with golden fruit, shining bright in the winter's sun, and a few "almendras," almond-trees, leafless, but covered with blossoms, exactly like those of the peach, and lading the air with their luscious scent. Though it is February, on a nearer approach you would hear the hum of myriads of bees. Right above these huertas the steep slopes for miles and miles are thickly dotted with the stunted ilex, or evergreen oak, here called encinas, and clothed with a short brown turf and aromatic herbs. They are wholly uncultivated, and the ground, strewn here and there with rocks, is far too precipitous, irregular, and broken to admit of hunting, though a sly fox may be seen in many of the glades, hardly distinguishable from the dog of the goat-herd.

Above us rose a huge round mound, like one of the Roman " barrows" of the Dunstable Downs, one mass of encina, and evergreens, and tangling brambles. Here I sat down, as the last valley opened before us, to enjoy the wild stretch of hill and forest. Right in front, some fifteen miles off, lay a peak of the brightest crimson hues, fading into dim purple on either side, while the rushy valley, covered with stunted evergreen shrubs, and wholly unoccupied and uncultivated, save for one desolate-looking stone shanty, spread for miles before us. Suddenly, winding along a rocky ledge just below us, half-hidden by the trees that, clinging to the rock, drooped over the narrow track, came along a crowd of thirty-six tinkling donkeys, whose grey backs contrasted prettily with the dark green of the ilex and chaparros (a sort of ilex). The gay, thoughtless, Andaluz donkey-drivers were singing the usual wild ditty of their race, with its monotonous refrain, " La, la, la, la, la, la, la, la, la."

This song, which is heard everywhere, in the campo, in the streets, on the busy wharf, or where the fisherman rocks out at sea in his tiny pareja, only consists, usually, of two lines, sung over and over again, and generally made up on the spur of the moment, the subject being some passing object, or some thought floating in the minstrel's mind, and longing to find escape. In this case the poor fellows only sang,—

"Here are two men sitting on the rock,
One man is tall, the other man is short,
La, la," &c.—

which ditty they all took up, until the silent defile rang with the tinkling of the donkey-bells and the ditty of their drivers.

Three things claimed notice in this wild, lonely, sequestered valley. At our feet, in the hollow, is a well, called the "Woman's Well." It is a square stone tank, about three feet deep, crumbling, lichened, and evidently very ancient—doubtless of Roman origin; and an arch of stone built over it, the brambles and evergreen completely covering up the tank. Into this tank or basin, which was just large enough for one person to lie down in, a tiny stream of water keeps flowing from the rock. Here, on a summer's morn, may be seen eight, nine, and even ten or twenty women, mostly poor, each waiting her turn to undress and lie down for ten minutes in the healing waters of the fount. They are supposed to be a sovereign cure for stiff joints, rheumatism, skin diseases, and lumbago. I bared my arm and thrust it into the water, and found, that though sheltered from the sun, it was quite warm, and of a yellowish hue.

Here, too, nestling in the ilices that hung up the slope, was an old Roman sandstone fountain, with a stone trough for the watering of the beast, and a massive, but small, ancient stone portico hanging over the well. Nailed against the stone was a black wooden cross, of the roughest description. I asked why, and was told that it was to mark where a poor muleteer, who had gone to water his beasts, had fallen in and been suffocated. These crosses are constant, to mark the scene of a murder or a death, in the interior.

The thick, dark-green hanging woods rising to our right, one mass of dark-leaved ilices and chaparros, the spreading downs to the right, with their brown turf and scanty evergreen trees and shrubs, the narrow deep defiles, and the valley, with its romantic, half-hidden Woman's Well, all formed a scene truly fitter for the artist's pencil than for the writer's pen. But in Spain, as elsewhere, no pen, however skilful, however graphic, can truly recall the charm of scenery. The inspiration of such scenery as I am describing must be drawn from that scenery itself, or from other within reach—much is, of necessity, lost on paper. The slow-sinking sun, the plaintive call of the plover, the vulture slowly wheeling overhead, all these things, with the damp scent of the wooded defiles, free from the dust and noise of the plains, or the tilled fields, give a sense of loneliness, of desolation, and of repose, that the passing traveller cannot resist.

We can adequately describe the effect of varied natural scenery upon the imagination and heart of man? What pen can really describe that scenery itself? Copley Fielding could portray faithfully the long grey sweep of the undulating South Downs, the mists that beat over them from the sea, the distant blue of the spreading sea beyond them, the villages nestling at their feet, the fleecy clouds that fleck the sky; but, beautiful as they are, his pictures cannot bring to mind all, or even a tithe, of the associations that a walk on those lonely Downs will conjure up.

Charles Kingsley has immortalized Devonshire

scenery, and one can almost see the rugged woodland, the dusky moors, the green ferny lanes, and the spreading blue sea of that coast, with its ever-shifting hues, and its brown-sailed fishing boats seeking, at the fall of eve, their several stations. But the charm of scenery must be sought in the place itself: to realize the fullness of its beauty and drink in its inspiration, you must wander on the down, or explore the woodland, or gaze out upon the tumbling sea.

At last, after our seven miles of weary, rocky walking, all the weariness of which, however, was soon to be compensated for by the grandeur of the scene on which we were entering, we drew near to our goal, the old Roman bridge of Badallano, close to Linares Station. Arrived at the station, where the scream of the engine and the grumbling of the trucks sounded strangely in the lonely valley, with the quiet, desolate hills belting it round, we soon, after striding across some rough, broken, stony ground, struck the river, the Guarizas, a tributary of the Guadalar, now, owing to the long drought, only a small and winding stream, eating its way between its sandy banks, some sixty feet below our path, studded with little islets here and there, covered with oleanders and other shrubs. At last we came into a pass or gorge of the river; on either side rose heights of rugged grey granite, looking as if giants' hands had piled the shattered masses of stone one upon the other. In every crevice of these grey heights grew the stunted chaparros in countless numbers, the chaparro and the barren, or wild, or bastard olive, its dark, dusky, sombre foliage forming a striking contrast to the grey riven blocks of granite peering out here and there from their foliage, or running sheer down, in shattered, naked, jagged masses, into the river.

Between these two rugged heights flowed the river; and, spanning it, all covered with loose boulders of granite, was the old Roman bridge, still connecting height with height. The bridge consists of one beautifully-proportioned arch, of red sandstone, standing some forty feet above the stream at low water. When, however, after the winter torrents, the floods come down, the water flows right over the bridge. Just now, there were only two small cascades of white, foaming water; but so rough and narrow was their passage beneath the bridge, that the roar was even then deafening. After the winter floods, it must be a grand and sublime spectacle indeed.

I clambered, or rather scrambled, over the loose boulders of grey granite,—here clinging round a sharp jutting corner of rock, here hanging on by some loose bush that had taken root,—and, looking at the dark, silent, deep stream, sheltered and ever cool in its narrow rocky channel, was fairly entranced by the barren and weird grandeur of the scene. The cold, abrupt grey granite walls rise, on one side, two or three hundred feet above the dark water-line, crested at the top with chaparro; here and there, half-hidden by the huge boulders of pale granite rock, lie still, shadowy pools of icy-cold water: it is just such a scene as one pictures to oneself the last home of the Covenanter Burley, in Sir Walter Scott's 'Old Mortality.'

Of course, it is not on nearly so grand a scale as the Pass of the Guadalhorce, on the line of railway from Malaga to Cordoba, or the magnificent defile of Despeñaperros, on the line from Madrid to Cordoba, where eight bridges span as many rocky ravines; but still it is as wild and grand a piece of barren scenery as one could desire to see.

As we retraced our steps, and crawled from block to block, the pale, large moon looked over the cresting trees of one height, and the pall of evening stole, in a few minutes, over rock, and river, and stunted tree.

CHAPTER III.

A MODEL SPANISH CEMETERY.

NEATNESS and trimness, more than absolute beauty, seem to me to characterize the best of the Spanish cemeterios. The great lack in them, to an English eye, is the absence of the rich green turf, which, in the churchyards and cemeteries of England, forms one of the most beautiful features—a lack which is only to a certain extent made up for by the trim garden-beds, the neat gravel-walks, and the shapely cypresses, or gorgeous orange-trees.

One of the best-kept cemeterios of Spain is that of Cordoba, beautiful not only in itself, but even more so, perhaps, from its antique and picturesque Moorish surroundings, and the natural scenery around it.

It was a calm, sunny Sunday morning in December when I started to visit the spot I am now about to describe. The walk was at once peaceful, interesting, and beautiful. Passing through the ancient quadrangle of the mosque, studded with its dark orange-trees, now showing their full wealth of green and golden fruit, we came full upon the El Triumfo—an ancient pillar, with its quaint stone figure of San Rafael, the patron saint of the Cordovese, surmounting it. On the right was the palace of the Bishop of Cordoba, built in 1745, and, hard by, looking over the peaceful Guadalquivir, the seminario, with its quaint, old-fashioned garden. Just below was the ancient bridge, with its seventeen arches; beyond the river, on the left, stretched the blue Sierra Morena, with its ancient watch-towers crowning its heights.

Leaving the broad, peaceful river winding slowly among its groves of alamos blancos (silver poplars), still in autumn russet foliage, and the rude Moorish water-mills, standing up out of the water under the shelter of the bridge, we passed through one of the land-gates, close to the cavalry barracks. Streaming up from the gate, with many a push and joke, came a party of mounted and dismounted Spanish cavalry, dragoons and hussars, their bright uniforms and clanking swords forming a picturesque contrast to the old grey gateway. One uniform struck me as specially attractive,—light-blue tunic, with light-yellow cord facings, and yellow tassel; cap of light blue with yellow band, and baggy, brick-dust trousers, enclosed, as is usual with Spanish cavalry, in shining black leather below the knee. The contrast of colours was very bright and pleasing, and suited the bright, sunny South very well. The men looked wiry and active, but rather small of stature. My guide observed, seeing me scrutinizing them somewhat closely,—" Chicitos, pero muy valientes!" ("They are very small, but very valiant!").

Passing through the last crumbling gateway, and under the last outlying fragment of Moorish masonry, we entered the stunted avenue of black poplars, near the end of which lay the cemetery, its white portals, and the stone figure above them, " salus infirmorum," looking quite sparkling in the morning sun. The two pitched and whitewashed patios, or little courtyards, into which you first enter, are very tastefully arranged and trimly kept. Four cypresses, bound together at the top, bend gracefully over a little stone well in the first, while orange-trees in profusion are trained up and along the walls of both. I noticed here a device which struck me as simple and clever. Nothing is much uglier than pitching-stones, but here the ugliness was to a certain extent redeemed by a simple and easy method. The stones employed were of three different colours, the common dark pitching-stones forming the background, on which trees or shrubs—noticeably one large tree, with spreading bough, called the "Tree of Life"—were picked out in the stones of lighter colours.

The little chapel—with its marble slab on which to rest the coffin, its tiny altar, with crucifix and lights—does not claim much mention. It was neat and bare, but it opens into a third little dark courtyard, seven yards broad by ten long; this was plainly pitched, and had three mounds in it.

"This," said my informant, "is where the Spanish Protestants lie."

A curious story was afterwards told me relative to this tiny court. A Protestant's body was refused by the Church its narrow strip of earth in the walls of the cemetery. The civil authorities decreed that it had a right to its home; accordingly, it was laid in this little patio, and not strictly within the walls of the cemeterio, though within the walls of its enclosure. Anything like the sequestered beauty of the situation of this cemetery, or the peacefulness of its shady patios, festooned with orange-trees, I have never witnessed.

Turning to the right, and passing forward, you enter the model cemetery of Cordoba. The bodies are buried, as is customary in the Roman Catholic cementerios of Spain, according to classes, first, second, and third, each paying a different amount for the funeral ceremony and for the ground occupied. This, as I have minutely described it in the first volume of this work, I need not further enlarge upon. On either side, as you enter, are the usual deep walls, with the little tiers of slabs at the head of each coffin bearing the inscription; but there are no formal, sandy quadrangles, as at Cadiz, and the whole place, or rather the part of it reserved for the first-class, has quite the appearance of a garden.

These little slabs, although they are only of just the same size as the head of a coffin, had letters of all colours, and were many of them preserved from weather by a glass plate in front, kept beautifully clean in most cases, and thus showing the inscription plainly enough. Some were quite like a tiny bow-window, within which, on either side of the inscription, or in front of it, stood vases of flowers, or tiny candles, some of which were lighted in honour of the patron saint's day of the person buried.

The favourite device on the tablets from 1830 to 1845 seemed to be, strangely enough, a skull and cross-bones; or, more frequently, a coat-of-arms or crest. Some of these tablets were of polished brass, under glass; some of black marble, with gilt letters. Most of them bore at the foot of the inscription the letters R. I. P. or R. I. P. A. Some few had texts of Scripture: the Book of Job seemed to be the favourite garden from which to cull these sacred flowers. On one tablet at the entrance I noticed, " Miseremini mei, miseremini mei, saltem vos amici mei," Job xix. 21, the conclusion of the verse, "For the hand of God hath touched me," being omitted. Of course, the "miseremini mei, amici," is a request for prayers for the soul of the dead.

I subscribe three typical inscriptions, copied on the spot.

(1.) At the head, a cross, with skull and cross-bones on either side; under the cross the words—

"Job xxx. 15. Aqui yacen los restos mortales
DE DON RAFAEL FERNANDEZ Y SANCHEZ,
que falleció
el dia 15 de Febrero de 1848,
á los 64 años de su edad.
R. I. P."

(2.) At the head of the inscription a simple cross. Then the words—

Propiedad.
D. RAFAEL OSCUNA Y GARCIA,
falleció,
el 30 de Julio de 1840,
á la edad de 17 años.
R. I. P.

(3.) Here is one, not uncommon, very terse and simple :—

DN. RICARDO AGUILAR Y HOYD.
R. I. P.

And many, like this last, had nothing but the name and the simple R. I. P. The absence of date struck and surprised me greatly, as did one other matter, namely, that whereas in many cemeteries one sees constantly the words, "His sorrowing parents," or, "Her bereaved husband," put at the foot of the inscription, to denote by whom the tablet was placed, here one rarely met with that.

The path, with its neat evergreen hedges, slopes gradually upwards; on either side are beautifully-kept flower-beds, rich with scented exotic shrubs and flowers, all growing luxuriantly. A few grand tombs and vaults were scattered about in the centre of this garden, some being very large and costly, but designed without much taste or skill: they were of marble and white stone.

The cypress-trees, the acacias, the trim evergreen hedges, and the gay flowers, all told of pains and care; and the blue Sierra Morena, with the Hermitage nestling in a cleft of its rugged side, and the bluer sky and bright sun, formed a scene strangely different from the damp green stillness of an English churchyard at Christmas.

As you pass up the central walk, on either side lie the white walls, with their numberless little tablets, which contain the bodies of the "first class," some of the inscriptions of which, taken at the entrance, I have above given. Many of these had lamps hung in front of them; on several I noticed the words, "The lawful wife." Immortelles were hung in front of many, and inside the glass of one of them lay a circlet of black and grey velvet, stuffed with some aromatic herb, and upon it, in gold letters,—

"Recuerdo: Eterno:
Mi adora esposa."

That is, "Thy memory is imperishable, my beloved consort."

So much for that part of the cemetery devoted to the dead of the "first class." One must use the words, yet how hollow and meaningless do they become when one reflects that their wealth and position can now give them nothing more than a stately tomb, or a velvet wreath, or a burning taper; and that they alone, poor or rich, will be *de la primera clase* in that House of many Mansions who have used, and used well, their means of grace and opportunities of usefulness!

At the end of the broad central walk stands what appears to be a small stone temple, with strong iron railings across its open front; it is the burial-place for the "canonicos" of the Cathedral of Cordova! Over the front is the inscription,—" Ossa arida, audite verbum Domini: Educam vos de sepulchris vestris: Et scietis quia ego Dominus. Ezekiel xxxvi." Around the walls inside are the usual little tablets, a bust (stone), and, I think, a few texts of Holy Scripture.

This division, this separation of rich from poor, of ecclesiastics from laymen, certainly does not commend itself to one's liking or approval at all; but it does not cease here, for, with a happier thought, the children who die quite young have, like their spiritual fathers, their own shady corner—and a pretty, shady little court it is, with its immortelles, its tiny tablets, and its bright flowers, in pots, standing around. To-day it looked very beautiful, and the inscription above it struck me as singularly happy,— "Departamento del angel," or, "The angel's part." It is sometimes called "The innocent's resting-place."

Then we wended our way to the home of the second class. They are chiefly plain brick squares, under-ground, but, although perfectly neat and trim, there are few inscriptions. Still I noticed some little tablets fixed on the surface of the ground, and one or two tiny wooden crosses, with a few flowers here and there, planted by pious hands. I cannot be distinctly certain, but I think, as is usually the case, these second-class bodies were all under-ground, and covered over with brick. The rule in Spanish cemeteries is, I believe, that the second-class bodies lie in rows, at the feet of the white walls which contain the ashes of their greater brethren. But here, also, I noticed another portion for children.

"And now," I said to my guide, "go we to visit the last home of the poor, the Entierro de la tercera clase?"—"Why go there, señor; there is nothing at all to see?" I believed him fully; but we went. The burying-place of the third class, although all its surroundings are neat, is a large sandy pit, into which the bodies are put. There is nothing indecent or irreverent about it; but one would like to see some little memorial of God's poor, who lie here *en masse*. Cypresses and a few rose-trees grew around, but that was all. Just above, was a small wooden building, used by the medical men to dissect or examine any body which might be picked up and brought there to ascertain the cause of death—at least, so I was informed; and as I saw nothing but a deal table and a washhand-basin inside, I conclude such is the fact.

Well, the last home of los pobres was a heartless one, I must say: but even its bareness and heartlessness could not deprive them of God's good gifts at the last. The same sun shone upon their last resting-place that was shining on those of their richer brethren,—the same blue, peaceful sierra sheltered them,—meet emblems, I thought, of the love that flows alike for all, rich or poor, from the "one God and Father of us all."

As I passed away, I noticed, recurring several times on different tablets, the text, "Miseremini mei, amici," from the Book of Job; also, that constantly the texts, though there were but few, were selected from that sacred book specially. Petitions, like those contained in the text just quoted, for prayers, and expressions of affection on the part of the bereaved, I noticed in many cases; but there were not many expressions of faith, and hope, and resignation. This cemeterio must take rank as a beautifully-kept one.

Poetry is not common in the cemeterios of Spain; but as we turned to leave, my guide said, "Here is a beautiful poem on this tablet,—" Una cosa muy bonita—you must copy it." So I did so, and I here append a translation, as it may interest some of those who read these pages. More than one uneducated person directed my attention to it. I was, and am, still at a loss to discern its beauty:—

> "Alas! and what remaineth of her now,
>   Whose grace and goodness once I called mine own?
>   Naught save the clay-cold limbs, the pallid brow,
>   Hidd'n in cold earth 'neath this unfeeling stone!
>
> "And had the Master's summons come for me
>   At that same hour—so alone we were;
>   Haply not one would have remembered thee,
>   The child of graces manifold as rare!
>   But I am spared awhile—and haste to grave
>   These words of truth, thy memory dear to save!"

The walk homewards was beautiful as ever, through the ancient city-gate, along the green sward beneath the rustling groves of alamos blancos, with the silver Guadalquivir stretching along to the right, and reflecting, in its clear placid waters, the sixteen arches of the massive bridge that spans them.

I subjoin one typical specimen of the funeral notices which are sent by the relations of the dead to be printed in the provincial papers, and are also printed on black-edged paper, and left on the table of the chief casinos and hotels:—

R. I. ✠ R. A.
Hoy juéves 20, del corriente á las cuatro de la tarde, será conducido al
cementerio catolico de esta ciudad el cadáver de
EL SEÑOR DON JULIO ARTEGO Y MOLINA,
Capitan de Caballeria
H.H.—G.G.
Su madre, hermanos, tios, tios politicos,
primos, primos politicos, sobrinos
director espiritual, demas parientes afectos:
Ruegan á v. se sirva encomendar
su alma a Dios ntro. Sr. y asistir
á tan religioso acto : favores que
agradeciran.
Cadiz : Novbre. de 1873.

I believe the H.H. stands for "He, He," *i. e.*, take notice, and the G.G., for "gloria"; but abbreviations are with difficulty understood by foreigners.

CHAPTER IV.

CORDOBA, AND ITS CHARITIES.

The ancient city of Cordoba, where the Kalif used to hold his court, and where the wonderful mosque, second only to that at Mecca, still remains a monument of wonderful workmanship, is fast going to decay and ruin. The first thing that strikes one, on getting out of the train, is the tropical appearance of the "Pasco," or public walk, for here grow and ripen the orange, the lemon, the citron, the pomegranate; and the graceful and lofty date-palm raises its tall head over the rest, and softly rustles its feathery leaves in the whispering breeze. There are two very tall palms standing in the centre of the city, which tradition says were planted by Abd-ur-raham as long ago as 788. Passing along the city-wall for a short distance, the town is entered through a handsome gateway of Roman architecture, and one finds oneself in a perfect labyrinth of narrow streets. So narrow are many of these streets, that on stretching out the arms to the right and left one can almost touch both sides. Under old arches, unmistakably Moorish, past new houses built of red brick, and past old houses that seem to have remained untouched as long as the palms in the convent-garden, one will at last, most likely after repeatedly losing oneself, come into the main street, which leads down to the river. As for myself, I only found this much-desired street by walking several times from one side of the city to the other at different points, by which means I at last hit upon it. When I had recovered my surprise at finding myself anywhere in particular, I walked down to the end of the street, to the river, and then I was repaid amply for my trouble. A splendid piece of water, as clear as crystal, deep and sluggish here, and running rapidly over shallows there, spanned across its greatest breadth by a splendid Roman bridge; and a little further down, below the bridge, situated in mid-stream, two old Moorish water-mills. To the right, as I stood on the bridge looking down stream, were the ruins of the Alcazar, or Moorish palace, with its garden of orange-trees laden with fruit; to the left, a landscape of fields and trees, reminding one not a little of English river scenery. All this made up a picture worth a good deal of trouble.

I found out, as I slowly wended my way back to my friend's house, that it is well to be careful where one puts one's feet in the streets of Cordoba, for a great many of the paving-stones are of soap-stone, which is very slippery, especially so in wet weather.

My friend, whose house was next door to the "Casa de Expositos," or Foundling Hospital, told me that, owing to the number of infants left at this charity, and the scarcity of wet nurses (four or five children being given to one woman to nurse), the mortality was about 75 per cent.; and that, in order to remedy this evil, he had asked permission of the authorities to allow him to try a sucking-bottle with condensed milk, with which he fed his own baby. To this proposition the authorities had very gladly consented, and if I liked to accompany him I could. My friend sent his servant on before, with the sucking-bottle and the milk and hot water on a tray, and we followed. We were received at the door by two extremely kind-looking, matronly Sisters of Charity, who showed us into a nice, comfortable room, and begged us to be seated. Here we met the two doctors belonging to the establishment, to whom my friend explained the mode of preparing the milk, &c. When some of the milk had been prepared, we sent out for a baby, and one was brought who had been left in the "turno" (a padded box, which is left open all night for the reception of foundlings) the night before. One of the Sisters said that she thought it was about two days old. I do not think any of us were very sanguine about the experiment answering on so young a child. If so, we were agreeably surprised, for the little mite of a thing took to it amazingly, and emptied the bottle without removing its mouth.

After this, I was shown over the establishment by two Sisters, who were exceedingly kind. I first went into a large room, which was used as a play-room in wet weather. One end of this room was fitted up with evergreens and rocks, amongst which were all sorts of toys—dolls, Noah's-ark animals, Christmas-tree candles, little groups of figures, some painted to represent butchers'-shops, and some of the religious, for example, Our Saviour in the manger. This was an immense source of amusement to the little ones, the Sister told me. We next went into the playground, where about seventy or eighty girls, ranging from about four years old to fourteen or fifteen, were playing. On seeing us, they all rushed up and swarmed round the Sisters, to whom they seemed very much attached, and who had kind words and bright smiles for all of them. In the kitchen were two other Sisters, assisted by two of the grown-up foundlings, cooking the dinner for all those little mouths. All the utensils were of bright copper, and everything was beautifully clean.

In the larder hung great sides of bacon, and around the sides were seven or eight huge "tinajas," or earthen jars, large enough to put two men in, full of olives. In a large chest or bin, divided into compartments, were garbanzos (a sort of pea), beans, flour, and other necessaries. If the dinner of these poor children was half as good as it ought to be, judging by the smell, they had not much to complain of, so far as eating was concerned. In the school-room we found a very pretty and young Sister of Charity occupied in teaching some two dozen little charges. The lesson was in writing, and I was charmed at the way she went softly round, bending over first one and then another, with a kind word and a willing hand to help. The room was hung round with maps and diagrams, illustrating, by pictures and figures, all manner of things for the aid of the very small pupils. From here we passed into the sleeping apartment; first of all, to those of the very small foundlings. This consisted of a long room, with whitewashed walls, on one side of which were some seven or eight French windows, making the room light and airy, although, on the day I was there, rain was falling heavily, and the room seemed somewhat cold and cheerless. On the other side were ranged along the wall some twenty or thirty tiny cradles, made of iron, in the shape of walnut-shells, which, with their scrupulously clean white curtains, looked very comfortable. We took a peep at one or two of the little faces behind the curtains. I think that, when I was there, there were only about ten or twelve very young infants. The other dormitories were arranged on the same pattern, only, of course, the beds were on a different style, and suitable for the occupants they were intended to contain. In one of these sleeping-rooms there was a sick child; and I was very much pleased to see that one of the elder girls was sitting at the bed-side with her work, and helping the poor little thing pass away the weary hours in that great lonely room. So much was I pleased with this thoughtfulness, that I asked one of my guides whether the girl came to sit there of her own accord, or whether she was sent; and the Sister told me that when a child was ill, no matter how slightly, it was customary for some one to sit with her, but that there were always volunteers, and that it was scarcely ever necessary to mention anything about it.

Next we went to see the "turno," which, as I explained before, is the turning-box into which the foundlings are put from the street. This box occupies a niche in the wall of a most comfortable room, where one of the Sisters always sits during the day, and, in the night, a spring is attached to the "turno," which rings a bell in the next room, where one of the Sisters sleeps. Anybody wishing to leave a foundling has only to put it into the box, which is nicely padded, from the opening in the street, give it a push, which turns it round, the bell rings, and the child is taken out; and the parent or relation goes home with a light heart, knowing that the child will be cared for. The date and exact time of entrance is then taken down in writing by the Sister in attendance, so that, should the parents or friends of the infant, at any future time, wish to take it away, the date and hour when it was deposited will serve to identify it.

It must not be supposed that these children are nearly all children of shame, for such is not the case, although, of course, they find a place and a refuge there amongst the rest. Very, very many of them are the children of very poor parents, who, not having sufficient to buy the many little things necessary for a baby, and most likely both father and mother being hard at work all day long, have not time to attend to it as it will be attended to here. Twice a week the relations are allowed to come and see the children, and they often bring with them little luxuries, such as they can afford.

Before we went away, we asked if we might send in some sweets for the children, and the Sisters said that they should be very glad. We came to the conclusion that an "arroba," 25 lb., would not be any too much; and on the following Sunday we had a large tray, filled up with a wonderful mixture of good things, carried into the casa before us. It was a pretty sight to see how the great and small seemed to enjoy their treat, and it was better still to see the genuine smile of pleasure on the calm faces of the Sisters of Charity—one of whom, by-the-bye, had a "sweet tooth" herself.

As I was leaving this very excellent institution, as is customary in Spain, I held out my hand to the Sisters, and said, "Estoy a los pies de usted" (I am at your feet); and I was not a little surprised to see that they appeared to ignore my proffered hand altogether, until at last the eldest of them said, with a kind smile, "You know, señor, we have a custom not to shake hands with gentlemen, so you must not be offended at our not shaking hands with you. May God take care of you!" This "Dios guarda á usted" is a very common form of adieu.

On the following day, through the kindness of my friend and one of the alcaldes, an American gentleman and myself obtained permission to visit the prison,—the prison of the Inquisition,—and the principal charities of the city. This alcalde, who spoke very good English, with true Spanish politeness, not only placed his carriage at our disposal, but accompanied us himself. At the prison-door we were met by the governor and the jailor, with a strap holding some hundred or so of huge keys slung across his shoulder. I was told, on entering, that it would be advisable to smoke; and I soon found that this was too true, for, on getting well inside the building, we became conscious of a stench, only partly corrected by the smoke of our cigarillos. The building seemed to be a square, enclosing the exercise-ground, as well as I could make out; but, unlike an English or American prison, there seemed to be a lack of arrangement in the plan of the place. One by one the doors of the cells were opened for us all along these corridors, and what we saw in one we saw in all. A small cell, about 15 feet by 10, with an arched ceiling, although some of them were just double this size. Each cell had a window looking out into the square which the building surrounds, and contained, that is, the smaller ones, generally three prisoners and their beds, which are almost always provided by themselves. These men were nearly all engaged in knitting stockings, making sandals of esparto-grass, or some other feminine occupation. It seems a pity that they are not obliged to work at something more likely to keep themselves in health, and take some of the expense of maintaining them off the hands of the Government. The friends of prisoners are allowed to come and see them through a grating, which opens to the street; and one often sees in Spain a reproduction of that splendid picture of Phillip's, where the Spanish girl holds up her baby to the prison-bars to be kissed by its father, and the great basket of bread, and fruit, and wine lying on the pavement. The money for the stockings and sandals goes towards providing this basket of good things.

I must not forget to mention that the American gentleman who was with us had been several years in China, and spoke Chinese, and we were therefore not a little surprised to hear that amongst the prisoners was a Chinaman. He was dressed in ordinary European clothes; but as we entered his cell, occupied by six or seven prisoners besides himself, the difference in the cast of his features soon betrayed him. The poor fellow seemed to be surprised and delighted at hearing his own language spoken, although my American acquaintance did not get along very fast, as one was speaking in the northern dialect and the other in the southern. The Chinaman seemed to have forgotten a good deal of his own language, for very frequently he would answer some question in broken Spanish. However, after a little while, which was taken up by the two in making strange sounds and still stranger gestures, we learnt from our interpreter that John Chinaman had emigrated from his home in the north of China to California; that in San Francisco he had become the servant of a Spanish gentleman, with whom he went to Peru, where he lived several years, and at last came with him to Spain, where he had robbed his master, and so got shut up in the prison at Cordoba. Upstairs was in no striking respect different from downstairs, and needs no special detail. We walked along the old battlements to a high tower, in which were some old and unused dungeons, circular, with a small hole at the side sloping upwards, so that about a foot of sky was all that an unfortunate prisoner could see.

In one of these dungeons a prisoner, some few years ago, made a resistance with stones from the wall of his prison against the door for two days, in which time he killed two jailors, but was at last shot himself. From the top of this tower, where a Civil Guard is always posted, overlooking the exercise-ground, and from which any prisoner attempting to escape could easily be shot, a splendid view of Cordoba, and its convent-crowned mountain, to the westward, is obtained. The river, the alcazar, the bishop's garden, the cathedral, the several other churches, and the cemetery, all lay at one's feet; and further away to the southward, on the highest hill-tops, were the old signal-towers which stretch from Cadiz to Madrid, and which served as a telegraph in the olden time. When we descended from this tower, we were shown into a room literally piled with old books, in manuscript, and with parchment covers. These contained the various indictments of the prisoners. Every one of them had its date written on the back, and we found on the shelves one with the date A.D. 1325. I have no doubt, had we examined carefully, we might have found much more ancient records. I was rather disappointed that the entrance to the torture-chamber of the Inquisition has been filled up, so that we could only see where the entrance was. It is supposed that all the instruments of torture, &c., are still there, and, in fact, that the place is just as it was left. One of the jailors said that he supposed, if Don Carlos came to the throne, they would have to open it again. I should add, as showing the shocking state of Spanish law, that in one of the cells a very decent looking fellow came up to the alcalde, his hat in his hand, and said that he had been there for three weeks without being heard. The poor fellow's only offence was, that he had lost the paper which all Spaniards are obliged to have when they travel from their native town to another. This paper is signed by the authorities of the town from which the traveller comes, and sets forth his name, address, respectability, and so forth. My impression of the prison, as a whole, was, that it was horribly dirty, badly ventilated, and unwholesome; and that the system of herding several criminals together in a den like wild beasts, with nothing to do, and often without a hearing, must be very demoralizing, and more likely to encourage criminality than correct it.

We were very glad to get out into the fresh air again, and next drove to the "Casa de Locos," madhouse. Here we were met by a Sister of Charity, who very politely put the house at our disposition, and accompanied us over it—at least, that part of it devoted to mad women. These poor creatures were all locked in their little rooms, which had a barred window looking on the passage. At most of these windows the occupants of these little rooms sat blankly looking out into the garden, which they could see through the French windows at the other side of the passage. Some of them seemed glad to see strangers, and wished to talk, whilst others retreated into the darkest corners of their rooms, and sat there muttering to themselves. One woman in particular, whose mania seemed to be dress, put her hand through the bars, and caught hold of the Sister, and begged her to buy a new shawl, exactly like the one she had on, only now. " Now, how much do you think it would cost?" she asked. And the Sister said, " About two dollars, I should think." The poor thing thought for a minute, and then said she did not think it would be so much, but, at any rate, she must have it to-morrow morning, and that she would pay for it. The Sister quieted her by saying she would think about it, and we passed on. I was behind, and as I passed, her thin bony hand caught hold of me, and, pulling me to the bars, she asked, in a mysterious whisper, if I thought she would really get the shawl ; and when I told her that I supposed so, she seemed satisfied, and smiled and winked in a very knowing sort of way. I afterwards learned that this poor wretch had asked the same thing for several years. At the door of one of the dormitories, where the less violent sleep, which were all very clean and nice, we were asked to wait, as there was a "furiosa" inside, whom it would be best to remove or quiet. When we entered, we saw no signs whatever of any violent maniac, and I don't know whether she was still there, or had been removed. On reaching the foot of a broad and handsome staircase, we were given in charge of a man-keeper, who took us over that part of the establishment devoted to men.

Here, as downstairs, each madman was sitting looking out of his window, and, on seeing us, a great cry was raised for tobacco—" Un cigarillo, por Dios." I gave one of them a cigarette, and was about to supply him with a match to light it by, when the keeper politely interfered. He said we should presently see how very nearly one of these madmen had burnt the place down a few weeks ago with a match supplied by a stranger. However, he lit the poor fellow's cigarillo for him at his own, and gave it to him, but said we had better not take any notice of them, as even lighted cigarettes were dangerous in the hands of madmen.

Some of the poor fellows were singing, some of them were surly, and others one could see rolled up in the darkest corners of their dens, who never spoke, so the keeper said, and never moved, unless it was for food. At last we came to the cell formerly occupied by the wretched man who had tried to burn down his door. All the woodwork was charred and scorched, and the walls were quite black. He had taken his straw bed and put it against the door, and then set fire to it with a match which he had concealed somewhere about him. We went to see him afterwards, and found him sitting at the window of his dark room. He immediately asked for something to smoke; and when the keeper told him no, and reminded him of what he had done, he did not seem to recollect anything about it. It seems a pity to box these poor unreasoning creatures up like wild beasts, and I cannot think that in such a condition there is any chance of reason returning.

From here we crossed over the way to the Hospital, exactly opposite, where we met with nothing but kindness from the Sisters of Charity in charge. In each ward were some ten or twelve beds, very clean and comfortable-looking. These wards are high and airy, and light streams in through the long windows, making them look very cheerful. Each patient has his ticket placed over his bed, with his illness described thereon, and the amount and class of his rations, &c.

E 2

In the kitchen three Sisters were preparing a great variety of dishes for the invalids, and the smell was a sufficient guarantee of the quality. The larder was very much the same as those in the Casa de Expositos and the madhouse, and requires no comment. In the kitchen we noticed a magnificent marble table, and also a large marble bath, now used for washing plates, &c. Another marble table of the same dimensions, viz., about seven feet by four, we found in the surgery. These tables and the bath were hewn out of one piece of marble, and are supposed to be very ancient. Everything here was orderly, clean, and comfortable; and I thought that I should not mind falling ill without friends so much, if I could come here, and be nursed and attended by those good and kind Sisters, who seemed ever willing and pleased to make the sufferer's lot more bearable. It is impossible to give too much praise to these good women, who frequently come from the best families of Spain, and devote their lives to the relief of sickness, to the education of poor children, and "to visit the widows and fatherless in their affliction, and to keep themselves unspotted from the world."

We next visited the Casa de Hospicio, or Refuge for old poor people. On passing through the outside door, we found ourselves in an open "patio," or quadrangle, in the centre of which grew orange and lemon trees surrounding a fountain; and round the outside wall of which ran a covered walk, floored with red brick. On the opposite side to the street-door, a flight of broad steps of soap-stone led into the interior of the building. On reaching the top of these steps, we were shown some very cheerful-looking dormitories, with numbered beds, each inmate of the charity having his number. The kitchen was, like the others, remarkable for its cleanness. Here were two very pretty Sisters cooking, and a boy cutting up mountains of bread. As basket after basket was carried out, I asked whether there were enough inmates to eat it all, and was told that there were about three hundred. (?) On one side of the patio was a room fitted up with towels, and some hundred or so of washing-basins, fitted in a double row, in a solid brick framework, covered with white china tiles. Each basin was full of water, and one of our party remarked that they did not appear to be much used, as there was no dirty water, and all the towels were clean; but, be that as it may, the fact that the poor old people could wash if they liked, showed the thoughtfulness of the founders of the charity.

As we left this capital institution, where the aged poor can, without shame, find an asylum during their old age, in thinking over all I had seen, I could not help feeling surprised that here, in Spain, where everything is supposed to be behind the times, the charitable institutions should be so thoroughly good, and should answer so perfectly the purposes for which they were intended. We afterwards visited the Ayuntamiento, or Council Chamber, of the city; but, apart from a very ancient portrait of the elder Seneca, who was a native of Cordoba, there was nothing worth seeing here.

What struck me most in the whole of our excursion, was the uniform gentleness of the different Sisters of Mercy we met in the course of our visit. Without exception, one and all brought a smile with them into the wards of the Hospital where sickness and death were struggling for the mastery—all had kind words for their self-imposed charges; and every little child in the Foundling, every poor creature in the Madhouse, and every suffering patient in the Hospital, wore a smile on their faces when one of the Sisters approached. Thank God that there are such women, who, to help their suffering brethren, will leave all behind, and suffer themselves, as we know they must suffer! May God reward them, and bless their work!

CHAPTER V.

"EL PAJARO," THE DECOY-BIRD.

FROM the heather-clad sierras of Galicia, from wandering, gun in hand, by its tumbling trout-streams, and among its sombre pine-forests, the haunt of the red-deer, the wolf, the boar, and the bear, to descend to the homely and unsportsman-like chase of the red-legged partridge with a decoy, or call-bird (el pajaro), seems a drop indeed. But when one has spoken of the "caza mayor," or chase of the larger animals, one must speak also of the tamer ways of hunting, the "caza menor," which includes the chase of the hare, rabbit, and partridge, and such small fry.

My object here is to present a faithful picture of Spanish life and character, especially in the interior, and no sketches of sport would be complete in which one short chapter was not devoted to the partridge-shooting in the Campo with a decoy. Every morning, in these towns, the spectacle is seen of the gentlemen of the town starting out on horseback, each one closely followed (as is the universal custom on a ride) by his servant on a donkey, carrying the gun of his master, and the small wire cage of el pajaro, or the decoy partridge.

Utterly distasteful as was the thought of this kind of sport to one who loves wandering with his gun and fishing-rod as much for the sake of the exercise and the scenery as for that of the slaughter, I yet determined to put my pride in my pocket, and go out for a day's shooting among the red-legs with the decoy.

The most successful at this sort of sport—if it be worthy of that name—was my own barber, who, although a keen sportsman in other branches of the caza menor, had made decoy shooting his *spécialité*. No one could enter the shop of Pedro de Dios without feeling that its owner was of a sporting turn. The walls of the long, dark, hair-besprinkled sala—where his four lads shaved and cut hair for all ranks of the town, from the herdsman in his sheep-skin to the señor in his capa—were painted with various sketches of the caza, both mayor and menor, in the most glowing colours imaginable. On the side of a sierra, of most unpoetic purple hue, a huntsman was potting at an impossible stag; on the opposite wall two hounds, of tawny red, were just making the final clutch at the tail of a poor frightened puss, while in puss's very path, as though to scare her from front and rear also, two men were giving the *coup de grâce* to a dying roebuck. At the two ends of the sala hung, in wild profusion, gaudy-coloured ducks, wild cats, foxes, and wolves, with a whole bunch of the "perdices" (red-legged partridges), forming the crowning feature of this gorgeous panorama, the "act the last, scene the last." In a dark corner of the room stood, in a small, conical-shaped wire cage, only just large enough for the poor creature to turn itself round in, the poor pajaro, or decoy-bird, a fine specimen of the male red-legged partridge. He stood upon a little carpet of dirty wool, which formed the lining of his cage; but his legs and feet showed signs of humour breaking out, his eye was dull, and his tail feathers nowhere. Close by his side stood the escopeta, or gun of Pedro.

Pedro, in common with all others of his special trade in the interior of Spain, added to his trade of barber those of "Dentista y Sangrador," *i. e.*, dentist and bleeder, which last appellations he deserved equally well with that of barber. He drew teeth and blood from all and any, and even went so far, in times of small-pox, as to add vaccination to his other surgical operations.

If you sat down in Pedro's shop to have your hair cut, just as he commenced, some poor, care-worn looking Spanish mother would appear at the door, and say, "Pray come at once, and bleed my child"; in which case he would smile blandly, and say, "Dentro media hora" (within half-an-hour), finish his task, and hurry off. For bleeding, which is the constant remedy in spring-time for the feverish diseases of men, women, and children, Pedro received only one peseta, a coin equal to tenpence of English money, and for tooth-drawing only fivepence! Constantly have I been sitting in Pedro's shop, and some unhappy creature has come in, seated himself beside me, and then and there been operated upon, the tooth extracted being handed round to be commented upon, and the instrument to be admired!

I fixed a day for shooting, or trying to shoot, the red-legs with the decoy; and on a bright, sunny morning in early March presented myself at the barberia of Pedro de Dios, ready accoutred for the rough walking of the Campo. An English sporting get-up is, perhaps, the best for an Englishman; but the Spaniard often wears a pair of canvas or flexible leather shoes or boots, or wraps several rolls of stout canvas round his feet and the lower part of the leg, binding it with thongs, and is thus enabled to keep his footing where there is much rocky walking.

The rocky, or rather stony, sides of some parts of the Sierra are terribly trying walking, especially when one has a gun and other traps to carry; and in dry weather even the sides of the hills, as you descend, from the dry, hard nature of the baked earth, are almost as slippery as the rocks themselves. In such places, the man who is flexibly shod has a tremendous advantage over his companion of the iron English boot, and will outstrip him both in ascending and descending the sides of a hill, or Sierra.

The goatherds, and ruder sort of cazadores (sportsmen), invariably, when engaged in their respective avocations in a rocky district, are shod with sackcloth or canvas, as above described, it being rolled so thickly as to preserve the foot from injury from glass or rock, and the leg from the prickly brushwood.

Pedro wore the soft, I the hard, foot-gear. He had just finished bleeding a neighbour's child, and was free for the day. He first took down his pajaro in its cage, drew a nightcap over the latter, and slung it over his back. Then he took his becerra, or gun-rest, and strapped it across his back, throwing a thick rug over the two. He shouldered his gun, and off we tramped for the puestos, or shooting-posts, which lay some five miles out in the Campo, or wild country.

Let me offer a short explanation of the three Spanish words here used. The word "pajaro" simply is an equivalent of the English generic word "bird," but with the prefix "el" (English "the") before it, it always means, in the rude phraseology of the Spanish interior, "the decoy-bird." The word "becerra" means literally, I believe, "snap-dragon," but it is used here to denote a gun-rest. This gun-rest is much like an English spade-handle, shod with an iron spike, but, of course, much shorter, so that when it is driven into the earth, the loop is just of the height of a man's head when he is sitting on the ground. In the loop of the handle, if I may so call it, is a small steel trough, just fitted to hold the gun-barrel, and moving noiselessly on a pivot, so that the gun-barrel can be turned to, and pointed at, any angle, high or low, to right or left. The "puesto," or post, is the ambush of the cazador, and will be presently fully described.

I have omitted mention of one very needful weapon which we carried with us, namely, a good stout billhook, for cutting off boughs of trees.

The walk, although the levante (east wind) blew keenly, and the March sun blazed down quite fiercely enough, was a very interesting one, so far as scenery was concerned. My companion was pleasant, but, like many fine sportsmen, very silent withal.

The country through which our road lay was of the wildest, only showing signs of cultivation at rare intervals, in the shape of an olive-grove crowning the slope of some hill less rocky than its fellows; or a field of sevada (barley), so dry and baked that the clods, like triangular bits of rock sticking up, absolutely bruised one's feet.

First, we passed through a wide plain of tawny red sand, and granite boulders here and there peeping out. It was completely dotted over with clumps of "gamon," or wild asphodel. (I am no botanist, but I give the names by which the several plants I speak of are here known; the botanical vocabulary of the interior is, however, very slender.) These clumps of asphodel are, as far as the leaves are concerned, exactly similar to so many clumps of garden daffodil; but, unlike them, each clump shoots up from two to eight or nine succulent stems, each clothed towards the top with graceful bell-shaped flowers, in size and shape like those of the English blue-bell—but pure white, with tiny pink or purple stripes, and pink stamens. The effect of these flowers spangling the arid plain for half a mile is very beautiful. In these plains there are no large trees. In the arid plains whence I write, a wood is unknown; the trees do not average more than twenty feet in height, and are stunted, dwarfed, and dry-leaved.

Here and there, from among the asphodels, stood up little stunted trees of the encina, or evergreen oak (*Quercus ilex*), one of the commonest trees in the Spanish interior.

Waste after waste we tramped across covered with wild thyme (tomillo), looking brown and withered, but sweet enough in a pressed handful, and also with every sort of prickly, dry, aromatic underwood, the small, stunted holly growing about two feet high, and interlaced with dry bents (this holly is called "cojoco" by the peasantry); the "dractarma," or mare's tail; the "lentisco," or Spanish mastich shrub (*Pistachia lentiscus*), supposed by the peasantry to be very poisonous; these, with the clumps of asphodel, the dry, interlacing bents, and the clumps of green "juagarzo," formed a splendid cover for hares, rabbits, or foxes.

So I remarked to Pedro. "Si, señor" (Yes, sir), said he; "but since the Republic, every one in Spain is a sportsman, and every one carries an escopeta, and so we find now neither hare, rabbit, nor partridge in the Campo,—no! hardly so much as a fox, or a wild cat!" It was true. Until Serrano's Government came, the name of the cazadores was Legion: every one carried a gun, and betook himself to the Campo.

The most picturesque scene upon the road, or rather no-road, which we pursued, was at a turn where we followed a winding path, known only to sportsman or goatherd, round the bend of some hills. Under a stunted encina, two goatherds were sitting down, in their sheepskin jackets, huge mantas, and with a gun and a dog beside them, their flock of brown, black, white, and sandy goats browsing all around on the crisp, aromatic herbage; above their heads rose a huge hill, with square blocks of grey stone or rock (granite) piled in wild confusion one above the other—so grey, so serrated, that one almost seemed to be looking upon—

"The rough rude ocean frozen into stone,"

and down these crags or boulders, or rather square blocks of grey granite, came part of the flock of goats, gambolling and skipping down from one slat to another, as though enjoying the feat. Growing out from every crevice and hole in these stones were stunted encinas and chaparros, their dark green or glaucus foliage contrasting beautifully with the quiet, grey colour of the slats of stone. Far beyond us, and all around, lay the blue serrated peaks of the Sierra Morena; and, at our feet, a tiny stone well, of the purest water, gushing from the rocks, with a well-worn hole for a man to stoop down and drink of the crystal stream. I was just kneeling down to slake my thirst, when my companion sprang forward with a stick which he carried. "Culebra," he cried ("adder"), as he aimed a tremendous blow at a spotted adder, that wriggled untouched into its hole just above the little well.

It was of a dark-brown colour, with bright yellow spots, and would have been in measurement about a foot-and-a-half long.

Spain abounds with reptiles, and at every footfall we scared a lizard, a scorpion, or an adder. The lizards (lagartos) shot away instantaneously into the nearest shrub; the adders moved more slowly, and we managed to despatch one on our return journey.

Along a ledge of rock, on one side of which was an olive-grove protected by a hedge of "pita" (aloe), the sword-like, spike-like leaves of which thrust their sharp points almost into our path—a path so narrow, so slippery, that, with my thick, English shooting-boots, and heavy load, and gun, I reeled over, and nearly fell three or four times; then up a steep mountain side, knee-deep in ground-holly, lentisco, bents, wild thyme, and the like—so we tramped along. At last we reached the top of the hill; and a more beautiful hill-top I never desire to behold. Splendid as cover for wild animals, bird, or beast, it was also equally splendid from its surroundings. Far away, in a belt, stretched the blue mountains of the Morena; at our feet lay the wildest of wild countries, covered with brushwood, from which rose up, here and there, slope after slope, bristling with grey slabs of rock. A few tilled fields, and dusky olive-groves, and goatherds, just reminded us that man was near; but all the rest simply spoke of desolation, wildness, and the chace!

We were on a table-land of short, thymy turf, dry as stubble from the long droughts, and dotted all over with thickets of evergreens and clumps of aromatic brushwood. The breeze, though cold, was delightfully refreshing after such a clamber; but, alas! that need, that *one* need, of suffering humanity in Spain, namely, water, was not to be had. We had both forgotten our water-bottle, and had not brought so much as an orange. So we knew our fate: we must wait till set of sun, with parched lips and thirsty.

But, fortunately, I had brought up a tiny flask of Catalan wine! The turf of this table-land was so short, the surface of the ground so level, that it would have made a first rate bowling-green; and then, the prospect—it was simply magnificent!

With a glass, we could see the shelving stones, the grey-granite slabs bristling up one of the hill-sides; and these, my companion said, were the haunt of numberless foxes. These foxes live and bring up their young in the crevices of these huge stones, and there is no "stopping *their* earths"; once run to ground, they are safe. But not only foxes, but wolves—a stray wolf or two from the Sierra Morena—often bear their young there; and, last summer, a friend of mine took, with great difficulty, a nest of three or four young wolves from their hiding-place amid the crevices of these grey rocks, and tried to bring them up by hand— by the bottle, as it were! He failed, however, for one and all of the young ones died within three months of their capture.

I thought of the litter of wolves—I scanned the grey rocks for the foxes. I gazed in admiration on the wild, barren scene around and below me; but my dreams and thoughts were soon dissipated when

Pedro handed to me the bill-hook, and bade me cut boughs!

We had come to one of the best of the puestos. The puesto, or post, is of two kinds; sometimes, in stony pieces of ground, it is a small circular enclosure of stones, loosely piled on one another, in which case a small crevice is left for the gun. Here, however, the puesto was of the ordinary kind—namely, of brushwood. The way it is made is this. A spot is selected where there are one or two clumps of evergreen brushwood, about eight feet in diameter, the brush being about two to three feet high. The sportsman clears a circular space inside, large enough for him to lie down in, and cuts a small opening in front for the rest. We chose a good puesto, cleared off the loose brushwood placed by the last occupant to thicken the walls of the puesto, and then cut plenty of fresh boughs, and cleared a larger space within; then we wove green boughs around the rest, and stuck it firmly in the ground in the hedge of the puesto. Round the old stump of a tree, called "the decoy-rest," we twined evergreen, to make it look "natural," as my companion called it, and put a screen of the same round the cage, so that, when placed upon the rest, the sides were hidden by the green fringe of lentisco, and the top of the cage was open to the blue sunny sky. We drew the nightcap off the cage, and put it on the top of the stump. In a moment, ere we could jump over the sides of the puesto, and ensconce ourselves within it, the decoy-bird (a male red-leg) began his peculiar call—calling, chucking, whistling, and crowing in turns. "Do-it-quick, do-it-quick, do-it-quick, chuck, chuck, chuck, crr-r-r-ow—chuc-chic, chuc-chic, chuc-chic—wh-h-h-h-ew!"

Just as we had fairly settled ourselves in the small circle of evergreen, up rode a Spanish caballero of the town, a famous cazador, his servant on a donkey close behind him, carrying his master's gun.

" What, you've taken the best puesto, you thieves!" He, too, had come out for his day's decoy-shooting, and was evidently chagrined, though he laughed good-humouredly enough as he trotted across the short turf and sand of the plateau to the next puesto, at finding his favourite lair pre-occupied.

I pulled out a few sandwiches, and offered part to my companion. "No," said he, "it is Friday, and we eat no flesh on that day in Spain; although, for my part, I do not see why flesh is worse for the stomach on Friday than on any other day. But, there, I don't know."

We watched and waited hour after hour. At last we heard the answering call of another partridge, and heard the whir of its wings as it flew a short distance towards us—the red-legs are not flyers, but run like greyhounds—and rustled about in the brushwood. However, it never came within sight or gun-shot, and not another bird was heard. A " slower " day's sport—if sport it can be called—it has never been my lot to have; and, lying cramped up in the tiny space, with a burning March sun overhead, and the chill east wind driving through the green walls of our little circle, I felt simply uncomfortable and dispirited; and talking and smoking are, of course, unallowable. It may suit the Spaniards, who are somewhat indolent, to lie ensconced in these tiny puestos and breathe the sweet hill air, and turn over lazily for a shot at fifteen yards, but commend me rather to a ramble over moorland or stubbles, or wanderings along many miles of quiet river, fishing-rod in hand, or a frosty night upon the edge of the mere, when wings come flapping heavily landwards from the stormy sea.

Homeward we tramped, for the pajaro had become sulky and would not call; and as we tramped across a bit of broken ground, Pedro consoled himself for his disappointment by bringing down a partridge. Then we beat some heathery ground for hare or rabbit, but without success; saw a stray fox or two sneaking home to his "earth," or rather, to his "rock," in the grey pile of stones and rocks; flushed a small flock of avefrias, a sort of plover, and saw a green lizard of large size—nearly a foot long.

My musings, as we tramped home as quickly as we could—for, although armed, it is by no means safe to be out on foot in the Campo after dusk—were all upon the poor pajaro, and the treacherous trade to which he is apprenticed.

I remember an old man, a gardener, in England, telling me, almost with the tears in his eyes, that his neighbour had succeeded at last in teaching his parrot to swear; "and," he added, to my infinite amusement, "it do seem such a shame, sir, to make the poor bird commit such a sin!"

If the pajaro be a moral agent, as was the parrot in my poor gardener's philosophy, it certainly is a shame to let him allure his fellows into danger or death, especially if, as is often the case, his victim be a widow, or a young maiden lady seeking for a husband!

CHAPTER VI.

FAIRS AND FESTIVALS IN SPANISH WILDS.

PERHAPS one of the most striking features in the character of the Spaniard is his exceeding cheerfulness — a cheerfulness that no adverse circumstances (save illness) seems to be able to daunt. And he is a man very easily contented. The rudest joke affords him a laugh, the simplest, roughest festivity can cheer and delight him.

Among Spanish amusements, the annual fairs and the festivals of Mother Church stand in the foremost places. Christmas, with its cold east wind, tempered by the ever-glowing sky; Holy Week, with its winding processions, ushering in the glorious Resurrection morn, succeeded by other spring and summer festivals,—add each their quota to the poor Spaniard's modest "roll of delights," until the harvest is reaped, the sacks safely stored in the cameras of the owners, the paja laid up for the horses' winter supply, when, suddenly, harvest and granary are forgotten, and one fair in swift succession succeeds to another. It may here be noted that, as it appears to me, the Spanish working-man's and tradesman's character contrasts most favourably with that of his compeer in England. In the latter country, both the "time to work and the time to play" (the latter, probably, because it comes so rarely) are not used, but abused; or, in other words, an Englishman makes it his business to gain

money, nay, even to grub for money, and he
begrudges every holiday or half-holiday, which loses
him, as he thinks, a certain portion of his labour and
his capital.

"Carramba," said a poor Spanish agricultural
labourer to me, when I told him that his grey-
smocked brothers over the water had only two holidays in the year, except the sober Sunday; "Carramba, what is the good of life at all, at that price?"

The remark struck me as forcible and true. The
Spaniard, as regards play and work, keeps to the
golden mean. He is never so absorbed in business as
to be unwilling to shut his shop and take a holiday
with his dependents; and, when taking his holiday
he rarely exceeds the bounds of temperance and
moderation, and is ready to return to work as lightly
as he went to play. If to "use this world without
abusing it" be the right rule of life, in this respect
the joyous Spaniard has the best of it.

Some description shall now be given of a few of the
Spanish holidays.

In one town where I was in the spring of last
year, I was surprised by a little crowd gathering round my door, and by a sharp double knock.
On opening the door, the gaily-caparisoned head of a
magnificent snow-white sheep was thrust in. Gay
ribbons and gold streamers covered her body, and
almost hid her well-combed hair. On her forehead,
in the shape of a cross, were bound, with gold ribbon,
three shining ounce-pieces of gold. A sweet-looking
young priest stood on one side of the pretty creature,
which tossed its meek head ever and anon, as though
proud of its trappings, and on the other the master of
the ceremonies, who requested me, in honour of the

Virgin of ——, patroness of the town, to buy half-a-dozen tickets, entitling me to join in the raffle shortly to be held for the sheep and her three gold pieces.

Each ticket cost two reals (fivepence), and some thousands were sold, the whole sum realized being spent in decorating the churches of the town, and giving a magnificent display of fireworks on the night of the festival of Nuestra Señora de ——."

There is another custom in Untrodden Spain chiefly to be found in the least-known towns of Andalucia. It is exactly similar to an Irish wake.

A little child has died, and is to be buried. The friends, fellow-workmen, neighbours, all come to the house where the little one lies, gaily decked out with flowers and tinsel, in its white flimsy coffin. There is music and dancing, there is eating and drinking. The mother is in the room, and receives, not sympathy, but congratulations, and at last, with joy, the little one, thus early delivered from the "waves of this troublesome world," is followed to its grave by the long and lively train of friends and followers.

It should here be added, that there is a peculiar sweet cake made specially for these funeral feasts.

However much the idea of festivity at such a season may grate upon some deeply sensitive minds, it must be acknowledged that this modest expression of joy is more in accordance with the sentiments of the English Church, expressed in her magnificent funeral service, than are the hushed voices, and darkened room, and mock tears, so familiar to us at the funeral of an English innocent.

The Spanish mother, tender-hearted and loving as she is, oftentimes, when spoken to sympathetically about the loss of her darling, will say that "It is better for the little one, and that, therefore, it behoves her not to repine;" or she will say, "It may be it is taken away from the evil to come." And by such speeches the exquisite German poem (Andersen's) has often been vividly brought before my mind, where a German mother, overcome with grief at the loss of her darling, is brought to resignation and calmness by the guardian angel of the little child placing before her tearful and bewildered gaze the book of what that child's life would have been had it been spared.

> "Then she saw her child, her heart's dear treasure,
>   Fated not to joy and peace, alas!
>   Fated, not to know a pure life's pleasure,
>   But through want, and sin, and shame to pass!
>
> "Then the mother knew her human blindness,
>   And, even through her tears, she brightly smiled:
> 'Blest,' she said, 'be God, who in His kindness
>   Bore from earth, and sin, and woe, my child!'"

I quote from the beautiful rendering of Mr. W. C. Bennett.

Speaking of Spanish mothers' feeling, it may not be out of place here to mention a most touching and pathetic epithet applied by some of them (of the lowest rank) to the life of one who has missed his mark in the world, and lain down in sorrow. Of such a one they say, "It was a broken life."

A beautiful sight, connected with the feasts of the Church, may often be witnessed on the eve of the feast in some of the least-known towns. You will be stumbling along the dark, unpaved streets in some dim-lit town, and suddenly you will see a little knot of men and women, of the poorest class, gathered under the oil-lamp that hangs over the crumbling door of some tiny chapel. You will hear, ever and anon, a little whir of murmuring voices, uttering in unison the same response. Look in, and on the right side of the small, old-fashioned altar, beautifully lit with wax candles, will be seen five or six young women kneeling two and two. Their heads are lowly bowed, their hands are clasped in prayer. In front of the altar three priests are praying, in Latin, that the sins of these five penitents, for such they are, may be pardoned and forgotten.

Standing out in marked contrast with the darkness, profanity, and bustle of the streets without, this little scene has much the same effect on one as the coming upon some moss-grown, crumbling cross, or the ruins of some ancient chapel, in the wilds of the Devonshire or Cornwall seaboard. It calms the spirit, it gives the too-weary mind a moment's repose, it lifts the heart awhile to heaven, and thought of better things.

In the town from which I write, a long succession of fairs commences in August, and hardly dies out until September has made its acquaintance. The town is roughness itself. The thermometer in the shade stands at 102° at mid-day! All the "seeing the fair," then, must be done either before 8 A.M. or after 5 P.M., and, indeed, both in fair times and in ordinary times, those are the hours when most of the business is done. From 5 A.M. to 7 A.M. more money probably changes hands than during the whole afterpart of the day.

The first fair, lasting one week, and held annually, is the Jarra Fair, or, as it is more commonly, but less correctly styled, the Jarro Fair. Be it remembered that, in Andalucia, the one great need of rich and poor—the one luxury which all can and will have—is pure, cold spring water. Now, owing to the intense heat, water kept in any glass or common crockery vessel grows tepid and unpalatable; and, therefore, the whole of the water for drinking purposes is kept in the light-coloured, porous Andujar jarras, or small pitchers. These being porous, a free evaporation is continually going on, and the dish in which they stand is filled with the water that filters through their porous sides. Just on the same principle, I suppose, that to perspire freely cools the blood, so the constant filtration through the sides of these vessels keeps the water within as cold as snow on the hottest day. The blessing of these jarras can only be known by experience, and I can only wonder that some enterprising spirit has not long since taken a cargo to England for use during the summer months.

These jarras are brought in huge cases, filled with straw, on the back of mule or donkey, some millions being annually sold at the fair. In shape, they are not only useful, but frequently most graceful, being made after the style of the old Roman and Etruscan pottery-ware. They vary in price, according to size, style, and workmanship, from one penny up to four or five shillings. Some are made to stand as ornaments upon the table of Dives; some can be slung behind the cart of the farmer; some can be carried, by a tiny handle, by the miner on his way to work. The sight, when all adown one whole long street the ground is covered with these jarras, in piles five feet high, of every size and shape, is a most striking one. All the housewives of the pueblo are here, wrangling about prices, and laying in their store of jarras for twelve months (for, remember, no jarras, no jewellery, no books, can be bought in this town until the fairs come again). We will say it is night; tiny oil-lamps, stuck here and there among the jarras, yield their dim light. There is no footfall heard, although thousands are thronging the street, for it is covered deep with chaff and straw; every now and then you see a space cleared, and, by the lurid glare of a fire on the ground, you see a cauldron of hissing hot oil, and three women and a man are plunging snake-like forms of flour and oil into the oil. These are the makers of the famous oil-cakes, called "bunuelos," which are in great demand at early morn and late evening. They are eaten hot, and, although rich and oily, are far from being unpalatable. Only look at that eager crowd of poor men and women waiting until the last made hissing batch of bunuelos has sufficiently cooled to allow of its being handled!

But, hark! one would hardly believe, in this town, secluded as it is, that at this late hour (for it is already past ten o'clock) one hears the whistle of an engine, and its snort and scream. Yet so it is. It comes from yonder dark entrance, from which falls one lurid strip of light on some grimed and eager faces. You push your way in, and are in the presence of gambling by steam!

Gambling surely has never before been brought to such rude perfection. Here is the engine, snorting and panting; in front stands the table, duly numbered, and parted into little plots. The gambling is conducted on this wise. A man chooses his favourite number on the table, and deposits on it whatever stake he purposes to risk; four or five balls are thrown into a sort of funnel by the master of the ceremonies, and one is instantly shot out upon the table, with a shrill scream, by the power of the engine. If it be our hero's number borne upon the ball, he stands to win, whatever it be, that number of the piece of money he staked. The table is only numbered up to seven, so that a man staking a real can never win more than seven like pieces.

It was, when I saw it, a striking sight, this old, barn-like room, its screaming engine, its crowd of eager gamblers, chiefly miners, peasants, olive-dressers, and artisans of the lowest class.

Gambling and cruelty to animals are two of the vices sucked in with mother's milk in this country. The little child of three years old is led by its mother to try its luck for a cake, chavo in hand (the chavo is half a farthing), on the street rouletta-table!

Immediately that the "Jug-Fair," as the English will persist in calling it, instead of by its own graceful title, "Feria de Jarras," is concluded (it lasts about a week), commences the fair general. The streets are covered over with a rough awning, and the booths are making a gorgeous show. The wholesale saddler, the wholesale jeweller, the knife-seller, the gun-maker, all have set up their stores, under booths of wood-work and canvas, or in some room of a private house or shop rented for the fair time, and a large amount of money changes hands. The stalls really make a beautiful show, and articles (as jewellery) of the value of twenty and even twenty-five pounds are bought. In fact, the whole town takes holiday, has saved up its money, and lays up a store of goods for the year. And, *mirabile dictu!* books can actually be bought!

To the general fair succeeds the horse, mule, bullock, and donkey fair. It is held on a sandy common outside the town walls, man and beast alike lying upon the ground, or under some rudely-constructed tent, for the night—no great hardship in this rainless clime.

Here you will see mules of enormous height; indeed, they make a far finer show than does the horse-flesh. Here, too, you will be assailed by the musical voice, deep-brown face, and outstretched hand of the wandering gitana (gipsy), come from the steppes of her barren La Mancha, eager to cull a few pesetas by telling you your *suerte*, or fortune. Marvellous is the accuracy with which these women will tell you, positively, facts with which human agency could hardly have supplied them. Indeed, how they find out what they say is, and ever will be, a marvel and a mystery to me.

But the feature that strikes me most in the fairs is the contentment, nay, the delight of the Spaniards, rich and poor, with a little. This contentedness of spirit is one of the brightest spots in their character. See the teeming crowds of rich, and poor, and middle-class, passing and re-passing each other in the gorgeous, sheltered street! All are sober, kindly, willing to be pleased, very courteous. The nobleman, from his "palacio," can stop and congratulate his grocer on having just secured his pretty bride, and married her civilly as well as ecclesiastically,—thus escaping, possibly, some conscription to come. There is no jostling, no rudeness, no pride of place!

By the way, my mention, just above, of a palacio may convey a very erroneous idea of the dwelling-houses so styled. The old-fashioned palacio is well worthy of description. It is still found in the old townships of the interior.

A long, low building, of one story; the walls made

of huge lumps of stone, and of enormous thickness; the floor of the rooms raised about two feet above the ground; five huge windows, with massive iron gratings, along either side. Such is the palacio, beheld from without. Enter it, and you will find that the house consists of very large rooms, opening, with folding-doors, one into the other,—the dining-room into the drawing-room, and the drawing-room into the bed-room, and so on. The rooms are high and airy, but always kept darkened. Above the ceiling is the camera, or granary, and (poor things!) one or two rooms for the female servants, the men-servants sleeping in the rooms above the olive-press! On one side, the windows open into the street, on the other, into a tiny garden, with luxuriant grape-vines and orange-trees. At the end of the little paved garden (for no grass grows in Andalucia) stand the olive-yard and olive-presses, the tanks of water, and the lofty stables. Such is the Spanish palace, of a type now fast going out! Perhaps mention should be made of the kitchen, where the ancient cook sits, in a room without ornament of any sort or kind, tending listlessly her charcoal fire on the hearth, and listening to the monotonous "Pip-pip-it, Pip-pip-it" of the quails, of which little cages hang all round the room; and also the "sunken room," as it is called, a room without a window, its floor sunk some three feet below the rest of the flooring, devoted entirely to the use of the mistress of the house in the burning, scorching heat and glare of the summer.

And now, as we leave my lady's dark and dismal, but, in summer, delightful bed-chamber, let us follow the crowd that is streaming on towards the Plaza de Toros, or bull-ring.

The bull-fight forms a prominent part in the programme of the fair's delights. Without it no fair were perfect. So often has this wretched sport been described (and so accurately, by an enthusiast of great experience, in these very volumes), that I shall say but little of it. But, to see all that was to be seen, I entered the bull-ring.

Unquestionably, the red, gold, blue, and green, gold-spangled dresses of the several orders of bull-fighters, trailing their graceful scarfs about the dusty arena,—the tiers of thousands of bright dresses and eager faces, one above the other,—the whirling of countless fans,—the enlivening strains of music,—the serried line of lancers, or cuirassiers, in front of the alcalde's stall, all seen beneath a glowing August sun, —have a most exhilarating, exciting effect.

But the first scene completely sickened me. The horses were posted,—weedy, wretched screws, valued at £3 a piece, and fit only for the knacker's-yard; each poor animal was blindfolded, the gates opened, the bull blundered into the arena. At last he fixed upon the weedy grey mare which stood just beneath me. The poor brute, blindfolded and tightly reined in, tried to move as the bull closed with it; in a moment his horns were deep in the cartilage of the front leg, and the animal was hoisted into the air. Then the bull was pulled off, and a crimson stream flowed down the poor brute's weedy, white, tottering legs. Two men thrashed it into the middle of the arena; the bull charged it again, tearing its bowels out to the length of two feet, throwing man and horse to the ground, and then, with crimsoned horns and forehead, rushing madly at another horse. A more disgusting exhibition I never have witnessed than the first act in the bull-fight.

In the second act, when the horses have been killed and dragged out, and the sand sprinkled over their blood, there is a real trial of skill, and real feats of surprising courage and agility are performed by the bull-fighters. But the bull-fight has degenerated; and, whereas formerly the great aim was to bring powerful and valuable horses into the ring, and to save them, by skilful horsemanship, from hurt or harm, now the savage joy seems to centre in seeing the horse—man's truest and noblest friend in the dumb creation—tortured, beaten, and dying, before the eyes of those whom all his life he has served, a lingering and cruel death. Commend me to shooting, hunting, fishing, but never again will I see the bull-fight!*

From the glitter and noise of the bull-ring we may wend our way at eve to some of the back-streets of our town, and gain admittance to a little house, whence comes the tinkling of the light guitar. Ask some of the rough and humble, but joyous and kindly women, to show you three of the dances of the lowest orders in Andalucia, and, although convulsed with laughter, they will do so. Dances rougher or more curious were most surely never conceived! Here is one (wholly unknown, I believe), called "El pimplon." It is danced (?) by two women. Each one squats upon the floor at one end of the room; then they commence jumping past one another, and back again, clapping their hands, and singing "Muncho trabajo, Muncho trabajo" (much labour), as fast as

* By far the best account of a bull-fight that I have seen, is that contained in the *Daily News* of September 11th or 12th, 1874, from the Madrid Correspondent of that journal.

they can, unassisted by the hands, and preserving their sitting posture. The exercise is fatiguing, especially when the bystanders are roaring with laughter at their frog-like movements; the perspiration pours down their bronzed faces, but it is a *point d'honneur* not to be the first to give in!

That dance finished, and a drop of common wine, strongly smelling of the pig-skin, handed round, they will commence a dance still more extraordinary and graceless. It is called "Los manjos de cinquo gidos," in the rude *patois* of La Mancha. Each woman clasps her clothes firmly beneath her feet with her hands, which are thus fully occupied, and, for decency's sake, cannot be moved. She then sits like a sack on the floor, gives a kind of shuffling jump, and rolls over on her back. She cannot, for decency's sake, move her hands, and so has a hard task, wherein consists all the fun of this extraordinary dance, to recover (literally) her seat! The last dance is called "El negrito." It is very similar to the "Fandango," the man and woman standing opposite to one another, holding up the fists, and dancing back to back and face to face, singing some words of love.

Haply, if you go to these back-streets and bye-streets at fair-time, you will see a black-eyed damsel daintily present some adoring swain with a small *calavaso*, or pumpkin. This is a privilege of the fair sex, and is a polite way of telling some lover that his attentions are no longer acceptable!

But rough, rude, and primitive as are the fairs in the secluded townships of the interior, it must not be imagined that they are at all so in the large towns, as Sevilla or Cadiz. At Sevilla the fair is, I am told, simply beautiful; and at Cadiz the August fair is, as

I can testify from personal observation, well worth a visit to that cheerful, joyous, sea-girt town to see.

It is held on the long Alameda, called "Las Delicias," and is only in its beauty at night. On one side of the long and imposing array of stalls, &c., the waters of the blue Atlantic are for ever lapping the stones. On the other side rises an avenue of trees and the fine barracks of the garrison.

Here, at night, for fourteen or fifteen days, is seen a truly delightful sight. Festoons of lamps of every size, shape, and colour, extending, perhaps, for nearly a quarter of a mile, meet the eye,—there were eleven thousand at the fair I witnessed; open-air theatres, bands of military music, stalls of all that is gay and sparkling, extended along the sea-wall; thousands of people wandered up and down, forgetting troubles, enjoying the cool sea-breeze from nine to twelve o'clock P.M., listening to sweet music discoursed by the three military bands, while their children danced to the strains upon platforms raised here and there. The lord met the peasant and the peasant the lord on equal terms here. There were no wine-shops, and no drunkenness was seen, the potations being chiefly ices and light "refrescos"!

And now I will conclude, with a few characteristic anecdotes of the autumn of 1874, what, I trust, has been a bright and joyous chapter for my readers. Although little felt at such large towns as Cadiz or Sevilla, yet the severe conscription, or "quinta," as it is called, put a damper on our last autumn fair in the interior.

Just before the fair, in August, 1874, the conscription was proclaimed. Men married by the Church only, and not by the civil authorities (the only exceptions being those who supported an aged parent), up to the age of thirty-four years, were liable to be drawn, the price of exemption being fixed at £50.

To my town, resistance to this severe, but, possibly, needful decree, being anticipated, came the Carbineros, to keep order. Their dark, serried line was drawn up daily outside the room where the lots were being drawn. One man, under the influence of liquor, said, while the lots were being drawn, "What babies you are to stand this!" and endeavoured to create a disturbance. The Carbineros were almost about to fire; but suddenly one of their officers appeared on the scene, a stout cudgel in his hand. He administered a sound thrashing, there and then, to the culprit, and sent him off to prison—so roughly are the lower classes threaped down and ill used at will by the Government officials in Spain at the present day!

This last quinta was badly arranged. Consumptive men, unfit for service, were drawn, and had to pay the £50. Men long since dead were drawn, and actually called for. In one case, the officers went to a house, and said, "Who is the master of this house?" On which the man's wife, a regular virago, said (and very truly), "I am." So she, too, was drawn!

Great dissatisfaction prevailed at this severe conscription. Many fled to the Sierra, saying, "If shoot we must, let us shoot boars, and not brothers." Others said, "If we are sent to the North, leaving our families, we will fire in the air!"

But, as a general rule, the poor Spaniards take all these things with singular complacency, and only a short time since I sat until twelve o'clock at night beside a young, cheerful-looking miner, who was composedly smoking his cigarette with me in a neighbour's house, and listening to a blind man's guitar. As we parted he said, " For the last time, señor, we meet ; at daybreak to-morrow I join the Madrid garrison. I am a conscript."

" And your four babes, and your wife ?" said I.

" I leave them to God's care ; it is His will, señor. Adios !"

CHAPTER VII.

ROBBERS OF THE SIERRA.

ONE morning my duties led me up to a mine some three miles distant from home. The September sun was then shedding down its fierce, leave-taking rays, literally scorching man, and beast, and tree, and parching the dusty, rock-strewn roads. Travelling, especially on foot, at mid-day was impossible, so I resolved to start at daybreak, and take breakfast at the mine.

While sitting in the darkened room of one of the mining captains, we were surprised by a grey beard suddenly appearing through the window, almost encircled, Bacchus-like, by the tendrils of the vine that trailed in profusion over it, and by an excited and quavering voice announcing that "Four men were lying in wait in the olives, and intended relieving some Englishman of his impedimenta on his way home."

The excellent doctor had just, on his Andalucian steed, passed by on his morning rounds, distributing his aid and skill or word of kindly sympathy at every lonely mine. For a wonder, his servant was not with him. I, too, had come up without Juan, my faithful little armed guard.

Unto which of us two did this startling message apply? I was safe, for I had, fortunately, not left the mine; but the doctor—alas! the kind, good, excellent doctor—had gone.

At this moment, the black, bead-like eyes and sturdy little figure of Juan appeared at the door. He had heard of my starting alone, and had (with that real willingness to serve and help which forms the brightest spot in the kindly Spanish character) ridden up, with his trusty escopeta, to guard me home. We instantly despatched Juan to stop the doctor, if possible, and bid him wait for a guard. As ill luck would have it, Juan, though mounted, and with his Moorish gun slung at his saddle-bow, had forgotten, in his hurry, his badge, the brass-plate carried on the breast, bearing the name of the mine of which he is the guardian. Now, with his badge, any one would have trusted Juan, but, without that official badge, it must be owned that Juan looked rather a suspicious character.

No wonder, then, that when Juan rode up neck-and-neck with the doctor, and bade him "halt," the latter thought he had evil intentions. But when, further, Juan imperatively demanded that he should follow him, for safety's sake, the doctor absolutely believed he was going to be led into an ambuscade, and, with a loud "Caramba, hombre," rode straight away from his would-be guardian.

A Spaniard loves nothing so well as a joke, and when Juan appeared among us at our breakfast-table, and related how he had been taken for the robber, he could scarcely tell his tale for laughing. Indeed, this recklessness of human life, this indifference to the danger of a brother-man, when once the danger really presents itself, seems to be part and parcel of the character of the Spaniard of to-day.

Here were four violent men lying in wait,—men who, probably, had often committed deeds of violence before this,—men, probably, driven out from the haunts of their fellows either for their crimes, or who, perhaps, had left their several pueblos, or townships, in order to evade the quinta, or conscription; lying in wait in order to rob, and possibly ill treat, some hapless man walking home alone,—and yet the little Spanish guard could actually roar with laughter while his friend went on into danger!

Two guards, armed to the teeth, accompanied me home on that day. One was Juan, who observed, with a sardonic smile, that "his escopeta alone was sufficient for any four olive-lurkers"; the other, a man noted for his fearlessness in disarming fighting-men of their naked knives.

As we walked, we scanned the glades of dusky olives far and wide. Not one soul did we see or meet, save one poor man and woman, sweltering along behind their laden donkey, returning, with the provisions for a week, from the nearest town. The woman, looking at our arms, turned pale, put up her brown withered hands, and, pointing to her tiny lodge on the slope of the olive-clad hill, said, "Turn in, caballero, turn in hither, I pray thee, and take a draught of Val-de-Peñas for your journey." I thanked her, and declined, and she dismissed us with the usual benison, "Vaya usted con Dios, y con la Virgen."

The olive-groves, as they are, have no claim at all to be called groves. They offer no shelter from the sun, no concealment at all. They are simply slopes, planted with regular rows, about ten or more yards apart, of small, stunted trees, and, with a good glass, a figure lying in the olives, unless beneath the shelter of the stone-walls which intersect them, would be seen at a considerable distance.

These four men, who would have robbed any hapless solitary stranger, were simple thieves, homeless fellows, living an out-of-door life, rifling hen-roosts, or robbing road-side ventas. They are not considered caballeros, or gentlemen, while the real bandits or robbers of the Sierra are admired, rather than disliked, by the Spanish peasantry, and considered rather in the light of heroes than otherwise.

Of such was composed the band of men who took captive an Englishman, very lately, in the neighbourhood of the mining town of La Carolina, in some of the wild and wooded passes that abut upon the Sierra Morena, where the stag and wild boar, and flashing trout-stream, overhung by ilex and chaparro, offer plenty of sport but little safety for the sportsman.

A minute account of this gentleman's capture appeared, from his own pen, in the *Times*, shortly after his release, on July 13th, 1874. It shall be here, in part, reprinted, together with the letters of the brigands demanding ransom for him, which are herewith appended, literally translated.

Here is Mr. Haselden's account of his capture :—

" On the 3rd inst. I started on horseback from these mines to proceed to Carolina, accompanied by my foreman. After a ride of two miles along a narrow path, surrounded by thick bushes and brushwood, two men, armed with Remington carbines, suddenly stepped out into the path four yards in front of me, and ordered me to dismount. My attendant, who carried a gun, found himself attacked in the same way by three others. Seeing resistance was useless, we dismounted. They searched us for arms, and took away our watches, which they eventually returned. They then led the way to a ravine, where the brushwood effectually concealed us. I was politely told it was only a question of ransom. I answered that I supposed so, but desired to know who was the chief of the band, as I did not wish to treat with all of them. On this, one of them told me he and another were the leaders. He then gave me a letter to read, in which they had fixed my ransom at £40,000. In this letter my brothers were repeatedly informed that I should be murdered if their request was not attended to. They also gave directions about sending the money. It was to be carried by a man dressed in black, with a white hat, and a red handkerchief in his hand. The man was to be mounted on a white mule. He was to go without arms and alone, unless he required a guide. The route was exactly laid down, with injunctions only to travel from sunrise to sunset. In case he should be robbed by other thieves, my brothers were to replace the money or I should be shot. I observed it was useless asking for such a sum—that we could not raise it. They, however, requested me to sign the letter, which I did. They ordered my foreman to take the letter to my relatives at Linares, entrusting him with our two horses, which were only in their way."

The party continued travelling all that day and night, their prisoner on a donkey, and they on foot; only resting for a short time on two occasions. On the road they fired three shots at a sportsman about three hundred yards off, who did not answer when called, fortunately without hitting him.

" We arrived at seven o'clock in the morning at the

place where they kept me all the time I was their prisoner. They formed a kind of hut by clearing a space of brushwood, joining the top branches, and covering them with more brushwood. The heat during the nine days I remained there was anything but agreeable. My bed consisted of brushwood and a manta, a kind of rug. They brought food, wine, and tobacco regularly. I was only threatened the first day, probably with the intention of making me write letters urging my brothers to send my ransom as soon as possible. This I refused to do, and seeing that their threats were useless they abandoned this system, and told me they did not intend to hurt me—that they were sorry to be obliged to place me under such restraint. During my captivity I was guarded by four of the robbers. One of the men who took me, and two others who showed themselves the next day, went forwards to secure the money. My guards were very cautious; they never put down a rifle without first withdrawing the cartridge. Most of the brigands appeared to be men who had not worked for some time back. Several of them expressed themselves well, although their chief subject of conversation referred to their former exploits and to the circumstances which had led them to adopt this mode of life. They disapproved of capital punishment. One of them said he was giving a good education to his son, and that if he thought he would take to his father's profession he would shoot him."

On the 13th, those who had been waiting for the ransom returned. Mr. Haselden then heard he was free, but was only allowed to start on his way back in the evening.

"The chief then gave me £6, saying I might require it on the road—that it would not be right for a caballero to go about without a penny. With Spanish politeness he excused himself for having detained me, and hoped I should find all my friends well at home. Not to be behindhand, I expressed the hope that the money would benefit them, 'que les aproveche a ustedes e dinero.' To one of them, a Malagueno, I said, 'Hasta otra vista.' He answered, 'Yes, but under less damnable circumstances.' The chief then informed me that henceforth I might travel about those mountains with safety, as they would be the first to take care no other band should molest me. I then mounted the mule, and, accompanied by one of the brigands, rode across the country for several hours. At midnight, on reaching a path which he said would lead to a house, he left me. About half-an-hour later I came upon some woodcutters, with whom I spent the rest of the night. Next morning one of them guided me to our mine, and thence I proceeded to Linares, where I arrived on the evening of the 13th. I then first learned the amount of the ransom sent—namely, £6,000. My relatives in Linares were nine days without hearing directly from me, with alternate hopes and fears, according to the different reports that went about the place, but without being certain whether I was alive or not."

The following is a word-for-word translation of the first letter sent by the bandits to Mr. Haselden's brothers, after being first submitted to him for perusal on the day of his capture, and signed by him. It runs thus:—

"Your existence depends upon four millions of reals, for we know very well that your capital amounts to more than one hundred millions of reals, and so, even if you give us this sum named, you will still have sufficient for your sustenance and that of your family; and this is done so as not to embarrass your capital. Now, you have surely heard of Chico de Portero, of the city of Ciudad Real, who was simply quartered because his parents and the authorities did not send the amount we asked for. Well, we shall treat you in like manner, if you (?) do not send the amount asked for. If you choose to inform the civil or military authorities, it is a matter of no moment to us, but you will pay for it with your head! Two courses are thus open to you, either to give the required money or to lose your life, and, in this last case, we shall commit an outrageous deed with you—one that will serve as an example for the future. The money must all be sent in gold, without sign or mark, for, if mark or sign be found upon the gold pieces, you shall forfeit your life. Adios."

Particulars of the route by which the money is to be sent.

"The conductor of the moneys sent must be a person in your family's full confidence. He must be dressed wholly in black, with a white hat; in his hand he must carry a red handkerchief, and seem as though he were wiping the sweat from his brow; and he must be mounted on a white mule. He must go, first, from Linares to Guarraman, then to Cuesta, to Cuesta del Carreton, Venta de Robledo, Huerteruelas, Molina de las Tuntas, Las Azeas," &c. (here follows a string of a dozen small hamlets), "and, lastly, to Arrobas. If we do not come forward to meet him on his road, he must return by precisely the same road. Whenever he does not know the road, he is free to take a guide from one of the villages, without, however, disclosing the object of his journey. He must ride from rise to set of sun. Where the setting sun overtakes him, there must he halt and pass the night, whether it be near a town or in the open campo, nor must he stay his footsteps at any of the pueblos (villages) above mentioned. If any one but ourselves should get hold of the money he bears, it will cost you (?) double the amount, or you will be shot. Therefore, it is to your interest to keep the affair secret, and not allow any one to accompany your messenger. If you do transgress these rules, you will be shot."

The use of the expression, "you will be shot," in a letter addressed to the family, must be explained in this way, namely, that the letter was, as it were, written to the unhappy captive, he being forced to sign and address it to his family, as though it were a letter from himself!

The letter was received, and a sum close upon £900 in gold was at once transmitted to these men. That sum, however, proved wholly insufficient to obtain the release of the unhappy captive. The only answer it elicited was the following, hastily written in pencil on a scrap of paper. The robbers, however, in it lowered their demand, as will be seen, from £40,000 to £10,000.

Second Letter of the Brigands.

"Received 100,000 reals, with which we can do nothing. If within five days we do not receive one million reals, be it known unto you that your beloved brother will be shot."

After eleven days' captivity the brigands accepted

the sum of £6,000, and Mr. Haselden was restored to his home and friends.

It will be asked, who are these robbers, and what steps were taken by the Spanish Government to capture them?

In answer to the first, reference may be made to another chapter in this book, where some account is given of them. They are sometimes men proscribed for political offences, who take their gun to the mountains when an adverse party comes into office, returning to the haunts of civilization when their own party is again in the ascendant. Oftentimes, again, they are men who have escaped from prison; still more often, men who have been pardoned (after lying for months, perhaps, under sentence of death) by one Government, but, with the advent of another, know well that their pardon will be cancelled. Many are convicts, who were released, as at Cartagena, by the Communists; some, again, have taken to the Sierra in order to avoid serving as soldiers against the Carlists. And, as regards the steps taken by the Government, the following may be said. Family influence or money will oftentimes procure a prisoner's release; and so, although one of this band was undoubtedly captured and confined for a night, yet ere morning he had escaped; indeed, when taken by the volunteers of the hill villages, he chatted gaily with them on his road to prison, and actually, a goat being killed on the march, he was appointed to cook the feast! No doubt his practice in the Sierra enabled him to perform his duty well.

CHAPTER VIII.

SOCIAL STATE OF THE HEART OF ANDALUCIA.

THE reader will, ere this, have formed for himself, from the foregoing pages, some estimate of the condition of the country which the writer has made his study. In this chapter it is proposed to give a bird's-eye view of the social state of the wilds of Andalucia.

Let me commence with the laws, and those who break them. The laws of Spain, theoretically, the laws as they are written, are excellent and most elaborate; the laws practically and in working are bad.

In each town of importance there are three administrators of justice at the present moment: the alcalde, or chief magistrate, and the sub-alcaldes; the juez, or judge of the district; and (in Spain of to-day) the military governor of the province, and his sub-governors. The office of the alcalde is something partaking of the nature of mayor and corporation, sheriff, and Inspector of Education and Nuisances. The alcalde is elected each year, or oftener, by the votes of the township. He may be a gentleman, or a tradesman, or some one of even lower grade. Generally there are two alcaldes and two assistant-alcaldes. The alcalde receives all the taxes of the town, and he is bound, out of this revenue, to keep the roads in good repair, to preserve public order, to pay for schools, and, generally, to look after the well-being of the pueblo which has elected him. He walks about the town, followed by a municipal guard, sword trailing behind him, his note-book in hand, and spies out all that is going wrong. But, alas! of the thousands or hundreds of pounds that find their way into the alcalde's strong-box, only a small portion, too often, is used for its proper purposes. The alcalde's office is unpaid, yet why are men so anxious for it, and why does many an alcalde, who was nearly penniless when elected, resign his office, after a couple of years, with money enough to start a *café* or build a dozen houses?

Then there is the judge of the town; the judge of the larger town adjoining it; the regent, or head of all the judges of the province; and, finally, the judge, or president of the nation, at Madrid. The first of these is called the juez municipal; the next, juez de primera instancia; the third, the regent; the fourth, the president of the nation.

The office of the judge is unpaid, save by fees, on a fixed scale, and (must I say it?) bribes. Civil and criminal cases, as a rule, are tried before the same judge. The first hearing is before the municipal judge. If it be a matter of too great importance, he sends it to the next above him, and so on.

Castelar has introduced, by a late edict, the trial of civil cases before a jury of twelve men. Before his edict, a prisoner, or claimant, however, might claim this as a privilege. The blots in the Spanish administration of justice are great indeed: a judge may constantly be bribed. Thus, in one case that I knew, the judge, a man of strict integrity, refused a bribe of £70; the case went to the higher court, and there the judge accepted it, and gave a verdict accordingly.

Here is a case illustrative of the ludicrous as well as the pernicious side of this system of bribery.

A lawyer, in my own pueblo, was, according to an old and barbarous law, condemned to have his right hand cut off for forgery. He escaped, being a man of property, by paying a bribe of £500 to the judge for the time being. Of course, however, his sentence was left recorded on the official list, and he received no formal acquittal; in fact, he walked about under a sentence of the loss of his right hand.

Another judge soon succeeded the first, and, being a strict disciplinarian, as most of them are for six months, finding the sentence against the unhappy lawyer still "recorded on the books," and seeing the man walking about with *two* hands, he proceeded to order execution. The poor lawyer drew out another £500, and proffered it once more to his foe: it was accepted, and he was free; but the sentence still stood recorded on the books.

Judge succeeded to judge, and each, in his turn, accepted the bribe. The lawyer's whole capital is now gone in bribes, and, when the next judge comes, next year, he will most surely lose the long-fought-for right hand! This story is given on the authority of a friend, but has not yet been verified by the author.

Another blot in the administration of Spanish law is the system of constant remands. You bring a prisoner into court, you appear against him; the judge, for no earthly reason, remands the man. Six months after you receive a summons to attend the court: the same weary routine of identification, &c., is gone through, and the judge says,—" You are remanded again." The poor, pallid wretch, guilty or not guilty, is carried back to the same lousy, filthy den called a prison, there to languish for another six months.

A third blot in Spanish justice is in the conduct of the lower officials. If they find a man drunk and incapable, they are allowed to beat him to a certain extent. This power they abuse in the vilest manner. A poor miner whom I knew (a teetotaller, by the way) was subject to fits. One night he was seized with one, and fell down in the street. The municipal guards came up, raised up his head, and beat him so cruelly with the scabbards of their swords, that one arm was broken. They took him to the hospital, and the doctor, a humane man, seeing what was really the state of the case, informed against the two municipales for " exceeding their duty." The judge, however, or alcalde, acquitted them both!

These municipal guards, who wear a sort of uniform, and always may be seen in the market-place, on the look out for a disturbance, &c., are a cross between an English policeman and a sheriff's officer or bailiff, and, consequently, they are thoroughly hated. A Spanish girl will, jestingly, say, "If I must marry either a butcher or a municipal guard, I think I would elect the former." And, be it remembered, that to marry into a butcher's family even is a terrible disgrace.

The civil guards, too, noble-hearted fellows as they are, are somewhat severe. Indeed, the whole principle on which the Spanish legal officials carry on their profession is this, that every culprit is a brute beast, a mad dog, and to be treated accordingly.

Here is an instance. A man (a miner) got excited with drink, and stabbed two men in the street. The civil guards, rifle in hand, pursued him, and ran him to ground in a courtyard. The guard who came up first presented his rifle at the man's head, and said,— "Give yourself up, or I fire."—"Never," was the answer; and in a moment the fellow's brains were scattered all over the patio!

Here is another instance. In other days the order, "Take special care that they don't escape," meant "Kill your prisoners on the road." One batch of convicts (political prisoners), on hearing this order given to the civil guards, said, through their spokesman, "Please shackle both our hands and feet, that you may have no excuse for shooting us."

Another blot upon the Spanish administration of justice is the proviso that every one who kills or maims another, even if the deed be a just one, and simply done in self-defence, shall suffer a certain term of imprisonment.

Here is an instance which happened to a mining agent, a personal friend of the writer's. A miner of his own mine conceived that Mr. H. had insulted him, and rushed at him with a knife. Mr. H., who was unarmed, rushed away, and met the guard of the mine, gun on shoulder. Breathless, he seized the gun, the guard held it doggedly. Up came the would-be assassin, and the guard knocked him off, and protected Mr. H. On being asked why he so acted, he said,—"If you had had a fair fight with gun or knife, all well; you both had, may be, gone to glory. But if you had shot him, you would have had two things, remorse and prison."

From the administration of justice, to those who come within the pale of the law, the transition is an easy one. A more lawless, desperate set than those who, to evade the law's sentence, or to escape being drawn at the conscriptions, betake themselves to the sierras, or mountain fastnesses, and there win a precarious existence by hunting, robbing, and other kindred pursuits, it would be hard to find. These denizens of the Sierra Morena are quite a race of themselves. Some are "ladros factiosos," or political robbers; some "partidos," which is much the same thing; some are miners and others who have committed murder; some are those who (to use their own phrase), "if they must shoot at all, prefer shooting deer to Carlistas"; some are common thieves and robbers. These men, many of them, own a kind of wild allegiance to some robber-chieftain, at whose bidding they will carry off any rich man, handing most of the ransom-money to their chieftains. They cannot be taken, owing to the thick brushwood, the wild precipices and crags, the caverns, and the wide extent of their mountain-home. Now and then, riding in the Sierra, you will see a man, quite like a savage and half-naked, who will fly like hunted hind at the approach of another human being, and be lost in the brushwood in a moment. Red-deer, quails, foxes, badgers, and partridges are plentiful, and a few bears, and these men are first-rate shots; so that they have enough meat, while the charcoal-burners and chicken-sellers from the hill-villages supply them with tobacco and skins of red wine.

Oftentimes, when these men get an exceptionally "good haul," they will get clothes, rig themselves out like caballeros, and take train to Seville or Madrid, to enjoy themselves, and then return to the hills, or stay in Madrid to become politicians!

Some of them are men of some attainments and

education, who, for political offences, have been outlawed. These, if their favourite Government should come into power, would emerge at once from their hiding-place, and accept office!

Sometimes these outlaws may be seen "groping for fish," wherewith to vary their diet. They descend to the plains, strip naked, and wade in the shallows of the river, putting a wary hand under every rock and boulder. One man stands on the bank, his fire lit, his frying-pan hard by, ready to cook the fish. Women, too, stand idly gazing, unshocked at these naked figures, until a few fine but coarse barbel are caught, when all sit down to the feast. They catch the barbel by the gills, and, as soon as caught, put his head into their mouths to kill him with a bite.

In the winter, the large shooting-parties of Spaniards and Englishmen who seek the Sierra for red-deer and large game (the caza mayor), often come across these wild banditti, and, if they fancy themselves likely to be over-matched, they strike tent at midnight, and make good their retreat to the nearest town. These shooting-parties generally consist of at least fifty men, all well armed.

"A Spanish prison," so says a Spanish *refran*, "is not a vineyard." Once inside its filthy walls, and manacled, you may never see daylight again, or you may be despatched to Cuba (if a political prisoner), or, in rare cases, you may be shot in the market-place of the town wherein your offence was committed. The prison diet is very coarse; its eternal round consists of the coarsest oil, beans, peas, potatoes, and rice, all given in homœopathic doses. No bed, save what you supply yourself, is allowed you. In winter's cold and summer's heat you lie manacled, chained to the filthy stone floor of the dungeon. Your companions are, usually, some eight or nine in number: their conversation is the filthiest, their habits the vilest. "This floor is harder than the feet of Christ," is their common blasphemy!

In some places, the prisoners are employed in constructing or repairing the Government roads of the first, second, or third class. At such times they may be seen, working in the full blaze of the Andalucian day, in gangs of forty. At every hundred yards stands an overseer, and a knot of soldiers, with loaded rifles. Each prisoner has a chain from the ankle fastened to an iron band across the waist. At night they are chained to each other, two-and-two. These men are called "presidarios." When employed on a road at any great distance from their prison-houses, a temporary barrack is sought for them in the nearest houses.

The indulgences allowed to Spanish prisoners are threefold. Firstly, on feast-days they may wander the streets, heavily manacled, to get what they can by begging of the passers-by. Secondly, their relations are sometimes allowed to bring them some little luxury, if the master of the prison be leniently inclined. Thirdly, were a man of influential position condemned for, say, ten years, his relations might get him off by having him bound as servant to some friend, who will be responsible for him to be "brought up when called for," and give him, in the meanwhile, food and clothing.

Besides the sierras, there are other retreats open to those who fly from justice, or from a world that has dealt hardly with them. Many of the "cortijos," or small lodges in the Campo, belonging to, and used as summer-houses by the landed proprietors of the country, are kept by these outlaws, and no one cares to interfere with them, or inquire into their past history, or, at least, these places form a home for many of them, who aid the regular guards in looking after farm, or olives, or vineyard,—assist at all the hunting-parties,— and, now and again, when very hard up for food, ask a moderate amount of pecuniary assistance from the landlord — a request which it is prudent to grant.

Again, those who have been disappointed in their worldly affairs, sometimes find a shelter in one or other of the few monasteries now remaining in the South, paying a fixed price for their humble room, working in the garden at early dawn to secure their vegetable sustenance, praying for the welfare of their fellow-creatures, idling and sleeping their sad life away. Theirs, to use the touching phrase of a poor Spanish girl, ever has appeared to me to be "a broken life,"—a life more aimless, if possible, and less manly than that of the wild denizens of the Sierra Morena.

The monastery called "Las Hermitas," at Cordoba, a short time since numbered among its inmates one or two men who had "known better days," and, among others, a world-wearied colonel in the army, who (for no crime) had retired thither to pass the close of a somewhat noble life.

The new levy of middle-aged men has made hundreds fly to the shelter of the Sierra. It is not that the Spaniard would not, but that he cannot, be patriotic, "For," says he, "for what am I going to fight?" And there is, it is to be feared, too much truth in what he says. Besides, in the army he is poorly fed. A short time since a fine young carpenter near me was "drawn," and went to the depôt. Three times within the first fortnight the warm-hearted apprentice wrote to his master. In his last letter he concluded with the words—" At last they have varied our meals. We used to have rice and garbanzos twice; but now, *gracias a Dios!* we have rice and garbanzos in the morning, and garbanzos and rice in the evening!"

Passing away from the Sierra, with its outlawed and unhappy inhabitants, and entering upon the cultivated plains, we shall find that, in all that relates to agriculture, Spain is well-nigh a century behind the age. There are many small holdings, and they are generally let on the following terms. Common (that is, rather sterile) land would fetch three or four dollars the fanega (the fanega=8,000 square yards, as nearly as I can calculate: I see the best Spanish dictionary calls it 400 square fathoms). Really good land would fetch about eight dollars per annum. I speak of arable land, for Andalucia knows no green pastures. An olive-grove would, in its perfection, be valued at an annual rental of four reals per tree, a vineyard not much more than a halfpenny or penny per tree.

Many farms are let on the following terms: the landlord claims annually one-third of the produce, or £50, say, per annum, and a certain number of pigs or sheep in addition. But the farming is of the roughest. It is needless to say that the English plough or the threshing-machine have not found their way into the wilds of Andalucia. The two mules dragging their quaint plough, just stirring the surface of the earth, wind slowly along the fallow; the unmuzzled ox treads out the corn upon the threshing-floors, or the mule or pony scuttles about it, dragging the primitive "threshing-machine," as it is called. The farmers are a rude, ignorant class of men; like English farmers, very conservative. The labourers are men who take little interest in the farm on which they work for the few months that working is possible. They are very poor, hopelessly ignorant, fare wretchedly, and dress sordidly. Still, they are ever polite, kindly, and generous to the stranger. About 1s. 6d. per diem would, perhaps, be the average amount of the agricultural labourer's wages; but he never strikes! He is ever " contented," if not "gay." True, his pleasures are very few, but he makes the most of them, and, where an English peasant would grumble, the joyous Andaluz laughs. He eats his bread and oil, he chews his lettuce, he makes and smokes his tiny cigarette; he earns a dollar, it is well; but to risk it is better. So, instead of buying clothes, or getting wine, or taking it home to the poor, hard-worked wife,—who once, remember, was a dark-eyed, handsome Spanish lassie, but, with hard feeding and hard breeding, and hard toiling in the field or at the wash-tub, is as much like a man as a woman now,—he goes to the nearest gambling-house, stakes his dollar, loses it, and walks out without a murmur!

Gambling, indeed, is a passion, and nothing else, with the Spaniards, high and low. If a man makes a large fortune, he never knows how to enjoy it unless he gambles at cards, or in the Government or private lotteries or at dice. In fact, the Spanish gentleman, if he does not gamble, seems to have nothing to do with his money: he hides it under the floor of his house, or sinks it to the bottom of his well, if times be troublous. The peasant, besides smoking and gambling, has his look at the bi-annual bull-fight; he takes a peep, on Sunday, at the cock-pit; he hurls the iron bar or throws the iron ball along the dusty road, if strong and active; or he plays dominoes or trugé (the simplest game of cards) for cuartos (farthings) with his companions.

But what, then, you will say, does this careless, improvident fellow do when his hair is more than flecked with snow, when his limbs tremble under him, and his strength departs?

He simply becomes one of the beggars. He literally begs his bread from door to door, and, morning, noon, and night, you hear his double-knock, and his everlasting salutation, "Ave Maria purisima, da me una limosnita, por Dios"; and there, at your door, his crooked staff in his hand, his half-naked frame covered with a ragged manta or rug, stands the worn-out labourer, artisan, or miner. He has long since left his house, and he herds with the motley company of beggars in the caverns and clefts of the rocks outside the town.

He is filthily dirty. He has lost all hope, all self-respect,—and why? There is no poor-house, where, however uncongenial the element in which you live, you, at least, are clean, sheltered from wind and rain, and fed; and there is no parish relief. In fact, begging in Spain is a necessary evil. The cripple borrows a donkey, and begs from its back; the maimed man thrusts the ghastly stump of his hand or arm in your face.

On Friday, which is generally the beggars' day, the houses of the charitable are thronged with a motley crowd of men, women, and children, of all ages, sorts, diseases, sizes, and descriptions. A noisy, wretched, forlorn, unkempt lot they are. They fight and push for the nearest place to the door. Many have come for miles to get their wretched chavo, or cuarto, or halfpenny, at the various houses. Then your kindly servant, her lap full of coppers, opens the door. The crowd surges up to and around her. At last all her store is exhausted. She draws back, and hastily bolts the door, against which a crowd of malecontents batter for five minutes, with loud cries of "Por Dios, señorita," *i. e.*, "For God's sake, my lady!" and then all is quiet. The blind, the lame, the halt, and the maimed have gone, and the house is quiet until Friday dawns again.

Sad to say, many strong young men and maidens, lost to all sense of self-respect, leave off their work habitually on Friday, in order to share and lessen the dole of their helpless brothers and sisters.

Well for you, when the beggars' hour is over, if you do not find a few fleas, and even lice, at your gateway; for, to use the very expressive word of a Spanish gentleman who was attempting to speak English, most of these people are, as to their clothes, "inhabited."

The education, or rather the want of it, claims mention in any account, however brief and necessarily imperfect, of the social state of the part of Spain here described.

Certain schools there are; and, in cases like that of the model schools of large towns like Cadiz (as described in a separate chapter), they are very good in theory, and work well. But the schools in the smaller towns are simply wretched, and those who teach in them inefficient. The rooms, too, although supposed to be selected and paid for by the alcalde and ayuntamiento of the town in which they are situated, are dark, close, ill ventilated, and crowded.

Besides this, many among the higher classes are very imperfectly educated, and write and spell badly, especially the women. In a town well known to the writer, one gentleman, whose daughter was heiress to some £20,000, refused to allow her to learn to write, lest she should indulge in some clandestine correspondence.

This vile system of never trusting, of always preferring physical to moral power, of using external precautions to prevent sin or indiscretion, instead of cultivating that moral sense which the Almighty has implanted in every heart, has ever struck me as one of the great blots in the Spanish national character.

Awful and horrible cruelty to animals again, an utter indifference to their sufferings, is another blot on the Spanish poor man's character, and one that stares you in the face at every step. To beat his ass till it reels, to stone slowly the dog he wishes to kill, to drown the captured rat by slow and easy stages, holding it by its tail in a pail of water, these sights are things of every-day occurrence.

Religion, again, has generated into superstition. It has lost its backbone, its reality, and, consequently, its hold upon the masses. The priests, too, in the country places, are greatly degenerated from what they were, as we all must degenerate, if oppressed, day and night, by the sense of a soul-eating poverty, especially in the case of those whose tastes lead them to desire, and even need, a certain amount of culture and refinement in life.

In the smaller villages, the priests sometimes do not even get their pittance of £20 per annum from Government, and they turn, necessarily, to other employments, such as making bee-hives, mending watches (in the rougher cases), to win their bread.

In one instance known to me, the priest of a small town, of some five hundred people, actually won his bread by making bee-hives and bird-cages, and in another case, by his gun and his garden, which, joined to the scanty offerings of bread, or skins of wine, of his poor flock, supplied his simple needs.

Naturally, with the decay of true religion, and the absence of useful learning, the tone of morality, both among high and low, is frightfully bad. Cheating and lying are absolutely thought trifles by the Spanish coal-seller, or water-carrier, and such classes; while married life among the rich will, in too many cases, not bear a very strict scrutiny.

My picture, you will say, is not a bright one. I answer it could not be bright and true at the same time, of this beautiful, wild, and picturesque, but most unhappy country. Still, with all their faults, the Spaniards have many qualities that render them lovable. Their warmth of heart, their excessive kindness and politeness to the stranger, their love of seeing others around them happy, their genial courtesy to their dependents and inferiors, their great sobriety, their ready wit, all help to make up a national character which, if not stable, is certainly not wanting in a certain attractiveness.

CHAPTER IX.

A SPANIARD'S ESTIMATE OF ENGLISH POLITENESS.

"I THOUGHT the Englishman was drunk when he knocked me down; but when he begged my pardon, I knew he was!"

The above is all I shall offer on this point; it speaks for itself better than any words of mine.

SPANISH BLACK COUNTRY.

PART II.

CHAPTER I.

INTRODUCTORY.

It is my purpose, in this Part, to introduce the reader to the mines and miners of Spain; to a portion of the country and to phases of character so little known, that these chapters (which will abound with strange anecdotes, and statements of facts hitherto unchronicled, drawn from daily intercourse with the Spanish miners) might well bear the title of "Sketches in Untrodden Spain." And I believe that the plain, unvarnished tale which I shall offer will be full of interest to all my readers, especially to those who love to study human nature under its strangest phases.

Perhaps there is no country in the world with a more varied, extensive, and widely-spread store of mineral wealth than Spain. It is truly a "land whose stones are iron, and out of whose hills thou mayest dig copper." Its hills, in many places, are pregnant with metal; north, south, east, and west, lead, copper, iron, coal, and quicksilver are found; but in many places, owing to the hilly nature of the ground, and the expense and difficulty of transit, these deposits are still untouched.

The question of Spanish mines and mining is a very wide one; and for an unprofessional man to attempt to treat it scientifically, would be not only presumptuous, but hopeless. Having, however, resided for some months in the heart of a Spanish mining district, the writer of these pages has taken great interest in all that relates to Spanish miners and mining, and has studied attentively, and with care, the life and character of the Spanish miner, with whom he has had ample opportunities of becoming well acquainted.

Let us first take a general view of the chief centres of mining interests in the country; then we will go to the mines, and spend a day underground with the Spanish miner.

In various parts of Spain the mines have yielded their treasure successively to the Phœnician, the Roman, the Moor, the Spaniard; and now "concessions" are being duly granted to the estrangeros, or foreigners, among whom English and German mining companies hold a prominent place.

Among mining districts, the province of Murcia, which lately gained from its unhappy city, Cartagena, so unenviable a notoriety, plays an important part. In native produce, both vegetable and animal, this province is rich; and the Carthaginians, despite its parching droughts, knew its value. Whole districts are covered with the esparto-grass—a tough, wiry, grass, something like the "spear-grass" of the north-east coast of England, which is not only largely used throughout Spain for ropes, sandals, mats, baskets, and the like, but has lately been largely exported to England and France for the manufacture of paper. The soda-plant, yielding alkali when burnt, grows also plentifully. Off the coast of Cartagena a species of tunny is also taken, and salted down for exportation; and salt is found nearly as plentifully there as at San Fernando, near Cadiz. But the chief trade of Cartagena is in lead and silver. So pregnant with minerals is the district, that the silt washed down by the wintry rains yields lead in abundance, with a small proportion of silver.

The province of Jaën, perhaps, comes next in importance, having many lead-mines, the lead of which yields a small, but very small, proportion of silver. Linares, its chief mining town, situated amid arid plains and slopes of stunted, dusky olives, boasts a colony of Englishmen, Frenchmen, and Germans, and without one particle of beauty, and with little comfort, is one of the chief districts of mining industry. This town is said to be the Hellanes of the ancients.

In the north-west, amid the wooded hills of Leon, where the pine and fir would recall to the passing traveller's mind memories of Scotland, and where are patches of verdant scenery almost Devonian, are the coal-mines of Arnao, the principal shaft of which is below the water's level; and not far off, in the same province, are the mines of Cangas de Onis, rich in copper and carbonate of zinc. The rough weather and deep snows of winter, however, detract from the working value of the mine, by making it inaccessible for weeks together.

In Aragon and Navarre are silver-mines. In the Basque provinces, near Bilbao, are two of the richest iron-mines in the Peninsula, although the hardy "caballero" peasant prefers poverty, rough fare, and independence on his tiny three-acre tenure, to the service of an Englishman; while Estremadura, the

Spanish peasant's "land of corn," the birth-place of Cortes and Pizarro, the land of locusts, and sport, and loneliness, and sweet jamones (the sweet ham of Spain), offers one of the largest quicksilver-mines in the world, and is a source of increasing wealth to the Spanish Government.

The mines of Rio Tinto give a fair amount of copper, while Ronda and Granada can also show their wealth of mineral, chiefly lead.

Such is a slight outline of the chief centres of mining work in this country. Some few of the above-mentioned districts I have personally visited, and it is to a mine and mining town, where, with the miners, I have lived on terms of daily intercourse, and, in our rough way, friendship, that I wish to introduce my readers.

Perhaps there are no towns in civilized countries where the whole atmosphere of the place is rougher —I know not how better to express myself—than in these mining towns. Exceeding roughness and an unheard-of primitiveness are stamped on everything: the country is rough, the people are rough, the talk of daily life is rough. In the lead mining districts one's ear is deafened and one's heart numbed and beaten down by the ever-recurring topics of "dineros" (money) and "plomo" (lead), day after day, week after week, month after month: "Plomo—plomo— plomo." "Alas!" said a scientific man, who came to live near me for awhile, "I should at last grow like the lead, as dull and heavy, if I had to live here." And so it is. From morning until night you hear nothing, see nothing, but lead: lead at the railway-station, lead-smoke (from the smelting works) in the air, lead on the donkeys' backs: plomo en galápagos, plomo en plancha, plomo primero o segundo (lead in pigs, in sheets, lead of the first or second quality). Lead and money, varied by money and lead, it is depressing alike to soul and body; and, gentle reader, remember there is a proverb among us, "Andar con pies de plomo" (to proceed with leaden feet); and a disease among us which is called "being leaded," and makes a man's eye dull, and his brain sleepy. So, if I seem to you to merit the application of the first, overlook it, and follow me patiently, and believe that while I am writing this I am "leaded," and, therefore, it is to be borne with me. But if you have ever done as I have, and struck out a few lumps of lead "underground," by the dim light of the Spanish miner's lamp, you will know that even the dull lead, as you strike it from its granite surroundings with the pico (pick-axe), or, as the miners call it, "picajo," sparkles; and so even the dull atmosphere of Spanish lead-mines is enlivened with Spanish salt!

Both among the mining-agents and mine-owners, as well as among the pitmen, the observant eye and ear will find a rich fund of originality, quaintness, and droll humour side by side with the deepest pathos and the most hopeless suffering.

After many months' residence in the heart of one of the largest and most densely populated mining centres of Spain, I sought permission of a Spanish mine-owner to visit personally the workings of his finest mine and go underground; and he gave me (*rara avis in terris* in the mining districts) a glass of first-rate vino de Oporto, the port wine of the English squire. As we drank it, and discussed mines and mining, he said that his wine always recalled to him "a truly touching anecdote." A young Spaniard had married a lady fifty years his senior, not a love-match, but a *dineros*-match. They called upon him together, and a bottle of the ruby port was broached. The old lady enjoyed, even (so he said) made music with her lips (? smacked her lips) over the grateful drink. Her adorer sat by her side, sipping his wine in silence. Suddenly the ancient dame said, " O señor" (to her host), " if you could only get me a barrel of that same wine I should live for another eighty years."— " And," said my host, " if you could have seen the pleading look the young man gave me, you had never drunk the wine without a sigh ! "

But this semi-pathetic, ever-ready humour is one of the redeeming points of Spanish conversation. You never converse with a Spaniard, high or low, without a laugh. In the course of the same conversation we were discussing the general state and internal management of Spain, and I said, " There are two things in England, in the cause of ' humanicacion,' to which I attach great importance, as showing that this humanization in marching onward, the Life-boat and the Home for the fallen woman. Are there any in Spain ? " —" As to the former," said he (and he was a man of education), " I do not know, not living near the sea ; as to the latter, I have heard of no homes for them, but plenty of homes of them." The latter statement, up to this time, I have been unable to verify, and I merely quote it as showing the ready wit of the Spaniard, even in the mining districts.

Here is a typical mining town. It is on the outskirts of the wild range of the Sierra Morena. It stands on the gently declining slope of a hill ; around it stretch plains of tawny sand, covered in spring with green crops of barley, broad-beans, and coarse wheat, belted in with olive groves, their dusky, stunted trees enclosed in crumbling stone walls, each enclosure having a small, dark-roomed shanty, the "lodge" of the olive-guard, in its midst.

The town is old, as many a fragment of crumbling Roman or Moorish masonry will show. It was built originally for some eight thousand people, and now at least forty thousand are packed within its walls, literally "like herrings in a barrel." The town is not Moorish, for the Moors knew well how to build the houses high, and with courtyards or patios for coolness within doors, the high wall on either side of the narrow street precluding the rays of the tropical sun from ever looking upon them. Most noticeable is this in Cordoba, where the old streets are so narrow that two vehicles cannot pass, and the high houses seem almost to meet overhead. The houses of the mining town are, at least a great proportion of them, of Spanish design, and consist of a one-storied building made of the huge thick blocks of the granite in which the lead usually is found, with very small iron-caged windows without glass; others of modern and wholly different architecture have sprung up in a thick and growing crop all around and among them. The streets are not paved, as a rule, but have been pitched at some remote period. In the summer droughts the loose stones roll about, and yield to your tread, often giving horse or man a nasty fall; in the winter the water stands in pools six inches deep, and streams of water rush, during the tropic rains, down the streets. Open drains abound in the suburbs; here is a long, sluggish, black stream, which flows from the "washing grounds" of the servants on the hill just above the town; it once was soap-suds, but has lost its beauty now. You never would believe that inky fluid had made your linen clean! As you approach the streets toward the suburbs, they, hitherto narrow and pitched, are broad, straggling, and of the natural soil; that is, in summer six inches of dust, which the slightest wind whirls into your face in dense and blinding clouds; in winter six inches of deep, black mud. Here and there it is "being mended," that is, huge lumps of granite are being carried to the worst places in panniers on donkey-back (the refuse of the masons), and are shot down into the mud, or pools of inky water, unbroken. Great, many, and loud are the curses of the muleteer,—the road-mender, the saints, his beast, his kin ("sangre," literally blood) all come in for a share of his curses.

I have seen these roads, on the outskirts of the town, sometimes well-nigh impassable for man or horse; only a donkey could be trusted to pick his way over the stones and through the pools of black, stinking mud. From these latter sometimes even a sensitive donkey will recoil with a face of horror, and shut his brown eyes if he must take the plunge!

The streets are generally called after the names of saints, Calle de San José, Calle de la Virgen; or from political events, Calle de la Republica Federal, and so on. The rent of the houses, wretched as they are, in these over-stocked towns, is very high. In the Spanish interior, generally, house-rent is very low; but in these towns a small house of four rooms and tiny courtyard will fetch £30 per annum, unfurnished. The roofs of the houses are of massive white tiles, and slope gently; the top story, with its tiny "cat-holes" (for the cats from the roof to enter by), being used as a camera or granary, the heat rendering it unfit for any other purpose. The walls, of grey or red granite, are made enormously thick, for the sake of coolness. Here and there one tiny bow-window, with lighted candles burning on either side of the brightly-dressed image which it enshrines, proclaims the house of a "religious" or strict Roman Catholic. At night, to a stranger wandering down these dimly-lit streets, the effect of suddenly coming upon one of these lighted up is striking. Saving this, however, the aspect of the town is not, as in many of the old country towns of the Spanish interior, religious.

The miners, wandering about the streets at night, may often be seen to stop and devoutly cross themselves before the images. Although not really a fervently religious set, they have a certain sense of the nearness of the world unseen, a sense probably inspired by the perils of their daily life. In my personal intercourse with them, I have on more than one occasion been led to mark a great similarity between the religious side of their character and that of the fishermen on our south coast of England. Both the fisherman and the miner see "the works of God and His wonders in the deep," both daily hold their life in their hand, both are irreligious in the ordinary acceptance of the word "religious," and yet both have a certain great generosity of character, a certain freedom from fear, a certain natural dependence, half-unknown even to themselves, upon the love and power of Him who made them.

The subjoined extract, relating to the Tarshish of the Bible, as is supposed, is from the note-book of a leading civil engineer and mine-owner in Spain:—

"In time of Strabon, century of Tiberio, the Rio Tinto, or River Tinto, so well known in Spain as giving a name to the celebrated mines (copper and iron) at its source, was called Hyberus, or Hir-beras. At this time Ura-berosa in the Basque, supposed to be one of the most ancient languages of Spain, means burning water, and the Rio Tinto was then, doubtless, as now, destructive to vegetation on its banks and injurious to cattle. It is popularly supposed that the province of Huelva was one of the first colonies of the Phœnicians, the Carthaginians, and the Romans in Spain; and it is not improbable that the Roman name of Hyberus was derived from Ura-berosa, and thence, from Hyberus to Iberia or Hiberia, the connexion does not seem remote. Another of the celebrated mines in the province of Huelva is the Tharsis. The country people still call the Sierra in the neighbourhood of that mine Tarsé; the Romans called it Tartésia, and its inhabitants Tartéssi. It is said here that 'writings of the time of Solomon state that a journey of three years was necessary to get to Tarsé to get copper, silver, and gold.' (?) It is supposed, with some foundation, that the Phœnicians associated the name of Solomon with wealth, particularly mineral wealth; and it is certain that many mountains, &c., in the south of Spain are so called: thus—at Rio Tinto is the Cerro Salomon (peak or ridge of Solomon); near Rio Tinto is the town called Salamea la Real (Royal Solomon); in Estremadura is Salamea la Serena, near a large deposit of lead slag; near Cordoba is another Cerro Salomon, also near a large deposit of lead slags; at and in the neighbourhood of the Tharshish mine are found remains both Roman and Phœnician, as is said."

These notes were taken by a leading civil engineer, after a conversation with a well-known Spanish antiquary at Seville.

CHAPTER II.

MINES AND MINERS.

STILL continuing my description of our typical mining town, let me say that its leading characteristics appear to me to be untidiness, noise by day and night, wine-shops, gaudiness of colour, and general picturesqueness of costume; absence of Spanish beauty among the women.

And, first, as to its untidiness. (I shall not detain my reader long on any head, but just give the detail of facts as I have seen them.) The huge pitching-stones are rolled on to the pavement, where there is a strip, by boys, for play, and left there; dead cats, and dogs, and fruit, in various stages of absorption, are lying in every direction—I say absorption, for decomposition and stench, owing to the extreme dryness of the atmosphere, are not found, as a rule, from such causes; the bundles of fire-wood (green) supplied to the houses are left out in the street often for twenty-four hours, and in the dark you fall over them; the *débris* of building materials is not cleared away oftentimes for months; donkeys take possession of the pavement, and, where you find a paved road, you are at free liberty to ride upon it and save your beast; beggars sit at every corner, and pursue you and seize your coat; begging children kiss your hand, and run by your side, with their unhappy, everlasting whine, "Una limosnita, por Dios, señor." I have known a Spanish horseman (a mining-agent) ride up one narrow street, down which I was walking, with an iron bar carried cross-ways across his saddle's pommel; it reached from one wall of the street to the opposite, within about two feet; the horse started, and went from side to side; a few minutes, and the man would be safely in the open country, so he held his bar firmly. Just as he neared me, one end caught in the iron bars of a small window of one of the houses, and as he managed to stay his horse, I too managed to get by. All the combing and dressing of the women's hair (I speak of the lower orders) is done sitting on low chairs in the streets, each person doing it for her next-door neighbour, or mother for daughter, and *vice versâ*. I think I have said enough on this head. What would a London policeman say, or rather, what would he not say, to all this; or to the sight of guitar-parties, or drinking-parties, squatting in the street, or sitting on low chairs right in the midst of the streets, to the great hindrance of traffic? "Obstructing the thoroughfare" is a mild term for all this; and as to "nuisances"—!

Next, as to noise, daily, nightly, as one of the leading characteristics of the mining town. An English miner, stealing forth to his work in the grey of dawn, would smoke his pipe in silence, and look at the clouds. The Spanish miner, even at five in the morning, commences that wild, peculiar, monotonous ditty which is the song, well-nigh the only song, of the Andaluz. As to the tune, it is ever the same. As to the words, he makes them up as he rides out to, or returns from, his work. His mule, too, is covered with bells hung on the collar round its neck. I once counted thirty bells on one mule laden with cloth; but five and six to each mule for music is nothing.

Then, as to music. Many people in England think of Spain, and speak of her, too, as the land of music and flowers, and the dance; and there is some truth in the words, but, like every general statement, it needs modification. In the interior, as regards music, the musical powers of the people are very slender. Still, in a rough way, by far the greater proportion of them are musical, especially among the lower orders. The guitar is the favourite instrument, and hundreds of the men play upon it, or, at least, get a few notes out of it.

But let me describe to you the sort of music that it is. We are in a Spanish mining district, and it is evening. We are passing down the quarter inhabited chiefly by miners, rough labourers who tramp from place to place for work. In some streets, every room of every house contains at night from seven to ten of these poor fellows, who wrap themselves in their mantas (large warm rugs) without undressing, and so get their repose. All down the street you hear the tinkling of guitars; every door is open, and you will be warmly welcomed if you enter in to join the circle of twenty or thirty who are sitting, some outside the room, in the street, some within, doing nothing but smoking their usual little paper cigarillos, and listening to the music.

One man is now holding forth. There is very little air in what he sings, none at all in what he is playing; all that comes from his guitar is "tinkle, tinkle, tinkle," the same note struck over and over again very quickly. It is an accompaniment, a relief to his voice, and nothing more. As for his song, it is nothing but a wild, loud ditty; the words are childish, but full of love :—

I.
"Black her eyes are,
And rich her hair,
Chaste is my girl,
And very fair.

II.
I love her well,
She loveth me,
Wait but awhile,
We 'll married be."

And so on. At the end of each verse, the man raises his voice in a series of rising and falling cadences, "la, la, la, la; la-la-la; la-la," several times repeated. The Spaniards will sit listening to this until midnight. I have often joined the party, and, it is but fair to add, that several times I have, in these rough parties, heard music of guitar and voice simply enchanting and beautiful. But that is not the rule.

The noise of the street-cries is also excessive. In the town of which I write, most of the trading is done in the street, and I have ever found that the itinerant seller of fruit, cloth, handkerchiefs, candlesticks, is more reasonable in his prices, and has a better and more varied stock of goods, than are to be met with in the shops. But, really something ought to be taken off from the price for the nuisance caused by these cries. From five o'clock in the morning until seven or eight at night, your house is never quiet. The cries are peculiar, the fashion being to prolong one syllable of the word cried until breath fails. "El toneler-----ro!"—here comes the travelling cooper. "El herrer-----ro!"—the blacksmith. "Pañuel----------os!"—here come handkerchiefs and cloth, strapped up to the height of four feet on the sides of a tinkling-necked mule, and wrapped in red, blue, green, and yellow waterproof cloths. "Muy buenos tomates y pimiento----------s!" —here comes a donkey laden with vegetables.

While at early morning, say five o'clock, or thereabouts, you are awaked by the cry of the goat-milk seller, "Leche-e-e-e-e-e!" I timed one of these last men, and found that twenty seconds was the time he kept up the cadence of the final *e*.

So much for noise. The muleteers shout; the donkey-riders sing, or hum their Andaluz ditties; the women sing at their work. Every cart-mule, every chief goat of a flock, and sometimes every goat, has its bell.

Then, as to the tiny wine-shops. The wine-shop is simply, in the mining town, one small dark room, with a heavy curtain across the door; within which stand a barrel of white, and a barrel of red, Val-de-Peñas. The room is rented of the owner of the house, and locked up at night. It is stone flagged, dark, and a little red curtain, half drawn back, across the door opening from it into the back courtyard, shows the women who keep the venta sitting on their low stools sewing, in the cool, out of the reek of the wine and tobacco. A few tiny shelves, in one corner of the venta, are studded with bottles of various colours; the white fluid (aguardiente blanco) predominates; then comes mentha, or mint-spirit; apio, or liqueur of celery; and, probably, a rough kind of plum-brandy and cherry-brandy; all of which cost four cuartos (farthings) the wine-glassful. Plenty of cooling vessels stand about, and green and yellow pottery.

Over the door is hung a tiny bush of wild olive, or chaparro, whence the proverb, "Good wine needs no bush!" and over the door is written, "Vino de Bal de Peñas, Vlanco y Tinto, Aguardiente Valenciano." The wine is sold in a vaso, or tumbler; the half-tumbler being called "caño de vino"; the full, "ration," in vulgar Spanish.

Every tenth house seems to have a venta; and, on the road to mines from any town, the ventas are little windowless, chairless, one-roomed stone shanties. The wine is vilely adulterated, as a rule; and it is best, when you are travelling, to ask at some private cottage for a drink of wine. If the cottager boast no barrel, he will at least possess a skin or bottle of wine, and will readily give you a draught.

Gaudiness of colour and general picturesqueness of costume, I spoke of as being also characteristics of the Spanish mining town. The drapery in the shops is of the brightest, coarsest colours; a rich light yellow, for the women's dresses, predominates. The handkerchiefs, worn over the head by men and women, are red, blue, yellow, and the three mixed. Many women, of the lower class, wear a yellow skirt of a kind of coarse woollen serge, with red stripes about four inches broad sewn on. Every one who flocks to the mining town for work preserves for awhile his individuality, and you see the Valencian peasant in canvas shirt, and baggy canvas trousers to his knee, tied round the waist with a piece of common cord; the Manchegan, in blue and yellow handkerchief knotted round his head, with skull-cap of fur, and huge flaps over his ears; the hardy peasant of Leon, with embroidered waistcoat, low-brimmed hat, and black cloth gaiters with steel buttons; the

Castilian peasant, with montera and tattered capa; the Catalunian, with his picturesque semi-Genoese dress;—these, and half-a-dozen other costumes, mingle in the Plaza with the pork-pie sombrero, short black jacket, scarlet faja, and woollen trousers of the Andaluz, and form a Babel of tongues, and lend a general picturesqueness to the scene.

As to the last characteristic of the mining district—absence of personal beauty among the women—I can only say that, with the exception of their magnificent dark eyes, and bushy, glossy, well-kempt hair, I never saw plainer features, both among rich and poor. Of course, Spanish beauty in some parts of Spain, especially Malaga, Cadiz, and the northern provinces, is marvellous, especially in the hair and eyes, and the exquisitely proportioned figure, and small hand and foot that strike you, set off, of course, by the graceful trailing dress, and that unrivalled head-dress, the mantilla. The Spanish beauty generally fails in her nose and mouth, which, toward middle age, often develope into actual unsightliness, the upper part of the face being still pretty. But in the interior the women are somewhat under-sized; inclined to be too much *embonpoint*, and not by any means so pretty as the English peasantry.

As to the shops of the town, they are of the roughest, but the drapery, cloth, &c., is marvellously strong and serviceable. There is the *Tienda de Comestibles*, where you can buy anything from a stabbing-knife to a sweet ham, bedsteads, goat's-milk, cheese, cocoa, &c.; the " Despacho de Aceitunas de Sevilla," or store of Seville olives—the finest in Spain; the " Despacho de Carne," or butcher's shop, where mutton sometimes can be got, tough as leather, in the summer, and in the winter, carne de macho, or goat's flesh—most distasteful to a foreign palate; the "Sombrereria," or hat shop; the stall, not shop, of "Refrescos y Gazeosas"; and the "Despacho de Dulces," or sweets' shop. As to shops for luxuries, books, articles of *virtù*, they do not exist; but every year a travelling-man comes, and, for six weeks, rents a front room; he brings really beautiful and good articles, and his shop, ere he departs, is empty, his pocket full. Shops wholly and solely for the sale of navajas, or clasp-knives—some of astounding size—are found in plenty; and saddlers' shops also abound.

And now, let us leave the town, with its dirty streets, its teeming inhabitants, its ever-recurring savour of garlic, and strong-smelling aceite (oil-olive used for frying), and get a breath of fresh air as we breast slope after slope towards the mines.

On a bright, but chilly and blowing, morning in February, I once passed out of the town, accompanied by a Spanish miner as guide, for one of the chief mines, distant about four miles. First, ere we left the outskirts, we passed the "Valley of the Washer-women." A stream and spring flowed through the sandy, rock-strewn hollow, the waters of which were collected at two points; on the one side, they flowed into a long, stone trough for the mules and donkeys engaged in the traffic to drink at, and overflowed into the hollow, making inky pools of mud; on the other, they flowed into a long collection of stone troughs, with sloping stones at the side of each, on which to rub the clothes. On either side rose a slope of olives, and all about the sandy, rocky ground were tiny stone-hovels, tenanted by every sort, shape, and description of persons. Gipsy, beggar, worn-out soldier, strumpet of the lowest class, men on tramp for work, all were sitting outside these, what in English landlord's phraseology would be called, " cottages on the waste." Hither, to these washing-grounds, flock the servants, washer-women, mothers of families, and, paying to the owner about a penny, more or less, per hour, they stand over their dripping linen from morn till eve. A more motley crew I never saw; their dresses of every imaginable hue, chiefly red, yellow, green, and striped; their bare arms, strong as those of a man; their uncouth, unceasing jabber; their hot words, for they often turn up sleeves and have a set-to with fisticuffs; all presented a strange picture. But, as a rule, they are a hard-working, industrious, honest lot. They may be described as what English soldiers call " Rough Christians."

The first half-mile of the road is made somewhat picturesque by the ever-recurring gaudily-painted stalls of the sellers of early coffee and aguardiente to the miners, as they pass on their workward road; by the donkeys, wholly hidden beneath their load of wild-olive boughs and evergreen oak, going into the town to supply the early bakehouses; and the rich hues of the morning sun, that, flooding hill and vale, lend a certain beauty even to the red dusty road, the shivered lumps of brown granite, the dusky olives, and the half-yellow plains of stunted barley.

Two little episodes, so wholly Spanish that I may be pardoned for introducing them, happened to enliven the earlier part of the journey—a journey otherwise only broken, as to its monotony, by the gay prattle of my guide, who gave me a long description of a midwifery operation he had performed the night before, and suddenly broke off from his Andaluz ditty to exclaim, " Caramba! I'll go to the end of the world with you, I like you so well," and the shouts of muleteer and donkey-driver, as we met or passed them, " Ar-r-r-r-r-e, moo - - - - - lo, ar-r-r-e," or " Arre, borri - - - - co," and the everlasting viaticum, which you receive and give as a matter of courtesy to all, " Vaya usted con Dios," sounds which seemed to go up like a chorus along the whole length of the road.

The two incidents were these. A lead-laden donkey had fallen in the road, and the driver could not get the poor beast up. He cursed the Virgin and the saints for bringing him such ill luck, and finally fairly wallowed on the ground with blind and senseless passion.

At a bend in the olives we came on four miners, fine muscular young fellows, stripped, their knives lying on the rock hard by, playing their favourite game of the iron bar. The iron bar is about five feet long, with smooth round handle, and weighs, I was told—of course I had no means at hand to verify the truth of the statement—from twenty-five to thirty pounds. Each man in turn steps forward, grasps it about the middle, gets a little purchase as best he can, and throws the bar in a horizontal position. Whoever throws farthest, wins the stakes. It is needless to say the game is always played for money. Amusement without the excitement of gambling added would be no amusement to the Spaniard.

The men offered me the bar, and I can only say that a man who threw it would, if unused to it, run a great risk of a rupture or strain. We sat down hard by, my mining friend and I, to make our simple breakfast of Val-de-Peñas and bread and bacon—Spanish fare; and on my proffering the bottle to Juan, he said, as he took a long and steady pull, "My father was a teetotaller, so it behoves his dutiful son to drink heartily, to atone for his one defect."

The stunted character of the trees; the clumps of prickly pear; the quaint wild figures; the shoal of wild-looking dogs at the road-side at one spot, some lying smeared with blood, as to their head and forepaws, and wholly surfeited, but looking very well contented with themselves, some lying half-inside the ribs, and tearing at the flesh, of a horse that had dropped; the utter absence of water and green, and all that one associates with the name of home, certainly strike an Englishman whenever he sees them.

As we crossed one more hill, the tall, smoking chimneys of the lead-mines, and the long ridges of granite thrown out (for all the soil about here is but two or three feet deep, and then comes granite rock, to an enormous depth, in which granite the lodes of lead run), and the clanking of the machinery rose close before us. My first impression was, what industry, what enterprise is here; for, remember, these mines are miles and miles from any railway, and, of course, there is no demand for the mineral on the spot. My next thought was, what a hopeless enterprise it must seem at first to commence mining, and in such a district. Foreign artificers and engineers, machinery, hands, all must be brought to, for they cannot be found upon, the spot.

CHAPTER III.

UNDERGROUND.

THE way of entering upon a mine is this: first, a competent person finds out at what depth, in what direction, and at what angle the "lodes" or veins of lead run,—all this can be judged with some little degree of certainty, but an opinion often proves ill founded; then the Government, which holds all these unclaimed districts of rock, and wood, and fell, is applied to for what is here called a "concession," that is, the Government are asked by the mining company to sell to them the "mineral rights" of such and such a tract of country. This effected, the mineowner's agent does what is called "denounce" (denonciar) the land—that is, formally lay claim to and take possession—ratifying his agreement with the civil authorities of the nearest town. And then he must get machinery and men—no easy task in many cases, owing to the exceeding badness of the roads, distance of the tract denounced from railways, and the hilly ground; but over all these drawbacks enterprise and faith have triumphed, and Spain is dotted with many little colonies of French, English, and German miners.

Perhaps, after all, at the commencement, the taking a mining tract does not require so much more faith in the man than ploughing the grey, slaty, wintry seas for fish, or casting the seed on the brown soil, not so much faith, perhaps, as is required of the little child when first told to say its prayers, and "keep on saying them, though you seem to receive no answer," as the teaching of the dame's school ran in other days.

I met the friend with whom I was to spend the day underground, and we repaired to the undressing-room. A glass of vino tinto and a cigarette repaired my nerves, which had been somewhat shaken by the contemplation of "breaking with the daylight," and we proceeded to put on the "underground dress." It consisted of a pair of thick woollen socks and list slippers, canvas trousers to the ankle, a warm sailor's jersey next the skin, and over it a short brown-holland (it seemed) jacket, lined with wool and flannel; on our heads we wore a tight-fitting linen skull-cap, and over that a "billy-cock" made of a composition of wool, felt, rosin, grit, hard as cement, and sounding, when tapped, like metal. This is to preserve the head in case of a stone or piece of rock falling on it. This last is a Cornish institution, and a most valuable one; but the Spanish miner works with his head unprotected save by the linen skull-cap, which, of course, is a protection against nothing but the dust and dirt.

Thus attired, we walked across to the mouth of the shaft, one of us, at least, not feeling very comfortable. The "shaft," for the first descent, was so narrow that, passing down the ladder, we could reach back, and lean against the opposite side. It looked like a simple well-head, and the ladder-head, standing a foot above the surface, was only one foot wide. "Which shall it be, ladder, or swing down by the rope?" had said my kindly companion, and I had elected the ladder. Down we went, I holding on like grim death. The arrangement of the several flights of ladders in this mine was very ingenious. At very short spaces each ladder came to an end, and there was a small space for a "rest," so that even were a man to fall he would only fall a small distance, ere he swung himself down on to the next, holding firmly with one hand to the former ladder. I should say that we each carried a common tallow candle for light, with a ball of clay stuck round just below the lighted end. As the candle burns down to the ball of wet clay, you push the ball an inch lower. This clay prevents the tallow from running over your hand, and so making it slippery.

The ladders are of wooden sides, and have iron spokes for the most part. They seemed firm and strong; but in some of the other Spanish mines—this was owned by an English company, and worked by Spanish miners—I am assured the descent is not so safe.

This mine was a very wide-spreading one. Wonderful indeed is it to walk through the dark, narrow galleries, and see, towering high above you on either side, the huge walls of solid granite. You hold your candle up, and, lo! the lead lodes, looking like the spatter left by a bullet on a rifle-butt, glitter and shine above, below, about, and around. On the first working you can sometimes see the distant daylight through some cleft above for a moment, and suddenly you have to climb through a low, dark passage, roofed with heavy oak trees and planks, capable of supporting five hundred tons of falling granite. This "roof" is placed in those places where there is a likelihood of a fall of granite.

We crept and stumbled along. Suddenly three

miners came hurrying round a corner, looking ghostly enough by the light of their flickering oil-lamps, and into our gallery. " Barreno, Barreno, Barreno," they shouted, and the hoarse shout echoed and re-echoed from gallery to gallery. In a moment, as they rounded the corner, a dull boom like thunder shook and made to tremble and vibrate the granite rock against which we leant, and nearly put out our candles; then another; then a third. This was the blasting, by which much of the work is necessarily done.

I noticed in this mine the " old men's workings," as the miners call them; they were the shafts driven in by Phœnician or Roman; but the mining companies of the nineteenth century have gone four times as deep below the end of the " old men's workings," and been rewarded with rich treasure.

This mine has four workings, each about forty fathoms below the other. In the uppermost the soil is dry; but in the lower galleries the miner has to work up to his ankles in mud and water, although the pumps are for ever at work, night and day. We had, in some places, in order to get to a working, to crawl through dark, dismal-looking passages on hands and knees, passages about two feet high by two broad; and the natural thought of a mind unused to this sphere of labour was, " How easily a block of granite might fall and cut off my retreat, and I hardly be missed in this labyrinth of darkness."

The darkness, the huge granite rocks, shivered about by pick and gunpowder, the pallid faces of the miners, lighted up by their little triangular oil-lamps, the dull boom of the blasting, the ceaseless, slow, measured, steady " pick, pick, pick," the utter sense of suffocation one experiences, the sulphurous smell of the blasting-powder,—all these must be heard and seen, described they cannot be in such a way as to give even a faint idea of the immensity of labour and force in rendering tunnels, and galleries, and chambers out of the granite womb of the earth.

The lead is found running in regular "lodes," or veins, from eight inches to two and five feet broad, and, perhaps, equal height — although this last has rarely been found — through the granite rock. It generally runs from east to west, at an angle of about thirty-two degrees. When a miner lights upon one of these veins, if large, he commences to blast, bore, and work with pickaxe at once; if small, the engineer or captain measures its proportions, and can tell in a moment whether it will pay to work it.

The losses and risks to the mine-owners are chiefly these; the vein is often lost for a while, or wholly, and the men's labour for weeks, in endeavouring to regain it, perhaps, without ultimate success, is lost. Then, again, it often takes weeks, even months, to find, in all the mass of granite rock, what is called a "paying" or "working lode." Strikes are unknown here, so there is no loss on that score.

There seemed to me to be two kinds of granite, one of a dark, tawny-red colour, and another of whiter colour—a sort of grey granite. I noticed, also, iron pyrites, and also frequently a border of white mica on either side of the vein of lead, separating it from the granite on either side. The lead is picked off in irregular-shaped lumps, like pieces of rock. By the lamp-light it looks quite silvery, but, above ground, just like the lead spattered on a hard surface from a rifle-bullet.

There are three kinds of lead: first, the vein, or lode of solid lead, just described, which is, of course, pure, and the most valuable,—this is taken straight to the smelting works; next, there is the second-class lead, or that which has a certain proportion of granite mixed with it, and needs crushing and precipitating in running water before going to the smelter; the third-class lead is that with a greater proportion of granite than lead, and also the flakes of lead that fly about and get mixed with the granite, dust, &c. All the lead yields, when smelted, a certain but very small proportion of silver. Half-a-crown in the pound is the average profit on the silver when it comes to market.

The amount of lead yielded by the mines has of late years been on the increase, owing, of course, to the increased efforts of different companies in working. As an instance, it may be cited that, on one line with which I am conversant, the value of the lead passed on was £15,000 during the year 1870, whereas for the year 1873 the returns showed it to be £60,000.

As to the miner's life and character. There are two sets, the surface-men and the pitmen, or miners proper. The former, who are variously employed, as shall be afterwards pointed out, in wheeling lead, crushing, washing, driving the mules, or managing the steam-engine, or turning the "whims," are not men of so distinct a class as the pitmen. The ranks of both these classes, however, are supplied by men chiefly of the province in which the particular mines are situated; but, attracted by the high rate of wages, men from every province, and in every picturesque variety of costume conceivable, flock to the mines, and swell the ranks of surface and pit men. Nor are men driven to mine-labour only by the necessity of winning bread. As of old to David at Adullam, so now to the various centres of mining industry flocks "every one that is in distress, and every one that is in debt, and every one that is discontented," forming a rough and motley, but, as a rule, by no means a disorderly or disagreeable set. Indeed, I have personally always found, both taken individually or taken *en masse*, the Spanish miners an open-hearted, honest, hard-working set of fellows. They meddle but little in politics, and prefer their cock-pit, music, and games to the more dangerous walks of life of Spanish artisans. "A short life and a merry one" is the rule with them, poor fellows. I fear, too often, it is short without being merry.

A man of moderate height, say about five feet five inches (for the Andaluzes are short and fleshy men as a rule, and they form the staple of the workmen at the mines from which I write), rather inclined to be stout, with singularly well-developed chest, and sometimes breasts almost like those of a woman, of pale, sallow complexion, with a keen dark eye, and bright fearless smile, hair cropped close to his head, fleshy arm, and small hand and foot, is the Spanish miner.

His dress consists of a short, but very thick and warm, jacket, of some dark coarse material, and lined with woollen, in length and shape like an English schoolboy's jacket before he attains to the dignity of a coat; a coloured handkerchief, tied in knots below the ears, the ends hanging over the back of his neck, a most wise precaution in a country where the swelling of the glands at the back of the ear is very common; a pair of thick woollen trousers; canvas shoes, or sandals bound with rope, or, if he can afford thirty-four reals for the purchase, a pair of light-coloured leather Blucher boots; generally over the head-gear above described, the thick felt pork-pie hat, or sombrero, is worn; a crimson waistband, containing knife (the famous navaja, or clasp-knife, for eating or stabbing) and purse; coloured checked shirt; with his "alforca," a kind of bag with two pouches, the one for small tools, and the other for provisions, slung over his left shoulder, so that it is evenly balanced, the one pouch being in front, the other hanging down his back; this, with a frying-pan strapped on his back, completes the miner's general appearance. When he goes underground, he puts on nothing but a tight-fitting brown-holland jersey, open at the chest, and lined with flannel, and trousers of the same, baggy, down to the knees. He wears canvas shoes or sandals, or works bare-footed, as he may choose.

In age the miner varies from about seventeen to thirty-four, and then his short life, as a rule, is ended, his children are fatherless, and his wife a widow. The poor Spanish girls say, "It is hard to marry a miner, for he must leave us so soon." In the quicksilver mines of Almaden, the sickness and death-rate, in great measure caused by excessive salivation, is said to be enormous; and at the copper-mines of Rio Tinto, very great. But in the lead-mines the mineral does not so entirely penetrate and break down the constitution as in these last-mentioned mines. The diseases to which the Spanish miner falls a victim, and their causes, are chiefly these:—

(1.) Pulmonary consumption, accompanied, as in England, with spitting of blood. This is the poor fellow's greatest foe, and hundreds fall a victim to it. It is probably induced by breathing the unwholesome, confined, sulphurous air of the mine; by working with wet feet for the eight hours, until the other shift comes to relieve guard for the night; by the exertion of climbing up the perpendicular ladders quickly and eagerly to get to the surface, which induces profuse perspiration, and also palpitation of the heart. The miner passes at once into the cold air of the surface, perhaps at five in the evening, when the chilly dews begin to fall. The perspiration is suddenly checked, and, with his thin and clammy underground dress on him, he walks across to the undressing shed to wash and smarten up. Then, in the cold evening air, he walks home, perhaps not over-well wrapped up. The exertion of running up the ladders is great. Sometimes, instead of sloping as ladders generally slope, they slope the other way, *i. e.*, outward, and climbing them is like climbing an ordinary wall-ladder on the under side.

(2.) Calentura, or fever. This is of three kinds, or rather has three stages, and probably is induced by the same causes as the above. The first stage is merely calentura. The second, intermitente, that is, it is tertian fever, with bilious symptoms. This stage is best treated with quinine, and many a man is deafened by the strength of the dose given. The third stage is perniciosa, from which recovery is well-nigh hopeless. High fever, sheer exhaustion, constant vomiting, and deafness, as of typhus fever, are characteristics of this last stage of the calentura. The spring and fall of the year are the most favourable seasons for this calentura, which, in many respects, answers to the "low fever with typhoid symptoms," so common among the peasantry of the English Midland Counties. In some cases, or stages, the tongue is black; in others, thickly coated with white. A medical man assures me that this fever is very closely akin to African fever, and other fevers which arise from living in a district where morass and swamp abound, with tropical temperature. The calentura of the interior often clings about the constitution for months, and its effects on a weakly frame are only with difficulty shaken off entirely. It is constantly brought on by a sudden chill, and, at its first appearance, is marked by alternating fits of heat and cold, shivering, bilious eyes, utter inability to keep food or drink on the stomach, great dryness of the skin, and exceeding mental depression. In its first stage the Spanish doctors treat this disease with bleeding and "febrifuge" pills, inducing profuse perspiration. What this "febrifuge" consists of I know not, but I have seen very great benefit derived from its use; indeed, I have myself derived benefit from it while suffering, at a distance from my English medical adviser, from a like attack.

There is a tree know in Spain among the lower orders as "calentura-tree." It is a tree of moderate dimensions, and is constantly found planted at railway stations, ferry lodges, &c., in districts scourged by this disease. The botanical name of this plant, I am informed by an eminent English doctor in Spain, is *Eucalyptis globulus*. It is, I believe, a native of Peru. Whether the febrifuge of the Spanish medicos is a decoction of the leaves of this plant, I know not, yet it is so asserted by the miners themselves.

(3.) "Dolor de costado," or "pain in the side," a term which is applied by the miner either to inflammation of the lungs or pleurisy. Both these last diseases are common, and when allowed to become fully developed, are most serious. Probably they are induced by the cause above named, the sudden change from the heated atmosphere of the mine into the chill air of the Spanish winter evening, or the cold damp of midnight. One "shift" of men comes to surface about 5 P.M., the second about 2 A.M. Working in the lowest shafts, ankle or knee deep in water, is also, of course, a fruitful cause of these evils.

(4.) "Leading," a disease which is variously called "being leaded," "lead colic," or "leading." Lead colic, however, is its proper designation. It is common to the surface-men, pitmen, and men engaged in the smelting of the lead. This disease is induced by the absorption into the system of a larger amount of lead than it has the power to throw off. Generally speaking, the bowels are powerless to act, and the vomiting is not sufficiently strong to throw out the offending particles. Sometimes diarrhœa is present. Violent cramp in the side and stomach, almost amounting to paralysis, is constantly present in this disease. In some cases, the sufferer is doubled up with agony, and is carried off in four-and-twenty hours. Two cases of this kind came under my notice, in both of which recourse was had to bleeding and violent purgatives, but without beneficial results, and the two poor fellows died, each within six-and-thirty hours of the seizure. But in these cases the attack was not a first attack, the constitution of each of the poor fellows having been previously enfeebled by the same disease. This colic, however, is not, as a rule, fatal. A person who is "leaded," or who is on the road to it, looks ghastly pale in face, his eyes are dull and the whites yellow, his appetite decreases, and his thirst increases daily. In certain forms of this colic, when the constipation is long continued and the agony great, croton oil is administered in infinitesimal doses, and generally with a beneficial effect. In others, where the bowel is relaxed, and continues unable to fulfil its duty, strong irritants, such as red cayenne pepper, are administered, and also with good results. The Spanish medical men constantly bleed patients suffering from the constipated phase of this disease, which is generally accompanied with fever.

Prevention is ever better than cure, and I have been told by two managers of large lead-smelting works that they found it possible to keep off the foe, in great measure, by exercise, if possible, great personal cleanliness, frequent doses of simple aperients, as compound rhubarb pills, and, above all, by a regular and judicious use of acids, which do much towards neutralizing the poison. A few drops of some preparation of sulphuric acid in water,—a bottle of this is put at the service of the miners at every mine; they come with a tin mug of water, and take thirty-one drops in it,—or lemonade, tartaric acid, and the like, they assured me they had found of the greatest possible benefit. The way in which the lead is taken into the system is through the lungs chiefly, the atmosphere being impregnated with lead, necessarily, in the smelting works. The very smoke you breathe there is lead, and, in the mine, the tiny particles of lead floating in the air, disturbed by the pick of the miner, are inhaled by him. The Spanish miner increases this risk by his mistake in blasting. An English miner, wishing to blast a lode of lead, would drill the hole for the fuse, and store the gunpowder, in the granite below the lead, and thus the cloud of smoky dust, which necessarily fills the cavern and hangs heavy in the air for long afterwards, will be, not lead smoke, which is poisonous, but granite smoke, which is comparatively harmless. The Spaniard, however, drills the fuse-hole and stores the powder in the heart of the load of lead, and thus the whole cavern is filled with poisonous lead-smoke, which he and his poor companions are inhaling for hours.

Apropos of "leading," I may mention a curious accident which befell the dog of a friend of my own, a large mine-owner in Spain. The dog, a fine specimen of the "bull-dog," or "bull-mastiff," of Spain, was cooped up in the town, and pining for air and exercise. For a week or two his master took him up to the mines, and on each occasion Juan took a plunge into a pool of water strongly impregnated with lead, and lapped a little of the water. He soon showed signs of illness; his eyes grew dull, his hair began to come off. His master, never dreaming of the cause of the poor fellow's suffering state, took him oftener than ever. At last the poor dog was seized with cramp, and howled with pain, paralysis supervened, and in a few hours from his last bath poor Juan's spirit had gone for ever.

This incident illustrates the second way in which the miner takes the lead into his system, namely, through the pores of the skin. In all probability, the quantity of the water alone, without the lead-bath, would not have been sufficiently poisonous to destroy life; and so, with the miner who perspires freely, the poisonous particles settling upon his half-naked body, and becoming absorbed through the open pores of the skin into the system, are highly conducive to lead-colic. Part of this latter danger might be avoided, were the miners forced to wash in warm soap and water, on leaving the mine, in a warmed shed provided for the purpose. But they are not by any means strict (to use the mildest term) in this respect. They use but little water, and soap is well-nigh unknown among them for this purpose, although, perhaps, from its power of uniting with the greasy substances on the surface of the skin, and forcing them to come off, it is almost as indispensable for health and cleanliness as the water itself.

Under the head of diseases may be classed accidents. The number of accidents, so far as I can ascertain, in a mine, or part of a mine, employing some two hundred men, would be somewhere about two per month, many, if not most, of which are due to sheer carelessness or negligence on the part of the men employed. Let me instance three such cases:—

(1.) A miner, rendered careless by habit, goes down the ladder, barely holding on with one hand. A little tallow has dropped on one of the spokes of the ladder, rendering it slippery; he loses his hold, is overbalanced, and falls some few yards to the next rest, breaking arm, or leg, or ribs.

(2.) Again, a miner knows that he is working in a dangerous working, *i.e.*, in mining phraseology, a place where loose fragments of stone fall from a height, say, of sixty yards. He works, nevertheless, with no protection save his linen skull-cap—this I have myself witnessed—a bit of *débris* falls, strikes his head, and he is carried up insensible.

(3.) Two or three miners are pursuing a lode in a passage, the roof of which is formed of trees and planking, firmly joisted in, capable, if left alone, of supporting some five hundred tons of granite rock four feet over the head of the workers. Knowing well the dangerous nature of a fall, which would absolutely make "the pit shut her mouth upon them," and, perhaps, leave them with a huge barrier of granite rock between themselves and the exit from the mine; knowing, too, the shock, the vibration that a blast necessarily gives to everything in its immediate vicinity (I have seen the naked rock tremble, the lamps go out, or burn blue, the men's frames near me shake like aspens), the miners, for sheer convenience' sake, determine to blast just underneath the props and planking. If a fall be the result, it may be they are dead men.

As regards deaths from accident, these are not common. In one mine that I visited lately, where two hundred men were employed, the captain told me that, in the past two years, only two or three had occurred.

To the honour and credit of the Spanish Government, it must be here said that their supervision of the mines, especially of those owned by foreigners, and the strict, unflinching scrutiny made, and inquiry held, as to the causes of any accidents that may occur, is almost unequalled. Instant notice of any accident must be given to the civil authorities of the nearest town by the mining-agents. The Spanish civil engineers are on the spot in a trice. Generally they declare the accident was the fault of the works, &c., and inflict a heavy fine upon the owners.

It should here be stated, that the remarks above offered upon the diseases of the lead-miner of Spain, are gathered as well from personal observation as from the information kindly afforded to the writer of these pages by two Spanish mining surgeons of eminence, of much experience among the Spanish miners,—men who have seen and sympathized with the miner in every stage of accident and disease; seen and tended him in the darkness of the mine, when stricken down by heavy misadventure, or when, wrapped in his manta, in the last stage of calentura, he turns his face to the wall doggedly and quietly, if not with Christian resignation, surrendering himself to his fate.

CHAPTER IV.

MINER'S MEDICINES.

HAVING spoken of his diseases, let me speak of some of the miner's own favourite medicines. He is a man who has a great faith in simples. Sage-tea is one of his favourite stomachics and cooling mixtures. In every case of faintness from a severe accident, the moment he comes to himself, he calls out, " A cup of tea, for the Lord's sake!" Tea is a luxury unknown to him save medicinally, and he has a marvellous faith in its curative and restoring powers. Probably it has a greatly beneficial effect in such cases, because it has never been used before, and, therefore, like the effect of a small quantity of stimulant on a person unaccustomed to the use of stimulant, it has a power which on the English tea-drinker would be lost. A decoction made of the leaves of the calentura-tree (*Eucalyptis globulus*), and drunk either hot or cold, is one of his remedies for fever. For biliousness, with feverish symptoms, his wife would give him the juice of two oranges, squeezed into a tumbler, with the value of four cuartos in magnesia. But there is one medicine which, in the heats of summer or the snows of winter, is ever within the miner's reach, and in which, for himself, his wife, and his children, he places the most implicit reliance for cleansing and purifying the blood and strengthening the system, namely, sarsaparilla. This medicine is taken in the form of a refresco by men, women, and children, at the little stalls of the coffee and aguardiente sellers. Wherever there is a little stall for bunuelos, a kind of snake-shaped cake fried with oil, aguardiente, and vinos, there is found the large bottle of sarsaparilla.

As regards the ordinary fare of the Spanish miner, it is somewhat as follows:—Suppose him to belong to the day shift, he starts from his home, dressed as before described, with his thick knotted stick, or oftener, perhaps, a thin iron bar with a crook, used as a walking-stick, and, if the morning be chilly, his rug over his shoulders; if hot, his jacket is thrown over his left shoulder, and he walks in shirt-sleeves. The women, with their hot coffee, and bunuelos, and aguardiente daintily spread on little boxes, are squatting along the road to the mines at their different points of vantage, and he stops at his customary "House of Call." He first drinks a wine-glassful of pure aguardiente, to keep the cold out. This costs two cuartos (two farthings) a glass, and has not much raw spirit, but mint, aniseed, and other aromatic ingredients. The aguardiente Valenciano is the favourite. It is pure white, rather like milk-and-water in colour, and is a capital stomachic, and for keeping the cold out invaluable. Then he eats a bunuelo or two, two of which cost a cuarto. This is, as has just been said, a kind of fritter, about the thickness of a man's thumb, and of a circular or twisted shape. It is made and fried in the streets, and would be nice were it not that the oil in which it is fried (with an egg or two, if the proprietress of the stall be a liberal soul) is so unduly strong. Then the miner has possibly a tiny cup of black coffee, with a dash of aguardiente in it, costing two cuartos more.

L 2

Thus fortified, he proceeds to the scene of his work, generally humming the customary wild ditty of the Andaluz, the words of which are simply a narration of any passing object that strikes his vagrant mind. Here are two of these extempore ditties, extemporized on the spur of the moment, and suggested by the passing sights:—

> " A big man walking with a sti - i - i - i - i - i - ck,
> A little man riding by his si - i - i - i - i - de!"

And again, as a poaching-dog glided out of sight among some dusky olives, with something unlawful in his mouth:—

> "Yellow dog with stolen morsel in his mouth - - - - - outh,
> Through the olives he go - o - o - o - o - es!"

The cadence at the end of each line is a series of rising, and then suddenly one or two low notes. It is a most wild, most monotonous ditty, and is peculiar to Andalucia in great measure. It meets one's ear from the fishing-boat, the olive-grove, the donkey-back, the shop, the street, until one's ear fairly tires of it.

Arrived at the mine at about 6·30 A.M., the miner joins his own working-party, one or two of whom have brought a frying-pan. Under the shelter of some tree or wall they sit down and make a fire. Each has brought, be it said, bread and fruit, the fruta del tiempo, or fruit of the season, whether it be orange, melon, or grape. Each one, again, has brought some vegetables, or meat, or olive-oil. " Without aceite" (oil), say the miners, " no comida." The frying-pan is filled with the humble stores of these poor, hardy, contented fellows. One slices half-a-dozen potatoes into it; another shreds a bundle of pimientos (capsicums); a third adds some lumps of goat's flesh, or baccalao (dried cod). The oil is poured over the savoury mess, bay-leaves are added, and then there remains nothing for the miner to do but to fry and eat the savoury mess in which his heart delighteth. All eat, with wooden or metal spoon, out of the frying-pan, which is placed in the midst of the little group. Breakfast ended, each takes out his clasp-knife (the famous navaja) and eats a portion of his bread and fruit, which last two comestibles always form the conclusion of the meals of the Spanish poor. The bread is coarse and cheap, and is sold in round flat cakes of one or two pounds weight.

On a chill, windy morning it is quite a picturesque sight to see a group of these miners, or of ploughmen, their primitive ploughs, each with its team of two mules, yoked abreast, standing on the brown, thistle-clad furrow in the field, huddled together under the lee of some crumbling grey stone wall, taking their breakfast, wrapped in their huge rough, rusty, chocolate-coloured mantas, and each with the inevitable cigarro de papel, or paper cigarillo, between his lips.

Breakfast over, the miners descend at 7·30 A.M., for the eight hours' work underground. They take with them nothing but fruit, bread, water, and tobacco for making the cigarillo. At 11·30 A.M., when four of the eight hours' work are over, they eat bread and fruit. At 4·30 P.M. they come to the surface, and are trudging home; eat bread and fruit again. At about 6 or 6·30 P.M. the miner is at his home with his wife and bairns. The greater number of these men, who earn (for Spain) fair wages, marry young, and husband and wife have the meal of the day, the evening meal, together, eating out of the same dish, crouched over the tiny "brasero" of charcoal, the niños having been safely stowed away in bed.

To describe the different dishes with which the Spanish girl rejoices her husband's and her own heart at night, would be out of place. But I will give one or two typical dishes, describing only those which I have seen, and of which I have partaken. Let me premise that, both at the tables of rich and poor in the interior, the meat from which the soup has been made is piled upon a dish, covered with vegetables, and called "cocida." It is, of course, goat's meat (carne de macho) or mutton; the former being the winter and spring, the latter the summer, meat of the interior, boiled to rags, much of the same kind of material to which the Guardsmen of London were condemned so long.

Beef, in the pastureless and arid lands of Andalucia, is an unheard-of luxury, save for the two days that follow a bull-fight, when, for obvious reasons, such as it is, it may be had.

The "cocida" of carne de macho is first placed on table, covered with garbanzos—a sort of nutritious dried pea *(Cicer arietinum)*, said to have been introduced into Spain by the Carthaginians, and, perhaps, rice. Then comes the soup, which is highly spiced with pimientos picantes (fiery capsicum), and strongly flavoured with bay-leaves. It is thickened with rice, or a rough kind of vermicelli, or sliced bread, and is very nutritious. Then comes the bread and fruit again. Then the friend drops in for a chat and a cigarillo; and with a glass of Val-de-Peñas, and the cigarillo and the guitar and the song, the Andaluz miner passes his evening. Here are one or two typical dishes, very savoury—I have found them too savoury:—

(1.) The pojera.—I know not how to spell it as it is called in the Spanish interior. It is a kind of hodge-podge; meat, soup, bread, spices, bay-leaves, and every sort of vegetable are stewed or boiled up together, and it is eaten hot from the stewing-pan. This is a favourite winter dish.

(2.) Gazpacho.—Arabice, soaked bread. This forms the bulk of the fare of the poorer classes throughout the fierce heats of summer. It is a cooling diet, and very wholesome. When nicely made, it is a luxury. It consists of onions, cucumber, lettuce, radish, garlic, pimientos, all chopped up fine, and put into a bowl full of oil, vinegar, and cold spring water, with slices of bread floating in it.

(3.) Baccalao-fry.—The baccalao is a dried cod, hard as iron, and requiring six hours' soaking in cold water before it is in any way palatable. It is cut up into small pieces, and put in the frying-pan with a lump of fat, with vegetables of the season, and pimientos picantes or bay-leaves; then, covered with strong-smelling oil, it is fried, and is, the miners say, "Muy rico."

Three sorts of sea-fish.—The only sorts which ever find their way into the interior, and, of course, that only in the cold months, are used as the staple for the evening fry. The atun, a huge fish, of reddish-brown colour, caught at Cadiz, weighing from 50 to 150 lb., the flesh is like that of the sturgeon, but somewhat coarser, perhaps; it is sold by the pound, and is very cheap and common. It is reported to be very nourishing. These fish come into the mining-towns from the nearest station on donkey-back, and, being strapped two on each pad, the long tails dangling and flipping along the dusty road, is an unusual sight. Then there are the "boccarones," or anchovies, caught off Malaga, and sent in shoals to the interior; and the "sardinas," a small, high-flavoured, silvery fish, like a sprat.

As to drink, the miner takes his aguardiente and his Val-de-Peñas wine, costing about threepence-halfpenny per quart, whether white or red, or Catalan black wine. The Val-de-Peñas, if good, is something akin to Burgundy, and is grown in La Mancha.

As to amusements, the miner knows but few. If athletic, he "throws the iron bar," or "rolls the ball," an iron or leaden ball, six inches in diameter, along the road. If not, he plays "rouletta" in the street, or cards at his own home. On feast-days the cock-pit is open to him, or he takes his gun and dog and wanders over the Campo to try and pick up a hare, or red-legged partridge, or bustard. Dance and song and guitar fill up his holiday. In the mines owned by the Spanish companies the Sundays are not observed, but the feast-days, in some measure, take their place. In the mines worked by English or German companies, the Sundays are kept as far as is consistent with the safety of the mine. Gambling, if it can be called an amusement, is a passion with many of these men, nay, with well-nigh all of them.

Of anecdote belonging to the Spanish miner I have not much in this place to recount. I have said before that the criminal, fleeing from the clutch of the law, the "suspected" person, *i. e.*, suspected of political leaning against the existing Government, the debtor, the adventurer, and the peasant who cannot obtain in his own province employment sufficient to support himself and his family, all flock to the mines for shelter, and support, and concealment; and it will readily be imagined that when so many strange elements enter into a large body of men, there are many of evil devices and unbridled passions, men given to drink, licence, and low debauchery. But this is far from being the rule. Still, we meet among the miners with many who, in England, would come under the appellation of " rough characters."

Here are a few trifling anecdotes, which came under my own personal observation, illustrative of certain aspects of mining life and character in Spain :—

When a late Government first came into power, not many months since, it was for a few weeks singularly lenient; soon, however, it became exceedingly severe. In one town, with which I was at the time well acquainted, no less than sixty persons, accused of political offences, were seized out of the population of 30,000, and, without a trial, were hurried off to the dreary exile of the swamps and savannahs of Cuba. " Better take them out on the Campo and shoot them at once," was the remark made to me by a gentleman with whom I was discussing the question. Confusion, sorrow, and heart-burning then reigned supreme, and man after man left his employment, his family, his trade, to seek shelter and work in the mines until the tyranny should be overpast.

In a mine that I knew of a political refugee sought employment and shelter. He worked underground, and his delicate white hand soon acquired, what with clay, tallow-grease, lead-dust, and hard work, quite a miner's horny touch. The civil guards heard of his whereabouts, and watched the shafts of the mine now and again. His ruse to escape detection was this:

when he ascended the shaft one of his most trusty friends went just before him; as he (the friend) emerged into the open air he scanned the country round, with keen, scrutinizing gaze, to see if the blue capa and red facings of a civil guard were lurking anywhere within eye-shot. If the enemy was at hand, this "advanced guard" simply looked down the ladder, and shouted, "Pedro, bring up that pick-axe that we have forgotten"; and it is needless to say that the poor fellow was underground again in a trice! Alas, his game was soon played out, and the ill-fated fellow has ere now shared the fortunes of his political comrades!

Tobacco for his cigarette is the miner's delight. He cannot live or work without it. Not the good, honest English cutty clay pipe, with its substantial "cut" of moist, aromatic shag tobacco, but snuffy-scented, dry powder, like a bad cigar pulverized, rolled up in the tiny papers sold at every corner, is the Spanish miner's joy. One evening, on the road to the mines, a gitano-looking man came up to me—it was at the close of a hot summer's day—and, in a most mysterious way, said, in a whisper,—" Cigarros, señor?" I was puzzled for awhile; and he then detained me by my arm, on which I bade him begone, and thrust him off. The man's dark figure and swarthy face followed me wherever I went, as I turned my steps homewards. I went into a venta, when I came out he was just outside; into a friend's house, he was fanning himself with a huge lady's fan just under the shade of some adjoining houses. I thought he meant mischief, and got a friend to walk the rest of my homeward journey with me.

The following morning I was called, ere dressed,

from my bed-room to speak to some one on important business. I hurried to the door, and there, with a huge sack half full at his feet, with his brass-earrings and his fan, stood my friend of the previous night. He was a contrabandista, or smuggler of Havannah cigars and tobacco, of which his sack was partly full. He explained that his business was brisk in mining localities; that he must be off speedily, and so on. I bought a few bundles of first-rate cigars for a very trifle, and bade him Adios.

Now and then a wild, lawless spirit sets a bad example among the mining population, and the bad example is followed by the younger men. At such a time the wine-shops will be full; the click of the navaja heard in the streets; and the hospital surgeons have extra work in dressing stabs.

Once, lodging in a street which was full of miners, I heard a desperate quarrel going on outside my windows, and the ominous click of the revolver or the knife. Fortunately, the guard came up, and prevented bloodshed. The two men, my next-door neighbours, had quarrelled, and turned out into the street at one in the morning, heated with passion and bad wine, to settle their dispute, which was, of course, about some wretched woman.

On another occasion, two bangs, louder than ever revolver produced, greeted my wakeful ears about the same time in the morning. On inquiry the next day, I found that some young miners, for a lark, had drilled a couple of holes in the stone wall of a poor old woman's house hard by, filled the holes with dynamite, and put a live fuse there. The dynamite explodes downwards, and so only a few fragments of the wall were blown out into the street. But it struck me, at the time, as a rough style of practical joking. The miners are very fond of using this dynamite for fishing. On Sunday you see them by river, and tarn, and pool, exploding this stuff in the water. The fish rise to the water stunned, and the men wade in and capture them. There is necessarily a large store of this explosive mineral in every mining town, and so this becomes a frequent pastime of the wilder sporting spirits. These miners, accustomed to face death and danger, have plenty of pluck and courage. During some of the Intransigente risings, our letters from England and France, and the North of Spain, were stopped, and lay, we heard, at a wayside station, some twelve miles from our town; whoever brought them must bring them through the very ranks of the foe. A miner volunteered; dressed himself as a melon-seller, and, unarmed, trolling forth his wild Andaluz ditty on the back of his donkey, his panniers filled with letters and newspapers, with a thin layer of melons at the top, he brought the letters to his town in safety. "I saw," said he, "the Intransigentes" (to many of whom he was well known) "sitting armed upon the rocks, just above one defile through which I had to pass."

And not only has the Spanish miner real courage, but he has a most loyal, most affectionate, and genuine feeling for his employers. I was once returning home late at night from some Spanish mines; one tired man, who was known to me, greeted me, and asked,— "Was I walking home alone?" On hearing that it was so, he shouldered his gun, and nothing would persuade him to leave my side until he had seen me within the precincts of the town where I dwelt. This is but one of the many instances of the Spanish miner's devotion to his employers, if kind and good to him; nor are instances wanting of the devotion and loyalty of these men to their employers, whether Spanish or foreigners, as a body.

For a Spaniard, the miner is rather given to drink, always commencing his morning with aguardiente, and ending the day with Val-de-Peñas; but I challenge any one to walk the streets of any English mining town, and find as little drunkenness as he would in Spain. Still, it must be admitted, that many of the miners—probably driven to it in great measure by their unhealthy life—indulge in too much stimulant.

The Spanish pitman is sadly underpaid; for his eight hours' underground work he only receives moneys equivalent to half-a-crown of English money daily; and, although provisions are cheap, and his manner of life, poor fellow, very simple, and his wants very few, this is most certainly far less payment than he is justly entitled to. He is paid thus little in this way. The captain of the mine measures out a mass of rock to be worked, by blasting and the pick-axe. It is so many square yards. A Spanish foreman of miners offers to do it for so much, his offer is accepted, he pockets at the rate of £5 to £7 per month for himself, but only pays the men two shillings and sixpence per diem.

CHAPTER V.

SURFACE-WORK AT THE MINES.

MARVELLOUS is the difference to any one who has studied carefully, as has the writer, the character of the Cornish miner in England and the Andaluz miner of Spain, between the leading features of character in the two. Sad as the mists that sweep his wintry wold, silent, contemplative, far-sighted, the rugged, independent Cornishman takes his way to his work. At evening he returns to his substantial fare, the loneliness of his cottage—for he cares for no noisy friends—and the study of his Bible, or some book deeply imbued with religion. Early the child of habit, he turns off to bed. Sunday comes, and he joins in the prayer-meeting, or teaches a class, or leads the sonorous singing of Wesley's hymns in his chapel on the grey hill-side. He is a man of few words on any subject other than religion; a man full of prejudices, full of obstinacy; a man who never acted on impulse in his life; a man who esteems lightly the trivial joys of life. Methodism and money are his all-in-all.

A very different being is the Andaluz miner. Bright as the sun that floods his morning path, noisy, thoughtless, impulsive, the courteous, ephemeral Andaluz sings his way to the mine, and plucks the wayside flower of the Campo to wear it in his button-hole or his sombrero. Life is a jest with him. At eve he returns to his home in the noisy town, to his light, savoury fry, or salad, or soup; and, that finished, he seeks some house hard by where the song and guitar and dance will help to while away the weary evening. He reads no book but the book of busy life around him, which he scans as keenly and reads as truly as any one. On his Sunday or feast-day he plays cards, or goes to the cock-pit, or plays the light guitar, to the singing of his black-eyed wife, or wanders over the Campo, gun in hand. He is a man full of talk and prattle and lively joke; a man who never speaks of religion, or very seldom; a man full of strong, fiery passion, but without a spark of obstinacy about him; a man who always acts upon the impulse of the moment, who will stab, or offer his dinner, on the spur of the moment's impulse; he is a man who turns everything into a joke, shuts his eyes to what is serious, sucks mirth and merriment from the veriest trifles; amusement and the news of the day are his all-in-all.

Enough has now been said on the character of the miner for the present, and the writer offers in conclusion a short description of the surface-work, or processes through which the lead passes when it is brought to bank, before it is melted, an operation which he also briefly will describe, as he has seen it in Spain. Only let him crave some indulgence from the reader if his words be heavy on these points; for he is conscious of having studied the miner's life and character with a far keener interest than the working of the mine.

The lead of the three kinds above described—first, second, and third class—is brought to the surface by means of whims, to be crushed, and acted upon successively by water, fire, air, and zinc. The history of the lead, after it is once brought to bank, is necessarily connected with the process of smelting, and, therefore, the scene shall be changed, and we will see the whole process as carried on at one of the largest smelting-works in Spain. Generally, the processes through which the lead passes at the mine itself are the being crushed and precipitated by the action of water; this done, it is put, in subsistence like gravel, into sacks, and sent on donkey-back to the nearest smelting-works; these last seldom being attached to the several mines.

But the smelting-works to which I now take you are situated on, and attached to, the mine whose ore they work upon; and, therefore, the whole process can be seen in its several consecutive stages. Situated in the remote wilds of the Campo, in a wild hilly district belted in with ridges of tawny red, crimson, and wooded sierra, clothed as to its every slope with thickets of encina (evergreen oak), chaparro, and other shrubs of the Campo, every slope covered with tough, or prickly, or aromatic shrubs, and dry bent-grass, the haunt of the hare, the wild cat, the red-legged partridge, the quail, and the bustard; where, as you wander, gun in hand, you see nothing, for mile after mile, but a few mine-chimneys standing up here and there and a few peasants cutting their donkey-loads of brushwood, and hear nothing but the wail of the plover; in a district where desolation is only atoned for by the rich tints of the naked sierra and the wild, rugged beauty of the scenery, stand the chimneys of the mine and the engine-houses of the smelting-works from which I write, the mine and works being superintended by a French company with Spanish *employés*.

Unsightly enough are the rude sheds, the tall smoking chimneys, the huge piles of broken granite in the midst of a scene which Nature has made so full of wild grandeur and desolate beauty. Here are the mouths of the several shafts of the mine, and all around them the smelting is carried on.

Save men and machinery there are no signs of life. Pool after pool, trough after trough, of yellow water is around you, water impregnated with lead; and chickens, cats, and dogs cannot live three months here; only men and rats can bear this atmosphere of lead; the mules are kept at a distance. The two or three horses, necessary for those *employés* who live upon the spot, look thin and dull of eye.

On a bright afternoon I went through the works with the manager, who had but lately come from the superintendence of a like establishment in Germany. He told me that he turned out, from the thirteen smelting-furnaces then at work, forty-eight tons of "soft," *i.e.*, finished, lead per diem, each ton consisting of twenty pigs, or oblong shapes of lead, which weigh 1 cwt. a-piece, and are strapped (two on each animal) on donkey or mule, and so sent off to the nearest railway station for transportation.

As we strolled from his house to the works my friend gave me some curious information on many points, which I shall here offer under the head of "Miscellanea."

And first, summing up the experience of many years of mining and smelting in Germany, England, and Spain, he assured me that for mining courage he considered the Spaniard had not his equal. "Why, look here," said he, "you may call it recklessness, but the Spanish miner will run like a cat up a nearly perpendicular wall of granite without fear, just grasping, with naked foot and hand, the little projecting pieces of the rock.

And as to ladders, why he doesn't care whether they are safe or unsafe." Then, in answer to my allegation that 2s. 6d. per diem, or even 3s., was far too little for such work as the pitmen did, he said,— "Well, it is not enough; but the Spaniard is not a man who lives for money, as does the Englishman; he can afford to sacrifice a day's wages for a day's amusement, and he cherishes his pride more dearly than his money." Thus I found that these poor fellows would sooner take "piece-work" below ground on their own account, and at their own responsibility—making, perhaps, only 1s. 8d. to 2s. per diem—than work under a ganger and earn 3s. per diem. They can then say, "I am my own master; I take piece-work!"

My friend told me that he considered no man should be allowed to work below ground until he had attained his twenty-second year. He also said that he had pitmen as old as forty-five working below ground; but that at that age they were worn out, and put to perform, so long as they could, the easiest surface-work possible for them to obtain.

In many of the Spanish Government mines the pitmen are, some of them, only of the age of seventeen! These, working before their frame is settled and their stamina fixed, die young, or have to turn to other work. In Germany, the system of Government supervision of mines is more strict and better than in France, Spain, or England. In each mining town there are a set of duly-qualified engineers stationed, sometimes as many as eight or ten in number, where the mines are numerous. These men each hold a book of mining regulations,—in shape it is like a large pocket-book, and bears the Government stamp,—

and supply a copy of the same to all the mine-owners, agents, engineers, &c. These men wear a recognized uniform, and have absolute authority to descend and explore any part of any mine; and should a boiler be dirty, a rope rotten, a ladder unsafe, or anything be found of neglect, they can fine the manager £20, or more, on the spot, and stop the mine if the fine be not paid and the defect amended.

Some Spanish surface-men were frying their meal upon the burning lead, thus eating a dinner impregnated with lead-smoke. My friend, who had warned them of the danger and folly of this, quietly, there and then, vindicated his authority by fining each of the culprits. Said one of them, " Well, but it's just the same to me whether I die to-day or next year!" I noticed a large reservoir of what looked beautifully clear water, and inquired if, in summer, a bath in it, for master and men, might not be advantageous. " Never," said he, " bathe in water near a lead-mine; it is strongly impregnated with lead. And in spring, never bathe in any stagnant water; it is sure to beget a calentura."

On the stone walls, which separated one part of the works from another, I noticed a quantity of blue-coloured blotches, and was informed that it was the oxide of lead from the smoke of the chimney, which had come down in the damp or rain, and settled there. From forty-five to fifty per cent. of this poison, for such it is, is contained in this smoke.

The lead is raised from this mine, here varying from 500 to 980 feet in depth, in large iron buckets, which are wound up to the surface by " whims." The three different classes of whims in work here are:—
(1) the primitive, or man-whim of the early miners,

in which three or four men turn the huge creaking handle, with a Spanish "Yo-heave-ho," like the cry of the fishermen turning the windlass on the beach of our South Coast fishing-towns: this is the man-whim; (2) the mule-whim, worked by two mules yoked abreast; and (3) the steam-power whim, which last, of course, is the latest introduction.

These whims are much like those used in the Cornish mines, consisting of a shaft sunk in the rock, generally found in Spain, as opposed to the square shaft of some of the Cornish mines, and a hollow cylinder of wood, turning on a perpendicular axis. While one bucket, or, as the Cornish men call it, "kibbal," is being raised full, the other kibbal is descending empty, so that no time is lost.

The lead of the first class, that is, lumps of the mineral taken from the pure, rich lode by pick or blasting, looking like shivered blocks of pure mineral, is shot out on the ground, and carried straight to the furnace. The lead of the second and third classes, the former being embedded in lumps of granite, the latter in dust and offal, is carried a few yards, to undergo the first, or water, operation of its purifying.

The water operation or process is as follows:—The lumps of granite are crushed into the consistency of gravel by huge iron rollers. This is put by shovel-fuls into huge troughs of water, or subjected to the influence of a running stream of water. If the troughs be used, they are worked up and down in small cisterns of water, and the water washing over carries away the stone and granite elements, the lead, from its greater specific gravity, being left behind. The men and women engaged in this work earn from 10*d*. to 2*s*. 6*d*. per diem. It is dirty, heavy work, and nearly all, men and women included, work up to their ankles in water, and work eight hours per diem.

There is then left a certain amount of lead, but still with a large admixture of stone, granite, offal, dust, &c. This, which looks like discoloured gravel or discoloured sand, is wheeled off to the first smelting-furnace, and we come to the second, or fire operation or process. Here are the master smelters, each one of whom, standing before his furnace with his two firemen, look red-faced, worn, and streaming with perspiration. All have a short blue jersey, sandals of esparto-grass or canvas, or bare feet, and thick dark serge and woollen trousers. The master smelter earns one dollar (that is, 4s. 2d.) per diem, the fireman, 1s. 8d. to 2s. The lead is shovelled into the heat. You wait a few minutes, and presently the mineral is red-hot. The master smelter opens, with a long iron pole, a tiny door,—an operation which, for obvious reasons, is called tapping,—and lo! into a huge cauldron, sunk in the ground at your feet, comes winding down from the furnace, in a long, winding, scarlet, or rather vermilion stream, coiling about as it comes down like a huge snake, the red-hot molten lead.

The cauldron looks at first—it is called, in smelting phraseology, not the cauldron, but the " pot "—like a huge vessel full of vermilion paint. At last it grows lead-colour, and then the fireman casts in a handful of dust from the floors. This is to purify the liquid molten potful of mineral. A cloud of thick yellow smoke, as he stirs the dust in, rises up, and with its sulphurous stench sickens, with its blinding cloud blinds you. You cannot see the men working at the next furnace, five yards off. This smoke is the most dangerous atmosphere of the smelting-works; it gives a heavy cough, sickens, and, if you are much in it, finally gives you lead-colic. The smoke clears away at last, and you see that all the particles of offal, of dust, &c., are lying in a thick coating at the top of the pot. This coating, an admixture of lead with dust and dross, is taken off with a huge iron ladle, and sent back to be re-smelted with the next batch of foul lead. This operation is called "skimming."

The lead in the pot is still molten and liquid. The master smelter comes up, with iron ladle; at his side, on the ground, stand several massive iron "moulds," or oblong shapes, with the stamp of the smelting firm, and the title of the mine, embossed in raised iron capital letters at the bottom of each mould. The lead is filled into these moulds, and, as lead will not stick to iron, in about five minutes the lead has cooled, and is in solid oblong forms, or "pigs," turned out of the mould upon the floor, and left to cool. Each mould of lead, of the larger size, weighs 145 lb., and sixteen of these pigs go to the ton. The price of this lead fluctuates from £17, which is low, to £25, which is well-nigh the highest price attained, per ton. In the shed where I stood to watch this operation four furnaces were at work, and the atmosphere was simply impregnated with lead. Three shifts of men are at work, each taking an eight hours' spell of duty; and thus, day and night, the furnaces are at full smelting power. The moulds of lead above described are about two feet long, four inches high, and five inches broad. These moulds of lead are what is called "hard" lead —that is, they have another operation yet to go through, namely, the process of "desilverizing," or extraction of all the silver from them, after which they are called "soft lead," and are sent into the English or French market.

I think I have mentioned that each one of the thirteen furnaces in operation on these works turns out forty-five tons of hard lead per diem! Whence comes the tremendous demand for lead? is a question the writer has often asked, and of which he has never received a satisfactory solution.

Hard by the furnace-house stands the shed for the "blast-engine," a small but powerful machine, for giving "blast" for the first process of desilverization. English industry and mechanical skill are represented even in these far-off wilds, for I noticed on this engine the words, "Ransome, Sims & Head, Ipswich, England."

We come now to the process of desilverization. On an average, every ton of lead from the mine in question contains twelve ounces of pure silver, and it is therefore worth while—" it pays," to use the mining phraseology—to extract it. The operation is thus performed, in two different ways:—First, the lead is re-molten in a furnace, to a certain extent; the blast from the engine is brought to bear upon it, and the lead runs off easily, while the silver remains fixed. This is the common means of "desilverizing"; but a later method, although only at present in use in one or two, at most, of the smelting-works of Spain, yet is a far superior method. It is briefly this:—The pigs of hard lead are again smelted in another set of furnaces, and poured into a large "pot," capable of holding ten tons of the molten liquid. A certain percentage of zinc, I know not what particular proportion or preparation, in powder is stirred in the lead, and it attracts and brings to it all the silver; the "pot" is then skimmed, and a "refiner" finishes the work at leisure. The lead is then poured once more into the moulds, and is "soft lead." It is strapped on mule or donkey back, and sent off to the nearest station.

There is but one more operation that I need notice. It is the "smelting" of the slag, or refuse from the first operation. It is done at what are called the "high-furnaces," and from this slag a certain proportion of pure lead is obtained.

The coal for heating the furnaces costs in Spain £2 10s. per ton, thus forming a most expensive item in the mining account. It is brought from England, or from the mines of Belmez, and finds its way to each distant mine, from the nearest railway station, in panniers on mule or donkey.

Coal is a luxury unknown to the Spanish poor, who still warm their feet over the tiny brasero of carbon or charcoal; even using the tiny charcoal made from the olive-trees, and called "picon," the fumes of which are rank poison.

I noticed, as we left the works, a shed full of lead in the rough state, i. e., partly admixed with granite; and on asking my companion how much there was lying there waiting its turn to be smelted, he informed me that each of the two sheds contained some 800 tons, more or less. I quote this simply to give some idea of the scale on which the lead-mining and smelting of the ore is carried on in this country.

Walking homewards in the bright evening of the Spanish spring day, for it was March, it was a striking thought that for upwards of half a mile the road was "burrowed under," and that one's fellow-creatures were winning their bread 900 feet below one's path!

Some mention should be made of the "runs" or

falls of earth and rock. I noticed several little valleys, as it were, of broken ground and rock, and my companion told me they were "runs," or places where the earth had fallen in upon the mine. And now the "day-shift" are on their homeward road with us, and we must say "Adios" to the men at the mines.

Two beauties of the dreary mines shall here be mentioned. The roof of the "old mines" (*i. e.*, those unworked for some time) is covered with the most exquisitely-graceful stalactites, of snowy whiteness, of carbonate of lime; and ferns of unimagined grace droop from the damp, dark soil of the unused shaft. Thus far, Nature throws her graceful veil over the deformity left by man. The second beauty has ceased, or nearly so. Until the decadence of religious observances, which came in with the fall of Isabella of Spain, there used to be suspended in each mine, on the first level, a tinsel image of Nuestra Señora (the Virgin); two tiny oil lamps (miner's lamps) were, night and day, burning before it, since each miner, as he ascended, poured, as a thank-offering, what remained of the oil in his lamp into the Virgin's lamps, which were thus ever alight. This spectacle is now but rarely to be witnessed.

CHAPTER VI.

CHARACTER AND SOCIAL STATE OF THE SPANISH CONTRASTED WITH THAT OF THE ENGLISH MINER.

THE two classes of men which it is here attempted to describe present a very marked contrast both in character and social state. And, first, as to the character of these two classes. No one can have been conversant with the English miner without having noticed how deeply the religious element—of a kind oftentimes mistaken, and sometimes amounting even to austerity—enters into and forms a leading feature in the character of the English miner. I speak specially of the miners of Cornwall and Wales, having not had sufficient experience of the miner in the North to justify me in estimating his character. And this religious element — which is common to the English peasant classes, whether a man be the old-fashioned, honest, simple-hearted churchman, who takes "the parson" as his oracle, sits under him, as a matter of course, twice every Sunday, and rejoices to hear "our parson deliver himself beautiful," or whether he be the austere, unreasoning Calvinist of the Sussex weald ; or the self-opinionated and harsh-judging, but earnest and ecstatic, Methody of Cornwall or the Midland Counties—this religious element seems to me hardly to enter at all into the character of the Spanish peasant or miner, the two presenting on this point, therefore, a decided contrast.

The phraseology of the English miner, his words, in health or in sickness,—if not downright offensively and obtrusively religious, as is oftentimes the case,—are, at least, tinged with the religious element. How often, in visiting the sick or dying among this latter class, do we hear, it may be from blanched and trembling lips, the language of a most Christ-like resignation, of a most child-like trust in the Lord of us all, a most bright and blissful hope for the future!

"It is the Lord's will; let Him do what seemeth Him best."

"This parting would be bad, if it weren't for the thought of Heaven."

Or, if the strong man be leaving all that he loves on earth, how often will his last words, as he leaves his wife and children to the tender mercies of a cold and hard-hearted world, be—"The Lord will provide. He never leaves those that trust him."

Again, how touchingly is the true nature and attitude of prayer depicted in the word used commonly by the poorer classes in the Midland Counties, where praying is invariably called begging; and to pray, to beg.

And, in health, the English miner takes a pride in his religion, and in all its accompaniments. His amusements are few, but his religious excitements are many. He pays to belong to the "connexion"; he leads a class, he is anxious to be appointed an itinerant preacher, and is ready to serve his apprenticeship for that purpose "on trial," and thenceforward to preach, and lead the sonorous, rough-cutting Wesley's hymn in the little stone chapel on the grey hill-side.

The following may be quoted as an instance of the religious element in the Cornish miner's character. One of these men told me that the two finest sayings

he ever heard were those of a dying man, who, on
being pitied, said,—" Don't pity me. Down goes the
body, up goes the soul to glory!" And that of an
infirm man, who, for want of room inside, was com-
pelled to ride upon the step of a Cornish coach. One
of the inside passengers asked of him,—" Is your life
insured, old gentleman?" And the answer was,—
"No; but my soul is!"

Again, the religious emotions of the English miner,
and others of different employments in his own rank
of life, often (far oftener than is supposed) finds vent
in a sort of religious verse, or rather doggerel, of which
the following lines, composed by a man of low estate,
are here subjoined from a heap of the same now lying
before me, as being eminently characteristic. They
are entitled—

Lines on a Fire witnessed September 21st, 1872.

I.

" Behold, our *newmerus* stacks of corn,
How beautiful they stand;
Like jewels they our farms adorn,
All over England.

II.

In them we all can plainly see
The Bread that giveth life
To all the human family
While in this world of strife.

III.

Of every sight they are the best,
Setting but one aside;
And that is Christ, who giveth rest
To all for whom He died.

IV.

But 'tis an awful sight to see
　Our corn to ashes burn,—
A lesson, sir, for you and me,
　If we can only learn.

V.

The wheat and barley, beans and straw,
　Was there consumed by fire ;
A sight which we together saw,
　But could not it admire.

VI.

Some in their hearts with secret prayer
　Addressed the heavenly throne ;
While others did profanely swear,
　And did their God disown !

VII.

This fire reminds me of a day,
　Which like an oven will burn,
When sinners will be turned away
　Who now salvation spurn.

VIII.

O, may we learn the lesson given,
　That, when our life is past,
We may receive the joys of heaven,
　Which will for ever last !

IX.

No fires there to burn our grain,
　No tears to whipe away ;
But perfict happiness will reign,
　Through one eternal day.

X.

There, with the Father and the Son,
　And the Good Spirit too ;
We hope to live, when we have done,
　With fires here below."

And not only are the ideas and the talk of many of the lower classes in England thus coloured and tinged, or even saturated with the religious element, but their hope, on the bed of pain and death, oftentimes burns with a lustre almost unearthly—a sure, blunt, matter-of-fact belief in Heaven and immortality as things tangible, unknown among men who are far their superiors in education, and, perhaps, even sometimes in moral conduct. Of this personal religion—of this child-like trust, of this calm, Christian resignation in time of suffering or death; of this bright hope of immortality, little—aye, passing little—is found in the character of the Spaniard of the same social position. He does not, it is needless to say, read the Bible—that rich store-house of thought and religion—it is not found on his shelves, and, were it put into his hand, not one in eight could read it. His conversation is entirely free from being tinged with the religious element, and when he touches upon these matters, so dear to the heart of his English brethren, it is too often with an admixture of levity which is strangely out of place. Thus a religious miner, whose boast it was that for many years he had never failed to purchase (the honour is paid for) the privilege of carrying one of the images in the processions of La Semana Santa, said to his master, a well-known Spanish mine-owner,—" I have had a bad time lately, and cannot afford to pay for the privilege of being one of the bearers of San Juan. Will you advance me the money? For I could not bear to miss the performance of that sacred duty; and won't I just shake him!"

Indeed, the religious indifference of the miner's character, compensated for, in some degree, in social intercourse, by his strict sense of honour and his easy good-nature, is as marked as the earnestness of the Cornishman. It is to be feared that his religion has lost its vital power, and has but little hope upon him. When the tinkling bell of the procession carrying the Host to some dying brother is heard coming slowly down the street, the miner, with his wife looking idly on, will merely say, " It is so and so dying. Bueno" (well); then idly light his cigarette, and dismiss the matter.

Sometimes, however, among the women of the mining population, will be found a really strict and simple religion. A Spanish nurse, whom I well knew, was one out of many instances of this. Whenever she had a few moments to spare, she would be found sitting on the door-step or at the open window, reading one of the books of the " Misa," or one of the multitude of printed prayers to " Nuestra Señora," or religious tracts, which are sold for a couple of farthings apiece at the corner of every street. Every night thrice she rose to count her beads and pray, sitting, half-audibly. One night her adopted child's fate was trembling in the balance, for he had been drawn for the army, but was seeking exemption on fair grounds. As the old church-clock tolled the hour each time, she rose from her bed, counted her beads, and prayed for her favourite's deliverance. The fatal morning dawned,—exemption was not to be his. I saw her on her return from the Governor's office. " How are you, Alfonsa?" I inquired; and the touching answer came from her quivering lips as the tears rolled down her careworn face, " Bien, con mucha pena," that is, " Well, but with many a pang." Nothing shocked poor Alfonsa so much as to hear it said, " To-morrow we will do this or that." She always, in an earnest voice, added, crossing her breast, " Si Dios quiere" (if God will). But she, poor thing, was very ignorant; and, on the sorrowful occasion just referred to, she deemed that her prayer was not granted, nor even heard, because God was angry with her for having neglected some religious ceremony of her parish church!

But such cases are the exception, and are far from being the rule. And if, in his carelessness about public worship, about his private devotions, and in the general absence of that definite personal religion, and sense of responsibility to his God, the Spanish miner presents so marked a contrast to his English brother, so also is the child-like trust in God, and the Christian resignation in times of trial, which characterize the latter, too often absent.

Seldom, if ever, do you hear those well-worn words, " The Lord will provide," or any word denoting the existence of trust in the Fatherhood of God, from his lips. In their place are found words and ideas which have a far different colour. " I suppose they will be able to rub on;" or, " It is bad, very bad, most unlucky." In fact, trust in his "luck" takes the place with him of trust in his God. True, no one is so cheerful, so joyous as the poor Spanish miner; but his joy is a surface joy, his cheerfulness is built upon no foundation. He is light-hearted rather because he refuses to think at all about the future, with all its unknown dispensation of weal or woe, than because he can leave it in the hands of a Providence which he feels to be all-merciful and all-wise.

And as regards Christian resignation, when days are dark or friends are few, but little is found in the

Spanish miner's character. His resignation is rather the resigning himself into the hands of a merciless necessity, than those of a kind and wise Providence. "It is hard, but it is my fate;" or, "Bad, but one can't control these things;" or, "Ah! life is a mule-cart journey, you must get into some ruts," are some of his common phrases. And of that bright hope of immortality which so often has astonished and delighted one when seen bearing its blessed fruit at the death-bed of a poor labourer or miner in some rude cottage or outlying hamlet in England, the poor Spaniard has but little share.

By his rude cuatré (small bedstead used by the better class of miners), still oftener by his rude litter spread upon the brick-floor of his one room, his wife and some other good woman will repeat, as he turns his face to the wall to die, the prayer to God, to Christ, to the Virgin guardian of the town in which he lives, but his lips hardly respond; he is thinking of his work, of his employers, of all that he is so soon to lose, rather than of all that he so soon may gain. But he does not complain,—and that is great praise; seldom does suffering of body wring a murmur from the blanched lips of the dying Spaniard. "If I am to die, what matters it whether it be to-day or to-morrow?"

There is, however, one point in which the Spaniard, with his indifference, his ignorance, his superstition, contrasts very favourably with the Englishman. "Cant"—by which I mean that excess of superficial religious talk so common among the Methodists of Cornwall and Wales—is a thing unknown to him; nor does he ever condemn, or even harshly judge, the religion of his neighbour. And in this last-named point, both among high and low, the Roman Catholic Church strikes me as grafting a more favourable, because a more modest and charitable, spirit upon her sons. Where all are under the Church and her decrees, there, then, is found not egotism, no exaltation of self, no religious pride. Perhaps the Puritanical spirit finds the grey skies and sombre mists, and rugged sounding shores of the Cornishman, better suited to its development than the bright skies and sunny plains of Spain,—though whether or no climate and scenery have, together with race, their share in fostering any special phase of Christianity in a country, is too deep a matter to be more than mooted here.

In another point the character of the Spanish contrasts favourably with that of the English miner. The former is, essentially, a sober man. Rarely is he "given to drink." He always commences his morning with a dram of aguardiente; but this is needful for the climate, to fortify the inner man; indeed, if you take the Spanish miner before he has had this potion, he is more inclined to be quarrelsome than at any other time of the day. The proportion of "drinking men" in any Spanish mine is about three per cent., whereas in England, although not more than that number may be regular drunkards, yet there are very few who do not sometimes "break out," and go "on the spree."

Again, the Spaniard is the very child of mirth, the Englishman of seriousness. The Spaniard sings as he goes to his work, sings as he returns from it, sings at his work; plucks the bright flower of the Campo to put it in his button-hole; loves society and good-fellowship, and spends his evening trolling forth to the tinkling guitar the wild ditties of his land, of love, and mirth, and jest.

How different is the Englishman! Life is no jest to him,—rather it is a serious reality. In silence he wends his way in the grey of morn to his work; silently he works; silently he returns homewards; silently he smokes his substantial English clay-pipe, and drinks his muddy ale, only now and then speaking a work or two, those words being the result of the musing of many minutes!

As regards contentment, the Spaniard, again, bears off the palm from his better-fed, better-housed, better-educated brother. No matter how small his wages, he never dreams of striking: coarse though his fare, it is eaten with a smile; comfortless though his lodging, he will welcome you to it as his "casa"; standing out in marked contrast to his brother across the sea, who is seldom, if ever, really contented.

Again, the Spaniard is the very child of courtesy; he is, as it were, one of "Nature's gentlemen." He could not say or do a rude thing. To walk with the stranger; to relieve him of any load he may be carrying for a mile under a burning sun; to offer you—and the offer is meant—a share of his simple meal, if you chance to come upon him when dining,—is simply his habit.

The story told of a rencontre between the late Bishop Wilberforce and a Berkshire peasant lad is not without its point under this heading. The Bishop's keen eye, during a confirmation, espied the countenance of a lad presented for that rite which he thought he recognized as the countenance of one whom he had previously confirmed, and, on his chaplain apprising the lad of that prelate's surmise,

"Him's a loiar, then," was the rejoinder of this wild bustard of the Berkshire Downs! A Spaniard would shrink in horror from the bare idea of using such language.

The impulsiveness of the Spaniard, again, comes out in marked contrast to the slow, calculating disposition of his English brother. As an instance of the two characters, the following anecdotes may be cited. A Spanish miner, with whom the writer of these pages was living, took umbrage at the conduct of some woman—of very shady character, alas!—towards himself, and, in his passion, turned the woman out of the house, saying, "She is a *mala mujer*" (a bad woman). I said nothing; but two hours afterwards he had invited the "mala mujer" to the share of his homely fare, merely saying, in answer to my look of surprise, "No one can afford to throw stones." An English miner, if my memory serve me correctly, acted very differently on a similar occasion. His neighbour's wife had grievously gone wrong in breaking the wedding tie, and it came to his ears. He slowly lit his clay-pipe, meditated for a whole evening, and then, having made out the bearings of the case entirely to his own satisfaction, and the unhappy girl's condemnation, he announced, as he rose to retire to bed, the conclusion to which his cogitations had led him in the following terse sentiment:—"Why, I'm saying to myself, you must be a naughty woman; surely you must,"—a conclusion on which he afterwards doggedly acted to the end of his days.

Sad as is the impurity before marriage, which most certainly does exist both among the mining and agricultural populations in parts of England, it must be confessed that it is more than equalled by the tone of morality after marriage in the Black Country of Spain.

It is no uncommon thing for a woman to have her "querido" (favourite, or darling), and the husband, in his way, being equally guilty, both are fain to wink at the delinquencies of the other. And although the mother guards her daughter from all opportunity of misconducting herself, by external precautions of the most stringent and tyrannical nature before marriage, yet cases are not uncommon where a mother will actually sell the honour of her daughter, a child of fourteen or fifteen, for the trifling sum of a few Spanish dollars. The indifference with which impurity is looked upon and spoken of in the Spanish mining-districts (and, perhaps, in others also) is something truly alarming.

I have said that a certain sense of honour and a great natural warmth of disposition aid in compensating for the Spaniard's want of definite religion and sense of moral duty. And instances of the former are not wanting in the daily life of the Spanish miner.

A short time since, two Spanish pitmen quarrelled below ground, and decided on repairing to the bank to settle their quarrel by the knife. The one went up by the ladder, his adversary, feeling weak, requesting to be wound up in the bucket, showing his perfect trust in the good faith of his foe. Most carefully, indeed with extra precautions, when he arrived at the bank, the miner brought his adversary safely to the surface. The two men fought, and the man who had so carefully brought his adversary into the daylight fell, mortally wounded, by his hand.

Again, you may see a crowd of three hundred

Spanish miners forming a ring around two of these combatants. The fact of a fight is soon known to the Municipal Guards, who, sword in hand, hasten to the spot, probably to find one being carried off to hospital mortally wounded. Should a single foul stroke have been given, the bystanders will detain the survivor, and hand him over to custody as a coward and a villain; but should the fight have been a fair one, the survivor, though wounded, will make, or have made for him, a safe escape, nor will one lip be opened to inform against him and betray his name.

To sum up what has been said in terse, but true sentences, it may be asserted that the Spanish miner is the very child of mirth, the English of seriousness. The Spaniard loves the song and the dance; the Englishman, his beer drank in silence, and his own fireside. The Spaniard loves to wander; the Englishman's boast is that he has worked on one farm for twenty years. The Englishman seeks to save money, and increase his wages; the Spaniard never saves, he lives but for the passing hour, and would think "agitation" too much trouble. To the Spaniard (of course, when I say Englishman and Spaniard, I allude to the peasantry), life is a jest; to the Englishman, a reality, and a stern one. The Spaniard is naturally polite; the Englishman naturally boorish. The Spaniard affects dressiness, even in his rags, and has a passionate love for gaudy colour; the Englishman affects a decent dress only on Sundays, and is content with the old grey, brown, or white smock-frock; or, in these enlightened days, when smocks are, I hear, fast disappearing, he is pleased with the customary suit of solemn black. The Spaniard plucks the bright flower of the Campo, and puts it in his button-hole; the Englishman, regardless of its charms, plods his way past his canker-rose or cowslip unheeding. The Spaniard is passionately fond of music and noise—his mule without bells were no mule to him; the Englishman likes quiet, and is not musical, as a rule. The Spaniard loves society; the Englishman, solitude. The Spaniard is ever contented; the Englishman, ever prone to grumble. The Spaniard has an abundant store of natural wit; the Englishman, *poco, poco*. The Spaniard is naturally intelligent; the Englishman naturally obtuse—what intelligence he has, he owes to the village school. The Spaniard is naturally demonstrative and affectionate on the impulse of the moment; the Englishman takes a long time to like you, and then he never lets you know it. The Spaniard has no sense of truth or truthfulness; the Englishman loves either. The Spaniard is uneducated; the Englishman, educated. The Spaniard makes the best of things—he is easy-going; the Englishman seeks to better them. The Spaniard never reads; the Englishman reads much. The Spaniard is very talkative; the Englishman, very taciturn. The Spaniard is passionate; the Englishman, morose or sullen. The Spaniard thinks nothing of cursing; the Englishman thinks it wrong. The Spaniard has no sense of personal religion; the Englishman, in all cases, a certain sense. The Spaniard, as a composer, composes profane, the Englishman, sacred, doggerel. The Spaniard uses the knife; the Englishman, his fists. The Spaniard has naturally the manners of a gentleman, be he ever so low; the Englishman has none, so far as I know, but what have been drilled into him. The Spaniard's skies are bright; the English, overcast. The Spanish cigarillo and wine are light and ephemeral; the Englishman's clay-pipe and beer are most substantial. The Spaniard's food is light; the Englishman's very solid. The Spaniard is loose in morals; the Englishman, strict. The Spaniard is madly enraged; the Englishman, doggedly brutal. The Spaniard is proud of his country and family; the Englishman, self-respectful. The Spaniard is reckless from not thinking of danger or of life; the Englishman, courageous—he weighs the issues, and makes up his mind to risk the stake at all hazards. The Spaniard is cruel to his beast; the Englishman, merciful. The Spaniard is generous on impulse; the Englishman, from principle. The Spaniard is thoughtless, and free from care; the Englishman, contemplative, and full of care. The Spaniard is boastful; the Englishman, not so. The Spaniard is somewhat idle; the Englishman, somewhat too industrious. The Spaniard lives in an untidy stone shanty; the Englishman, in a neat cottage, with a garden and a beehive. The Spaniard meddles in politics; the Englishman leaves them alone. The Spaniard seldom shows his religion by word; the Englishman, very often. The Spaniard is a sober man; the Englishman, prone to drink. Very affectionate, very warm-hearted, with a certain keen sense of honour,—bright, cheerful, genial, sober, and full of courage,—the Spanish miner's chief faults, perhaps, are his untruthfulness, his passionateness, and his want of purity. And, as to his social condition, it will hardly bear comparison with that of his brother in England.

Good education, good fare, good lodging, are ever offered to, if not accepted by, the English miner; and, in addition, his wages are constantly on the increase. Not so with the Spanish miner. His education is nothing at all. True, the Spanish Education Department theoretically provides that every son of the soil shall be compulsorily educated, but the practice differs widely from the theory. Not one miner in five can read or write, and, if he can, his choice of books is very limited. The books offered him are either superstitiously religious or violently political. Such a flood of true religion and useful learning as is offered to the English poor, in the cheap literature of the day, is wholly unknown to Spain of to-day.

And the Spanish miner's fare is most ephemeral compared with that of his English brother. It may be here noted that the Spanish miner has just begun to drink and value English beer. He says,—"It nerves my arm; it cures my cough!" Truly the beer, potatoes, dumpling, and pork of the sturdy Cornishman will build up a stronger frame than fruit and light acid wine, than soup and savoury fries!

As to the lodging of the Spanish miner. In one close, ill-ventilated room will sleep ten or twelve strong men. Many, for the summer months, sleep in tiny shanties, thatched with rushes, flocking into the towns when the winter rains commence; or, if the miner has a tiny stone house to himself, it has no windows, it is stone-flagged, it is crowded with pigs or poultry, too often not his own; and, should the cold hand of sickness be laid upon him, his fare and treatment in the hospital of his township is poor indeed. Not long since, in an hospital with which I was acquainted, it was proposed to vote twopence per diem as an allowance for the food of each sufferer!

How different, how far more blissful, the lot of his brother in England! Even as I write fancy brings before my eyes the regular work, the high wages, the ample fare, of the English miner, and, standing out in bitter contrast to that of the Spaniard, his neat cottage, with its glass windows, maybe his trim garden, his village school, his grey and lichened church. True, his lot may have, doubtless has, its hardships, but it is bright compared with that of the poor Spaniard,—and more, it is, by contrast, a blissful lot.

Drawing this chapter to a close, my mind cannot help following the poor Spanish miner to his hospital bed, and his last, long home. To be bled by unskilful physicians, after the long journey in the litter from the distant mine, the scene of his accident; to lie gasping out his last with little definite hope for a bright future; to know that, "when all is o'er," no decent, comely burial will be his, but a rough passage to his last resting-place, and a shallow grave, —all this is sad enough, yet over it all the poor Spaniard triumphs, surely in some strength not his own. Cheerful he lives, uncomplaining and grateful he turns his pallid face to the wall, and allows his spirit to pass, without fear, into the hands of Him who gave it.

CHAPTER VII.

AMUSEMENTS OF THE SPANISH MINER.

We have now accompanied the poor Spanish miner in the dull routine of his daily or nightly toil; we have followed him to the mine and through the mine; we have seen him hewing or blasting in the dim smoky light in the granite womb of the earth. His diseases, and their causes and remedies, the accidents to which he is liable, have all been briefly touched upon, not, the writer hopes, without enlisting the interest and sympathy of all his readers with the cheerful, warmhearted, heedless worker. We have followed the lead from the lode, or vein, to the surface, and seen it in its various stages, from the dressing-floors to the furnace, until it pours out, in a crimson, livid stream, into the moulds to be shipped for the market.

It is but a plain unvarnished tale that has been placed before the reader's eye of the Spanish miner as he is to-day, as he will be to-morrow. His living, his dress, his coarse ephemeral fare, his peculiarities of disposition, have been dwelt upon; and his general happiness, his contentedness, his courtesy, and his keen sense of honour have (Chapter VI.) been contrasted with the discontent, boorishness, and seriousness of his English equal, together with his dogged and persistent habit of condemning others less blessed or weaker than himself. The writer has written wholly without bias; he has drawn no conclusions, he leaves it to his readers to do so.

Little, however, has been said about the amusements of the poor miner, when at winter-time the evenings draw in,—here night falls suddenly, like a pall, on the dreary landscape,—and when the wintry rains pour down in tropic torrents, and the streets are ankle-deep in black mud, rendered even blacker by the sickly flicker here and there of a tiny oil street-lamp. And when winter comes; when the wild wind from the Sierra sweeps the barren plains, and howls its mournful dirge through the windowless shutters of the poor miner's dwelling, enfolding one in its damp chill embrace as it is encountered at the corners of the straggling streets; when guitar and song are no longer heard in the streets, which echo sadly to the step of the lonely traveller; when the dark-eyed, gracefully-draped Spanish girl opens a little way the caged window, and looks anxiously up at the sky, only to close sorrowfully, and with a sigh, the shutters of her cage, and to go to bed, murmuring, with a shudder, "Ahi! Dios mio, que malo tiempo hace; no vendra!" ("Alas! what wretched weather! He will not come!")

No, little Novia; he will not come to press your white soft hand in his own, and think himself happy to stand at your bars for hours! Go to your bed, and may your dreams be pleasant ones!

Where, on such a night, are all those young fellows who, on a fine night, make the streets of a Spanish mining-town to ring again with their coarse jest and wild Andaluz impromptu song? Are they at home? Some of them, perhaps; but the some, it may be, are but few; nor shall we find them until we go to the *café*, the gambling-room, and, alas! the brothel.

Each of these places, on such a night, will be crowded with these fearless, long-suffering, courteous, devil-may-care fellows, who go through life acting, only too literally, on the command, "Take no thought for the morrow."

The low *café*, where he sips his coffee and aguardiente in congenial company, hears his dearly-loved tinkling guitar, and can laugh at the coarse jests (very often jests at the expense of the priests, alas!) of the comico on the stage; the gambling-room, where he can satiate his keen appetite for speculation, and where the complicated game (which is the favourite) gives ample scope to those who desire to mulct him of his hard-earned wages; and, lastly (oh que no!), the brothel, where he sits, even until the first streak of dawn looks in reproachfully upon him, listening to the sad-gay banter and loose jests of prostitutes. These three resorts are the haunt of the Spanish miner. He cares nothing if he lose the whole of his day's wages, paying down the money with a smile and devil-may-care air; nor is he ashamed to be seen coming from the haunt which is worse than the gambling-room. In these places he enjoys himself after his fashion. Noisy and boisterous in the two, in the gambling-saloon he is ever silent and keen-eyed.

The amount of gambling and prostitution is awfully large; it is immense. Yet, be it added that the sins and immoralities of these poor misguided men are, more than half of them, sins which he does not consider to be sins at all. He has been face to face with them from his earliest childhood; he has committed them under the eyes of his parents, unchecked, as early as he was capable of so doing. Sins which are fostered oftentimes by the example of his father, his mother, and sometimes even of his priest.

In Spain the peccadillos of these last form a constant subject for the coarse jest and ridicule of the lower orders; but, as a priest, you may never criticize or decry what he says or does in church. There, at least, his office sheds rightly a halo of protection around him; there, he is God's appointed minister, and not to be criticized.

Taking all this into consideration, it is hardly wonderful that the Spaniard, child of impulse as he surely is, should obey his passions blindly, and that the self-control which he has never seen exhibited should be a stranger to him.

Arrived at his one room at evening from his mine, the miner sits down to his céna, or supper, which is possibly rice and goat's flesh boiled to rags, served up in one large dish or pan, into which all the other occupants of the same room also dip their spoons, sitting around the tiny deal-table in a circle. The regularity with which each, in his turn, takes his morsel, the regularity with which the spoons move dishward and mouthward, would surprise a stranger at first sight. This meal concluded, the poor fellow drinks a caña or two of Val-de-Peñas wine, lights his paper cigarette, and sallies forth to the places of resort above mentioned in the following order:—the venta, or wine-shop, the *café*, the house of ill-fame. The venta has been described in a previous chapter; it is enough to say that on a dirty night these tiny dark cells are thronged. At about 8·30 the wine-cup is laid aside, and the miner, with marvellous regularity, wends his way to the *café*.

The charge for entering the *cafés*, of which there are four in the town from which I write, is, on common nights, *nil;* on feast-days, a trifling sum paid at the door, namely, one real (2½d.), entitles you to a ticket for refreshment to that amount. The appearance of the *café*, with its saloon and small tables dotted about, is much like the saloon of an English gin-palace, and holds about 200 to 300. The room is so densely filled with smoke that you can scarcely see the stage at the farther end. A rude curtain falls in front of the platform, hardly concealing the rude attempts at scenery. All around you are miners sitting at the tiny tables, and your ear is half-deafened by the click of the dominoes; every one plays, and they are furnished gratis by the proprietor.

The time for which these men play this weary game, without even looking up, reminds me of a characteristic of the Spaniard which is greatly to his credit—he is essentially a patient man, never tired of waiting; he will light his cigarette, and sit on your doorstep, hour after hour, waiting your convenience, and, when summoned, will appear with a smiling face. The following anecdote may be cited as an instance. I told a Spanish miner to wait outside my house, and quite forgot that I had so done. Five hours afterwards, on starting for my ride, I saw him still waiting. Apologizing for my apparent rudeness, he said, " I am very much at your disposition, señor." And one could not forbear inwardly drawing a comparison between this poor fellow's perfect good temper and courtesy and the probable rough bearing of an English pitman under similar circumstances.

But it is time to seat ourselves among the homely, cheerful crowd at the *café*, and learn more of the

Spanish poor. Around us are men of every variety of provincial costume, every variety of occupation. In Spain the bitter distinction between class and class is unknown; the servant who waits at the table of the nobleman joins in the conversation of the table; the gentleman smokes his cigarette with the shopman; and so a few gentlemen are sprinked here and there among this motley crowd of miners, shopmen, water-carriers, olive and vine dressers. Women are absent, save a few brightly-dressed gipsies, who set town etiquette at defiance, and, once seated, you (Oriental fashion, is it not?) clap your hands for the waiter, or make that hissing noise so common to direct attention in Spain. Coffee, milk, aguardiente, maraschino, rum, brandy, and lusciously sweet " gascosas" (soda-water, lemonade, &c.), can be had, although the rum and brandy are execrable. " Refrescos" of sarsaparilla, lemons, almonds, &c., and other sweet and cooling drinks, are the fashion.

If you know the miners, one of your old friends will instantly hiss, and put a chair next to himself for you; he will insist on treating you, and be offended if you refuse. These poor fellows would sooner spend their last farthing than allow the Englishman to pay; and, frequently, when you have not seen him, your friend will have seen you, and paid the waiter for all you have had. You ask for your account, and the answer is " Esta pagado" (it is paid for); nor will you ever know to whom you are indebted, the waiter being bound in honour not to disclose the payer's name! With such little outbursts of natural kindness, with such little amenities, do all, from the rude miner to the nobleman, soften and brighten life as they glide idly down its swift-flowing stream.

Sit down with these four men at the table in front of the stage. See, one has already " given the sign," as it is called, to the waiter that he means to treat you because he knows and likes you. Try and " give the sign " before him to the waiter, signifying that you yourself wish to stand treat, and you will invariably find your own pitman has been beforehand!

And now all round you are waiting for the tattered green curtain to rise, and time is hanging somewhat heavily on hand. Some one orders a bottle of lemonade, the cork of which, flying up, drops amid a group of dominoes; the miners are delighted with the joke; every one orders a bottle of the same, and the corks are popping all over the room; the lemonade, however, is left untouched, for the most part, these simple fellows having thus paid fivepence a-piece for this amusement!

Perhaps you have come without tobacco for your pipe. I did so once, and in a moment three pouches were lying on the table, the owners severally entreating me to " do them the favour of using it." So courteous, so easily pleased, so kindly is the Spanish miner.

The curtain rises, and the music begins, or the acting, as the case may be. Accompanied by a pianist, a dark-eyed girl, in flaunting dress, with ribbons of many colours, commences first one, then another, of the wild provincial ditties of Spain. The Malagueña, or Malaga song, a great favourite; the Manchega, which makes the eye of the miner of La Mancha sparkle as he thinks of the wine-skins of those desert, yet wine-producing steppes; the Sevillana; the Gaditana; the Granadina, also a great favourite. The same wild, monotonous air, the same melancholy modulations, prevail in each song—songs so peculiar in their music that the notes could not be written, nor could an Englishwoman acquire the art of singing them correctly.

The Spaniard is passionately fond of these wild ditties; they have a strange hold on his heart and fancy; and English music he despises. "Of course, no Inglés can sing our songs; for in England they sing quite differently." The singer and player both receive 2s. 8d. per night, and wine, &c. Sometimes some real, wandering gipsies will be paid for the night, and beguile the time with the dances of Andalucia, accompanied by the guitar and castanets. Every one in the audience who can do so is expected to keep time by the clapping of his hands; and every one shouts, "Holé, holé-é-é," at the top of his voice. So exciting is the scene that one can hardly refrain from joining, as every nerve of the dancers quivers and vibrates, and the beads of perspiration fall down their faces.

But better than the song and dance—for are not these ever at hand?—the Andaluz miner loves the theatrical representation. It may be one of the capital Zarazuelas, which are great favourites, and, although rude, spirited. The bell has rung; the curtain goes up; the pianist is at his post; the prompter's whisper is heard from the box. In front of a huge looking-glass sits a withered and repulsive-looking old woman. Her doncella, or lady's-maid, a dark-eyed, graceful girl, is preparing her mistress for the theatre, to which a certain Don José is to escort her. The old crone "fancies herself" to a tremendous extent; and when rouge, scent, paint, and cosmetic have been freely applied, she looks truly hideous. But she loves herself, and love, they say, is blind!

Don José is dear to the old lady, and she firmly believes that she is dear to him; but he has merely courted her to win the person of her maid! Don José comes: he looks at the old woman, with a sly under-glance at the young one. With a cold shudder he shuts his eyes, and kisses the old crone's painted hand fervently.

The sweetly pretty daughter of the old lady now enters. She is to be left at home, while her old-young-lady mother goes to the theatre. She kisses her mother, and with tears welling from her expressive, lustrous, black eyes, sings a touchingly pathetic song, which brings down roars of applause from the two hundred miners and peasants:—

> "Vamos á dormir, vamos á llorar,
> Mientras al Teatro se va mia mama."
>
> "We to our beds must go, we both must moan,
> While to the theatre mother has gone."

Don José deposits the old lady at the theatre, slips away, and comes back to dress his hair at the looking-glass and make love to the lady's-maid. She enters the room and offers to finish his hair-curling, &c., for him, which she does with a comical mixture of bashfulness and love, the two singing a really pretty duet, "Thanks to Heaven, the old lady has gone!"

But to pursue the scenes any further would be useless and waste of time; enough to say, that the love of the Don is found out by the old lady, that he pulls down her false hair, that wit and grotesque action abound. The Spaniard is always ready to applaud anything good, and to hiss mercilessly any piece of bad acting. But spirit, broad wit, and extravagance are his idea of what is good acting.

And now let us leave the *café* and the stage, and pick our way to a sad and sin-stained house. Fain would I leave unmentioned this, the last part of my subject, relating to the most objectionable phase of the miner's life. Only let me say, that while I relate the naked truth, hideous as it surely is, my readers must recall what I have said ere this about the great disadvantage under which the Spaniard, in this respect, labours; namely, the evil example set before him in his boyhood.

Immorality in England, if I may be allowed the expression, is not immorality here. Here, impurity is talked of not with bated breath, but as though it were a matter of course, and universal in the daily talk of social life.

Houses of ill-fame, alas! abound on all sides, offering their temptations freely to those who require little temptation enough to lead astray their wandering steps, and make them fall; and the gay banter, and lit-up rooms, and freedom of these unhappy homes, seem to have a marvellous attraction for the poor, hard-worked pitman, who spends most of his day at the end of some dark level underground, in a space six feet in height by four in width.

Alcahuetas, or procuresses, are a well-known class—wretched old women, who walk about the streets to entice young girls from thirteen to sixteen into their vile dens, from which, to speak figuratively, there is no return. Over such hellish portals well might stand the poet's words :—

"All hope abandon, ye who enter here."

Mothers, too, forgetting natural affection, honour, and

duty, not unfrequently take their daughters to these evil houses, sitting down quietly to chat with the scarcely less vile ama, or mistress of the house, while her young daughter is being seduced in the next room, the mother receiving, as blood-money, perhaps three or four dollars, or less. Blasphemy, too, is added sometimes to this unnatural crime,—a woman known to me, as she left her daughter at one of these houses in the embrace of some lewd debauchee, saying, "Vaya usted con Dios y con la Virgen!" ("God and the Virgin accompany you!")

Another mother whipped and starved her two daughters until they yielded to her unnatural resolve, and, it is needless to say, falling, they never rose again. But, truly, one's heart bleeds, and one's blood boils, at such things; and, for the poor fallen girl, as well as for the poor miner,—taking into account the fearful strength of their early temptations, the dreadfully polluted atmosphere in which they are brought up from early childhood, their no religion, and few ennobling influences,—taking, I say, all this into account, one can but feel that they are of those who, having received but little, are of those on whom there is no room for harsh judgment.

God forbid that such things should be; but they are, and the facts here chronicled are merely such as have come under the writer's personal experience, or have been verified carefully by him.

Tyrannically is the Spanish girl guarded until her marriage, fenced in by external precautions, taught little or nothing of that inward guide which alone, if cultivated, is stronger than the magnet's force, harder and safer than the bar of iron, truer and sterner than the guardian mother. Bitterly, when bolt and bar are withdrawn by her marriage, does she resent her former treatment, and wildly does she throw down the reins of self-control, even, alas! in some cases, conniving at the sin of a younger sister. I speak of the few, of the lowest classes.

The married life, alas! has too often its degrading blots, the husband and wife having each their "querida" or "querido."

But this is the dark side of the picture, and gladly I throw down my treatment of this part of the subject, a part which, to be truthful, and present a faithful portrait of the Spanish miner, I could not dismiss unnoticed.

CHAPTER VIII.

CORNISH MINERS IN SPAIN : A STUDY OF CHARACTER.

To transport Cornwall into Spain — the land of fantastic, drifting mist, and iron-bound coast, and sounding sea, to the sunny, cloudless skies, and dusty plains, and sweltering olive-groves of the Spanish Black Country—to bring the thoughtful, grim, Puritanical, repelling Cornishman to the reckless, light-hearted, easy-going, and attractive Andaluz, seems a strange course at first, and it will naturally be asked, " What has Cornwall and the Cornishman to do with Andalucia and the Andaluz ? " To many who read these pages it may be unknown that Cornwall, with her old spirit of enterprise, and Devonshire have formed in the wilds of Spain, wherever mineral abounds, several colonies of their stalwart sons, consisting of mining agents (called here " captains of the mine "), engineers, pitmen, dressers, smelters, and others, who live, surrounded by Spaniards, on the lonely, and oftentimes unhealthy, mines, bound together by a sort of natural freemasonry, suffering often great privations,—such as the lack of good food, the scarcity of books and newspapers, and the want of society, —but working pluckily, and with a perseverance and skill unknown to the Spaniards, and still, to a certain extent, preserving intact their national, or rather provincial, characteristics, while adding to them, imperceptibly to themselves, but surely as the blazing sun of Spain bronzes their face, a certain quaint, Spanish humour and drollery, a certain liberality of thought and opinion, which go far to fill up the blanks of the Cornishman's always fine and manly, but somewhat unattractive, character.

Taking, in his own land, his character very much from the surrounding scenery of rugged rock, and gnarled trunk, and barren grey moorland, and drifting mist, and breaking sea, the Cornishman here loses much of his inherent ruggedness of character. Perhaps the bright sun melts off some of the angles; certainly, the novelty of the surroundings, and the magnitude of the scale of scenery, and the intercourse with foreigners, broadens his mind, and he learns at last to believe that Cornwall is (possibly) in England, and not "England in Cornwall." "I never thought a Catholic could be a good man," said a stalwart pitman to the writer the other day, "until I came to Spain."

The writer's duties, for a long time past, have necessitated his spending much of his time among the Cornish miners, employed some by English, some by French, some by Spanish, some by German Mining Companies in Spain; and although his work has oftentimes been very weary, yet even when baffled by disappointment, when scorched by the tropic sun, when drenched to the skin by the fierce tropic rains, or beaten back by the fierce, cold *levante*, or east wind (that scourge of the pedestrian in Spanish wilds), the thought that he was in duty's path has ever sustained and even cheered him; while the warm, hearty, iron grip of the Cornishman has welcomed, and the gay, witty prattle and courteous speech of the Spaniard has enlivened, his path; the study of the two very opposite phases of character occupying, in contemplation or writing, many a dull and idle hour.

Certainly, if an Englishman " in society " desires to learn how he may come to value mankind, and " honour all men," he should serve a few months' or years' apprenticeship in the wilds of the Spanish Black Country, for there he will learn to value and love those who, at first intercourse, are apt, whether Spanish or English, to be abrupt and even repulsive in manner, while at heart most loving, and full of sterling good qualities.

It may be worth a passing thought, the question how far many men are spoiled by the blessing of living, as it is called, " in society,"—by which the writer means in a place and among surroundings where they meet daily so many, that they pick out, as it were, the most attractive for their friends, and too often pass by many from whom they might glean the best things—cleverness concealed under eccentricity, great warmth of heart under semi-rudeness, great forbearance and patience under dullness or apparent mediocrity.

One, men say, is not " in society " (perhaps he is the better man for that!); another is (so they choose to think) " rather eccentric "; a third is too " uninteresting." And so men pass by one and the other, neither doing any good to, nor receiving any good from, them.

Of all the many whom we meet in our daily walk of life, we value but few, too often simply because we know none; and we know none thoroughly, because in the number of acquaintances offered to us in a country like England we find, or fancy that we find, a compensation or substitute for a few true friendships, thus valuing quantity above quality.

Such was not the method of Him, who, walking among His fellow-men with an all-discerning eye, could call no one "common or unclean." So did not He.

It is true that we often seem, on a superficial survey, to have nothing in common with the majority of men whom we meet; but may there not be among them many whom a closer knowledge would enable us not only to value but to love?

My walks around the mines, which, at the spot whence I write, lie dotted over the country from a mile to four miles apart from each other, have been most uninteresting as regards sport and scenery. True, one may carry a gun and get a chance shot at a snipe in the hollows, or a plover on the barren slopes, or a raven, or half-gorged white vulture, on his return to the crags and mountain fastnesses of the Sierra; but such chances, in a country singularly treeless and open, are few and far between. The scenery, too, is devoid of water and of wood; dusky glades of olives succeeding to slope after slope of broad beans or barley; in the distance, the magnificent serrated ridges of the Sierra Nevada, Sierra de Jaën (this last a very fine range, unmarked on the best maps), and the Sierra Morena, now red with the morning sun, now blue, purple, and crimson in the hazy heat of the noon-day; the road beneath one's feet either knee-deep in dust, or flooded with streams of down-pouring rain—a road that knows no " happy mean "; blocks of granite sticking up here and there, and low-roofed ventas (boasting bad wine and worse company), built of the same material; these, with now and then a rather fine tumble of bare granite rocks, were the not very interesting surroundings of the writer's walks.

And if the walks, as regards scenery, are barren of interest, certainly the chosen companions of his tramps were even more so. These were the "guards of the mines." In Spain there are "guards" of everything: the guard of the "campo," the guard of "the olives," the guard of the rich man's "casa." Generally, men are picked out for their good conduct to fill these posts, and who generally combine a keen love of sport with their jealous care of their owner's property. These men wear a brass plate upon the breast, bound over the left shoulder with a broad leather strap, the plate bearing the name of their mine or master. Gun on shoulder, they wander about the premises at night, and hesitate not to take a pot shot at any luckless intruder.

My favourite companion, a night-guard on an English mine, always rode behind me, an attendant being necessary in this country, both for appearance and for safety, whether you be afoot or on horseback. Juan, with his cigarette in mouth, esparto-grass sandals, and long Moorish gun slung at his saddle-bow, cut a singularly eccentric figure. But his donkey, a white male, was as eccentric in character as his master in appearance. Whenever he espied a lady donkey in front, he bolted (only, however, directing his attention to those of his own spotless colour), and, if sharply reined in, gave utterance to a roar so long, so loud, so pitiful, that every donkey within a radius of half-a-mile would express his ostentatious sympathy with him. The bit is not used for donkeys or mules in the interior of Spain, an iron band across the nose serving the same purpose. Even in Cadiz and Malaga one constantly sees a pair of high-spirited carriage-horses with no other curb than this noseband, and the thought has suggested itself to me that this is the meaning of the Scriptural phrase, "I will put my hook in thy nose."

Very forbidding is the approach to a Spanish Government mine—the long, dusty, rock-strewn road, lined with its ambling, lead-laden donkeys, each carrying 2 cwt. of mineral in a couple of small sacks. Now and then a litter resting in the middle of the road on its way to the hospital, the four sturdy bearers wiping their perspiring brows. Here and there, half-hidden by wild thyme and rosemary and tangled bents, hard by the road-side, you will come upon the shaft of some ancient mine, usually of an oblong shape, denoting its Roman or Phœnician origin. Strange to say, although oftentimes seventy feet in depth, these disused shafts have no railing around them, and nothing to warn the traveller of his danger.

The mine here alluded to is a Spanish Government mine, one of the wealthiest in the country. It consists, so far as architecture is concerned, of one large, low-built granite quadrangle, wherein live the governor and the *employés*, the house of the former being easily distinguished from the rest by the small patches of white paper pasted over the doorway upon the outside. These are the multas, or papers denoting the pecuniary mulcts or forfeits of those miners who have neglected their work, with the names of the offenders appended. In a Spanish mine, these fines are very severe, and, the money being stopped from the week's pay, there is no escape.

The Spanish "working-engineers" are certainly clever artisans, to judge of the many by those I have known; and the Spanish civil engineers and mine inspectors are among the best educated and most skilful surveyors, and most pleasant companions (many are men of high family), that one could wish to meet with; yet the Spanish Government mines constantly prefer to employ, as their working engineers, Englishmen.

The two maquinistas on this mine, Paul and Michael, were both typical Cornishmen, and vividly recalled some of the characters in "Westward Ho!" to my mind—the one deeply religious, the other with an innate love of adventure almost amounting to recklessness. They both "hailed from" the western wilds of Cornwall, and lived together in a tiny one-storied shanty close to their engines. Michael, or Don Miguel, was a splendid specimen of the powerful, dare-devil, adventurous spirit of the West of England; he had been pitman at Botallack, shared in the pilchard fisheries, had come to Spain, not so much for the higher rate of wages as for adventure. "Though I have got a wife and a child at home, I don't mean to join them until I have been to South American mines. Perhaps I'll die abroad, as grandfather did; he always said he would, and so do I. It runs in the blood, I s'pose."

To show the rough character of these really hearty and honest men, Michael's first greeting of myself may be quoted. "Come at last, have ye? The right time, too!" Then (seeing I hesitated),—"Come in and take the luck of the pot; no lies about it; you won't be asked a second time. If it were the Queen of England, I wouldn't say more, and we shan't see she." The sturdy, independent spirit, tinged with religion, found utterance in the older man, as we ate our Dutch cheese and crisp endive, and drank our Val-de-Peñas wine, while an unsightly Spanish woman prepared a bowl of gazpacho for our delectation:—" There were twenty men tried for my situation, but I didn't care for twenty, no, nor for twenty hundred. Why should I block my fancy for others? But," he added, with real seriousness, " I *du* think 'tis wrong to spend my Sundays as I du."

Of course, on the Spanish mines no difference is made between Sunday and week-day, the festivals being the only general holidays; and each man can claim a holiday either on the day of his own patron saint or that of one of his mates. These poor fellows' lot is somewhat hard, owing to the causes above mentioned; and, leaving a wife and young family at home, their hearts are often wrung by the black-edged letter that comes to tell them of the loss of one of their loved ones. Such a missive came to one of the Welsh captains of a mine which I visited; and the poor fellow—a stalwart, handsome Welshman, who, in his few years " on the mines" had saved several thousand pounds—said to me, as he spoke of his darling's grave,—" Write an epitaph for her, sir; and, mind ye, it is to be something strange!" He meant, I suppose, uncommon! But whether this enforced separation, with the meeting of husband and wife but once in three years, led, as in this man's case, to a tightening of the strings of love, or whether, as in others, alas! it leads to immorality, and to their loosening, it is equally hard.

Several points in the peculiar character of the Cornish miner in Spain must be now briefly dwelt upon. Among others, it must be mentioned that he is full of anecdote when a stranger visits him. In fact, his loneliness and isolation forces him to bottle up all his stories until the rare opportunity comes of retailing them. And, I must say, I have heard more stories full of dry humour when sitting with these men than anywhere else; stories spoiled, however, by the slowness of their narration, the *modus operandi* of telling them being two words, a mouthful, a collection of thought, then two words more. One or two of these men's stories are worthy of being repeated.

The older man of my two entertainers aforesaid (Don Pablo) had worked in England for a certain Mr. Dunn, a rigid Quaker. Mr. Dunn one day asked Paul to take luncheon, and Paul refused; but afterwards he repented, and went to ask for the food. "No," was Mr. Dunn's answer, "you said you would not, and I never allow any lies to be told in my house."—"So," said Paul, "I lost my dinner." Next week, Paul returned to his work, the thought of his lost meal still rankling in his mind. Mr. Dunn asked him again whether he would take some luncheon, and, determined this time not to be done (forgive the play), Paul said "Yes." A huge Cheshire cheese was set before him uncut, and Paul inquired of his host, "Where shall I cut it?"—"Just where you please," said Mr. Dunn.—"Then," said Paul, "I'll cut it at home, and—you won't have any lies told in your house, you know."

The moment one of these men tells a story, it is a *point d'honneur* that his fellow should cap it with another.

When this story was finished, another "English artisan in Spain," of the same ready wit and rough-hewn calibre, joined us. He was a smith by profession, and, in appearance, the very type of him who stands "under a spreading chestnut tree." This poor fellow, originally of Tynemouth, had lost twelve children in Spain and his wife; he had been twenty-four years in the country, and had had what is commonly called a rough time of it. When his children were born he had hesitated to have them baptized by the Spanish priests, owing to the belief, prevalent among these poor, and oftentimes ignorant and prejudiced, men in Spain, that, if baptized by the Spanish clergy, his children might be called upon, as Spanish subjects, to take up arms for their country. And so the poor fellow had buried his unbaptized children in the mountains, taking their bodies up at night, slung upon a mule's back! Very pathetic were the simple words in which he commented upon this sorrow: "I can tell ye, it went uncommon hard with me to have to do it; it oftentimes nearly made me throw" (*i. e.*, vomit). For seven or eight years he had been engaged in making a railway in the north of Spain, and his experiences, when related, were most interesting. He used to sleep, week after week, his rug rolled round him, in a disabled railway carriage; once, for three months, he never undressed, and never interchanged a word with any one save his two hundred Spanish workmen! "But," said he, a tear rolling down his rugged cheeks, "I experienced, when I laid up ill in a tiny, hill-side cottage in the north, more kindness than I have ever received before or since. The peasantry used to leave, by night, skins of wine outside the door, and, to this day, I have never found out who were my benefactors." Thus testifying to the warm, generous nature of the peasantry of the north of Spain.

This man had been so long in Spain—all his children, too, had (naturally enough, being born in

Spain) spoken Spanish so much from their youth up, that his English—a mixture of the North Country dialect and the patois of the Spanish miner—was almost unintelligible to me, as he recounted, as his contribution to our round table, how "he never refused to take a boite with any one, because once he left grandfeyther's mooton to run home and be in time for a bit o' roomp-puddin' at whoam. When he got there, the other childer was doin' apple doomplin'; so he took and axed sister to bring back the roomp-puddin', and she took and give him such a hidin' as he never had before; since which he had never refused a bite, whenever, however, and wherever he could get it!"

This story met with great approval from the rest of us: it was such a simple, rough, and pathetic tale, and told with real difficulty, in the nearest approach to his native dialect which he could command.

These men very soon become considerably Spaniardized themselves. They stay in the country, perhaps, for twenty or twenty-five years, until they have, by sheer hard work and fair fighting, amassed a few hundred pounds, when they either, tempted by the bright sun and the high wages, settle down among the Spanish mines, or else return to the old country, to find the home broken up, the friends dead and gone, the links too often snapped, and their constitution enfeebled by the Spanish heats, and wholly altered,—utterly unable to bear well the damps of Cornwall or the cold of the North Country. Their grown-up children constantly marry among the Spaniards, and make Spain their home, talking, at last, a jargon (when they essay to speak English!)

so strange, that it would puzzle even Professor Max Müller himself.

In marrying a Spanish girl, the Englishman in Spain either takes his chosen spouse to the Cathedral at Gibraltar, to be married after the rites of the Protestant Church, or else, as is too often the case, he makes, to save trouble, a "recantation" of his old faith, and is received into and married after the rites of the Romish Church. For the Protestant marriage of a Spanish girl is not recognized as such in Spain; and even the officials who take the annual census of the names and ages of the several households in any town, persistently call the lady thus married by her maiden name alone, and enter her as such on their list. Sometimes, but not often, an illicit connexion, ending in marriage, springs up between the English miner and some dark-eyed Spanish lassie; but it may be they marry after all, and the Spanish law (offering, as it does, a good field of study for English jurisprudents) legitimizes all the children born before wedlock the moment the marriage is concluded.

Having spoken of these men's lonely and isolated life; of their warm hospitality; of their rugged, broad wit; of their extraordinary patois; of their hardships and their frequent intermarriages with the Spaniards,—a few lines shall be added with regard to their intercourse with the Spanish miners under their command. The state of the case, briefly put, is something like this:—The Englishman has no courtesy and very little tact, and quarrels and "desgustos" arise between the two from the following causes: (1) because the Englishmen, for the most part, do not understand or speak the language really well, and so make mistakes, and give and take offence; and

(2) because they do not understand, and make allowance for, the peculiar temperaments, ideas of caste, and notions of the Spaniards. The Englishmen are too matter-of-fact for the Spaniards. The Englishman thinks to himself, "Have not I treated that man fairly?" whereas the poor Spaniard, with more refinement, if less truth and solidity, says to himself, "Has he not spoken rudely to me?"

One is constantly reminded of the story of a Sussex peasant and his wife, who, in the following anecdote, typify exactly these two phases of human character. A poor wife goes to visit her husband in the stocks, on the village green, and says to him, "They can't have put you there, John?" and the poor fellow, with Cornish matter-of-fact, says, "But they have, though!" But though he is—according to Spanish ideas—discourteous and too matter-of-fact, the Spanish miner looks up to his English captain for his dogged determination and pluck, for his truthfulness, for his strength of limb. The Cornishmen are self-possessed, mentally and physically powerful; and the Spaniards respect them accordingly for their *sang-froid* and their strength.

As an instance of the *sang-froid* of the English miners and captains in Spain, the following may be quoted. The smith above referred to said to the writer, "I've been twenty-four years in the country, and I've never met with any contradiction from a Spaniard, barrin' as my life has been twice attempted."

Again, a Spanish miner, discharged for a third offence, once came at this man (who had no weapon) knife in hand, to deal him a deadly blow. The North Countryman folded his arms, and stood like a rock.

The Spaniard, seeing his right hand near his breast, and surprised by his coolness, said, "Ah, you have a revolver!" "Well, then," said the North Countryman, eagerly seizing the suggestion, "I am the best man! And," added he, telling me the story, "I reckon I did not tell any lie either!" And any one, looking at his muscular frame, and cold, stern eye, would have believed that he was "the best man."

This same man told me that once a man of his own gang drew his knife upon him. They closed and wrestled, and the Spaniard was thrown and his knife taken from him. "Good-bye, señor," said he, as he went away. "Of course it is good-bye for ever; I shall be turned off now."—"Not at all," said the Englishman. "I bear you no ill will, and only threw you because you forced me to it. If you don't say a word, I never shall."

But it is time to leave the "Bed of Rosemary" (these mines have strange names,—"The Omlet," "St. Peter," "The Broad Shaft"), and to wend our way across the rocky, broken ground towards a little, isolated, desolate mine, on which lives "Captain Jack, the Preacher."

These Cornishmen are most of them Methodists, and some of them are rendered still more severe in character by an admixture of teetotalism; the characters formed out of, or braced by, these various conflicting elements, forming the most marked contrast to that of the thoughtless, ephemeral, tolerant Andaluz.

A good man, according to his light, a true and brave man, but one without real liberality and without real human sympathy, so self-opinionated as almost to "divide the world around him into 'my idee' and humbug,"—such, if you can conceive of it, is Captain Jack, the Preacher.

Captain Jack had been leader of a class in the wilds of Western Cornwall, and he could never forget it, nor could I. Never did I cross the sandy, rocky, thyme-covered waste which led to his lonely cottage, without a cold shudder; for I knew well that, however tired and thirsty I might be, no refreshment or rest was forthcoming until after a good argumentation. Of " living nearer to God," of " sins blooded out," of " buildin' upon the Rock," was Captain Jack's daily converse.

A short, thick-set, uneducated man, with a keen, kindly eye, a hearty grip of the hand, and a prayer for all, such was Captain Jack. The very isolation of the mine where he dwelt—a very small one—had tended to make his character sterner and his opinions more fixed than they would otherwise have been. That the Preacher tried to do his work, I know well; that he succeeded, I am not so sure. There was in his character a sad lack of human sympathy, and, without that, no man can win men.

Religion of a certain sort makes some really nice characters strangely offensive, and I was always glad when the Captain laid aside the "spiritual man," as he called it, and, after the sermon and prayer, became once more the "natural man." I loved to see his kind, bright smile and old self come back, as he lit his short black clay, and poured out a bumper for the " old woman," and me, and himself.

For the sturdy, middle-aged Cornishman who comes out here from his own solitudes simply to live a few peaceful years of hard work, and save a lump of money (by high wages, coarse cheap fare, and living on the mines rent-free), the life of the mining captain in Spain may be very well; at any rate, it is harmless, if he escapes calentura, and may do good. But for any educated gentleman, who has not many resources in himself, and has been accustomed to society at home, and books and papers, to come and live upon these mines,—and many, even now, are trying the experiment,—I should give the advice *Punch* gives "to those about to marry," namely, "don't." The climate is disagreeable, and, if not absolutely unhealthy, very trying; the society is uncongenial; the country is most unsafe; the sport wretched.

And, as regards the middle-class mining captain, it is questionable whether he very greatly benefits himself by leaving his native shores. True, the wages are fair; for an agent, £150 per annum, with house (such as it is), servant, firing, and lights free, being about the average. But we cannot look at life only from a financial point of view. The agent has to run the risk of calentura, or fever; also he is in a strait for years until he has acquired the language of his new country. Then he has to leave his wife and children behind him, only seeing them once in every three years for three months (the time and period allotted by the companies). True, he has permission to bring them, but he must pay their passage; and, when here, his wife has no society, his children no opportunity of getting educated.

CHAPTER IX.

EL CARNAVAL IN A SPANISH MINING DISTRICT.

THE Spaniard of the interior treats life as a jest, and never loses an opportunity of showing that he does so. While his sun shines brightly, while the castanets click and the guitar tinkles, he lives—lives for the day, forgetful of the morrow. Should the sun be overcast, should illness come on, he creeps into the darkest and most remote corner of the room, and curses the "unkindly fate" that tempers the sunshine of his life with the shower, and spreads the dark cloud of illness over his house as well as over the skies of his land.

The seasons of his Church's festivities are true gala-days to him. He throws himself into every amusement, and spends his last penny on glitter, music, and better fare.

Ask him why he does not lay by for a rainy day, he will say, "I don't know that it will ever come, and I certainly shall not be happier for thinking of it." Or ask him why he does not save for old age, and he will tell you, "Perhaps I shall never reach it."

Carnaval-time is with him a season of amusement—a scene of noise, and glitter, and mirth, in the rude, strange revelry of which he is quite at home, and with the childish delights and amusements of which he can fully feast his mind. In "Los dias del Carnaval," or, as they are called by the higher class, the "Carnestolendas," his soul delights: in the prospect of their coming, in their delights when they have come, in their memory when gone, he lives, and smokes, and smiles.

What is it to him that but last night a batch of political prisoners went guarded closely past his door, for whom Carnaval had, and will have, thoughts and memories all too joyless? What to him that the poor lassie next door is going to fast, and sew, and weep, for the conscripts have been drawn again, and her Novio has been drawn for service?

Long before the streets were placarded with the huge posters, or, as they are called here, "Los Bandos," saying that the 15th, 16th, and 17th, being "Los dias del Carnaval," masks and mascaradas may be worn in the streets "until set of sun," and a general holiday observed; long ere this, the town of which I write— a large country town under the ragged woods and barren granite peaks of the Sierra de Jaën—was waking up: making dresses, buying masks, idling, gambling, smoking, dressing up figures in all sorts of strange costumes, laughing, or working, if needful, to save a few pesetas for the Carnaval.

On Sunday, February 8th, the scent of the coming festivities hung not lightly in the air. At eleven o'clock two bulls, dressed out in gayest streamers, headed by a brass-band playing its loudest and its liveliest, and followed by a crowd of gaily-dressed men and women of the lower orders,—peasants, muleteers, artisans, gitanos, in every conceivable costume,—promenaded the streets, and then proceeded to the bull-ring. The bull-fight then took place—a subject already sufficiently described. Thousands thronged the ring;

even the poorest had his peseta ready to pay for admittance.

Next day entered my trusty Manchegan servant, her pensive face bright with smiles. " Good news for the English officer! Mañana, carne de toros en la Plaza!" (Beef in the market to-morrow!) Never, by any chance, do you get beef in the interior save after a bull-fight: it cannot be killed, owing to the heat and its bulk, in the summer; and, owing to the absence of fodder,—I mean grass and herbs, the Campo being barren and often treeless,—no cattle are seen in the winter months. So, mañana, for the first time during my residence here, since the last bull-fight, nearly eight months ago, we had beef. Joyous sound! joyous smell! Thoughts of a good dinner, after living on coarse fish, and goat's flesh, and dry hares, and still drier red-legged patridges, for months, to get a slice of beef. I thought, " I will eat it; I will close my eyes; I will stop up my ears; I will put an English pipe between my lips, and I will resolve that I am in England!"

It was not to be. The beef was like boiled shoe-leather, and smelt badly.

Not contented, not satiated with the bull-fight, the cock-pit must also be open for the Spaniard. It is simply one pitched room, in a small house on the outskirts of the town; and thither, about once a fortnight, flock the partisans of this cruel sport. The tinker, the miner, the small tradesman, the fondista, will keep his cock, and back it, on Sundays, for an ounce of gold; or, if he cannot afford that, for a dollar or so. The passion, in Spain, is not for sport, but for the gambling which is a frequent concomitant of the sport. With all classes gambling is one of the recognized and lawful pursuits, or, at least, pleasures of life. You shall be sitting in a small public gaming-room, devoted to "rouletta," in will walk a peasant, who has been hoeing beans all the week at two pesetas (20d.) per diem; he will stake a dollar, lose it, and walk out with a smile. The cocks may be seen in little wicker coops, side by side with decoy-partridges, standing in the sunny street, their masters sitting beside them on the pavement outside their house-door. The best fighters come from England, and an English cock is backed readily at two to one. The tails of these cocks are cut off, and, with their feathers clipped and docked, they present, eating their wheat or barley and shreds of raw goat's flesh, a pitiable and disgusting sight. The fight generally results in a death!

Throughout the week before Carnaval gaming was everywhere to be seen. The small itinerant carriers of "rouletta-boxes," which are about the size and look much like the organ of the itinerant organ-grinder in England, flocked into the town, each box being well filled with biscuits—the same crisp, well-curled, flimsy biscuit that is eaten with an ice in England—and instilled into the veriest child the first idea of gambling. The wheel and numbers are on the lid of the box: the child puts a farthing on the box, and says, "Numbers 3 and 5"; the wheel turns, and, if it stops at 3 or 5, the child gets a pennyworth of sweet biscuits. Frequently I have seen a mother give her children—perhaps of the age of five or six years!—a farthing a piece, and lead them through the throng to the rouletta-box.

Games of the very roughest kind were the order of the day. Here is a description of one or two. A heavy water-pitcher was slung upon a rope, fastened, from window to window, across the street in which I live; traffic—traffic means only pannicred donkeys and mules, and an occasional horse or lumbering mule-cart —went on uninterruptedly, for, as soon as a muleteer wanted to pass, the two tallest girls or women, who were amusing themselves with the rope-and-pitcher play, lifted it over his head with a small, forked stick. Imagine this in one of the chief streets of an English country town of 30,000 inhabitants! What would Policeman A 1 not have to say to it? "Thoroughfare obstructed.—Disorderly lot!"

The rope-and-pitcher game is this: one of the party is blinded, and allowed to make so many slashes in the dark at the pitcher; but he cannot see, and the party tell no tales, so one of the hoydens who stand by ties a string to the pitcher, and when the blindfolded boy is just getting near the mark, she pulls it along the rope to the farther end. Whoever hits and breaks the pitcher wins, and then the fragments are used for an all-round game of ball!

Other games and amusements were of the following kind:—In the Plaza, or Market Square, where the scene is always a strikingly picturesque one, day and night, summer and winter, a young fellow, who had lost one leg in the war of the north, played the game of "Bull."

This was the game; and the crowd around his play-circle was so dense, that I could hardly elbow my way into quarters sufficiently close to admit of my seeing it properly:—The man—a fine young Manchegan, of some twenty-three summers—took off his wooden leg, and poised himself perfectly, standing still, or hopping about, in the circle, on the uneven, half-pitched ground. His companion, a boy about eight years of age, put on his head a huge pair of bull's-horns, with eye-holes, &c., and, thus accoutred, rushed and butted again and again at the *ci-devant* conscript, who, hopping nimbly aside with his one leg, and also with the help of a glaring scarlet handkerchief which he threw, if hard-pressed, over the boy's eyes, most neatly avoided the shock. This butting and hopping aside, sometimes round and round the ring, hotly pursued by the boy with the bull's-horns, sometimes merely letting the horns almost touch his stomach, and then deftly stepping aside, throwing the scarlet over the bull, would last as long as ten minutes. Then, taking off his cap, the hero solicited and received cuartos or dineros of the better sort. The Spaniards were delighted; the Plaza rang with their shouts of "Olli!" "Olli!" and their laughter.

The game was strangely rough and rude; but, remember, we are in the interior. The surroundings, however, were picturesque. The Plaza, or broad open square, dotted all over with the fruit and vegetable vendors' tents, changes its general hue from month to month. In the melon months its general hue is dark green. When the chestnuts, walnuts, and common nuts form the chief store, then the prevailing hue is a soberer one of russet-brown; but the moment that the naranjas, or oranges—the grand fruit of Spain—and lemons come into season, the whole place changes its colour, and the prevailing hue in January, February (this last the chief orange month—every child, every peasant, has his orange in hand or pocket), and March is the rich golden yellow of the orange. They lie in heaps all over the market square, and can be bought for less than a cuarto a piece; *i. e.*, four for a penny.

It has been well said, by an Englishman once well known, who has passed to his rest, that "of all the birds, he loved best the robin, because it always trilled out its plaintive ditty when the leaf of autumn began to fall, and the other birds ceased to sing."

"Sweet messenger of calm decay."

And, further, that "of all the fruits, he respected most the orange, because it came, with its cooling acid juice, cheap, and within the reach of every fever-stricken pauper in cottage or hospital, just at the time when other fruits could not be procured."

The Spaniard thinks the same; and he will tell you, "for bile, for calentura, for inflammatory attacks, God has sent an antidote in the orange of Spain." The great medicine for biliousness, costiveness, and for other complaints, among the Spanish peasantry of the interior, is the juice of an orange squeezed into a glass, with two farthings'-worth of magnesia.

The Spaniards believe firmly that the fruta del tiempo (fruits of the season) are the only proper medicinal agents, and they act upon their belief. Every mother gives her child daily three oranges; every peasant eats an orange three times a day, with a slice of bread, after his meals; and whether he be riding his donkey or driving his mule-cart, the peasant will not miss his orange.

If the one-legged man, and the mascara de toro assaulting him, were a great source of amusement to the simple-hearted, rude, and ephemeral crowd that daily hemmed them in, no less so were a tiny dog, who, shaven and shorn as to his hind-quarters to look like a poodle, danced to the squeaking of a fiddle—this latter, as rare here as a guitar in England—and the wooden figures, stuffed with bolsters, which were set up, dressed out, outside several of the houses, to be looked at, pelted, and thrown over, amid roars of laughter, or carried on the shoulders of women up and down the street, in the midst of an admiring and vociferous crowd.

Such was the aspect of our town until the morning of Sunday, the 15th, dawned, and saw at every street-corner the huge posters announcing the advent of El Carnaval. Sunday, the first of the three days, was wet and cold, and only the very roughest and rudest masks were seen promenading the streets. Here was a man, dressed simply in his wife's embroidered petticoat, put on like a surplice, and a huge, triangular paper hat, black in colour, and two feet in height, with no mask on, but his face blackened, or painted scarlet. Here was another, dressed as a woman in her deshabille; the dressing-gown being a chintz window-curtain, loosely wrapped round him. He wore a mass of false hair, and a paper mask, a woman's face. In such-like rough costume, followed by a cheering crowd, did the few most resolute and determined masqueraders, of the lowest classes, promenade the dripping streets, embrace in the street any one they chose—it is not etiquette ever to attempt to discover who your saluter is—and enter houses to offer their congratulations in squeaking, falsetto voice.

The smaller ventas (wine-shops), with their cool, dark, den-like shops, their tiny dripping counters, green basins, and two huge casks of wine of La Mancha, the rough-red and the satiny-white (Val-de-Peñas, tinto y blanco), were thronged. But there was no drunkenness to speak of, for the Spaniard, ill cultured as he is, is no drunkard.

On my return to my house from my dreary Sunday's walk, the middle and some of the better classes were all turning out in masks to a huge ball at the casino, which commenced at ten on Sunday night and ended at five on Monday morning.

One incident occurred, which may here be mentioned, at this ball. Men, of course, went, many of them in the dress of women; and no one could tell whether his partner was man or woman, for every one talks in a shrill falsetto. A friend of mine went to the ball, and selected the prettiest girl in the room, as a sensible man would naturally do, for his partner. They danced together three or four times, and at last he met an acquaintance unmasked, and asked if he knew who his partner was. "Well, then, if you want to know, you've been dancing all the evening with your own old cook,"—a lady who not only had passed her fortieth summer, but who had acquired the habit of drinking too much aguardiente at times, so that her name had become somewhat of a bye-word.

Monday dawned chill and wet. Towards two o'clock, when, on a sunny Carnaval-day, the streets would be thronged, rain fell heavily, and only a few draggled mascaras (mascara is both the mask and the wearer of the mask) picked their way through the streets, where pools of water stood, and streams of water ran down.

"A very bad Carnaval," said an old peasant of La Mancha to me, as he brought me in, in a common washhand-stand basin, about three pints of Limonada de vino. This is the Carnaval-drink of the peasantry of La Mancha. It is simply a mixture of water, orange-juice, spice, and white Val-de-Peñas wine. It is brewed in an ordinary bed-room basin, and each person dips his copa (wine-glass) into it, and drinks and smokes the Carnaval nights away.

Many weddings took place in the three days of Carnaval. The poor are married at the church. The higher classes in the interior are married first by the priest in the drawing-room of the bride's casa; that religious ceremony over, the civil judge of the township (the Juez) performs another civil or ceremonial marriage. He holds a book with the form of marrying, the couple stand before him, and he decrees " that the children born of such a marriage shall be legal heirs," &c. Then, in the evening, comes a supper and a merry dance.

Tuesday was a typical Spanish day, and in the joyous sunshine, at noon, every house (poor or rich) sent forth its crowd of mascaras to promenade the uneven streets until set of sun. The very servant who, an hour before, has brought you your dinner, comes up to you in the street, screams in your ear (often saying something vastly impertinent, because she wears a "cara," as the lower classes call the mascara), and calls you Don Juan, or Don Jaimé, in shrill falsetto voice. All, in fact, who like this rough play —among the middle and poorer classes, men and women too; among the higher, only men—put on whatever costume they like, of the roughest sort, and walk the streets, saluting every hapless stranger whom they know by name, grasping his hand, and absolutely "button-holing" him, until he is deaf with their screaming in his ear. Sometimes the mascaras "hunt in couples"; sometimes surround you in a body of six or eight; sometimes—constantly, indeed, for this forms a great portion of the fun—they enter your house; you cannot tell who on earth it is, for they are dressed as a bride, as a Hussar, as a Moor, as a miner in his underground dress; and it is considered "ill-form" to attempt to unveil your guest or pry into his secrets.

What is seen in the streets of the interior, then, at Carnaval time is this:—A motley group of people, in every variety of costume, but, be it known, of the very coarsest and the very gaudiest that can be imagined, strutting up and down the streets, screaming out in falsetto, like parrots, entering houses, *sans cérémonie*, and greeting every one they know in a somewhat demonstrative and alarming manner. The streets are simply one mass of colour, glitter, and noise, for many of these groups have castanets, tambour, guitar, and many sing loudly. At every street corner you will see the "fandango" being danced—the typical dance of Andalucia—by a man and woman in costume. Here is one dancing pair that I noticed especially. The man was the type of an Englishman (!), wearing a tall black hat, long black coat, and grey trousers; his face was blackened. His fair partner was dressed in a short white linen skirt, with tawdry lace, cherry-coloured jacket, bare feet, and hands laden with brass and silver rings. A more grotesque couple I have seldom seen. And with what spirit they danced, in the dirty road, on the uneven, pitching stones, until the perspiration streamed off their faces!

The "fandango" is a most peculiar dance. The two, each with the hands over the other's shoulders, in every hand a castanet, which they keep on clicking, stand close to one another (face to face), and dance in an active, unceasing, untiring series of little tremulous shuffles, the whole frame seeming to tremble. At the end of every minute the two pirouette round, and, face to face again, with clicking hands and whole frame vibrating, the guitar of their accompanist going tinkle, tinkle, tinkle monotonously, they commence another dance.

Here are some of the costumes which, while church-bells called to prayer, and beggars cried for "Una limosnita, por Dios" (an alms, for God's sake), and extra guards, with clanking swords, told no tale of peace or joy, thronged our streets:—A woman's petticoat, put on like a surplice, and a triangular hat, three feet high, and "shorts" and bare legs; mask, either blackened or scarlet face, or any sort of paper mask, long nose, or deformed nose, or no nose at all; woman's face, with woman's hair, and paint. These might be counted by the dozen. Spanish soldier's private dress, *i. e.*, long blue coat, and brick-dust coloured baggy trousers, and gaiters, green facings. Hussar uniform (all these faded or ragged)—light blue, yellow facings; black leather from the knee to the boot. Woman's dress—white skirt, with scarlet border a foot broad, yellow shawl, esparto-grass sandals, guitar or castanets; another—white dress plastered over with patches of yellow, red, and blue paper gummed on to the skirt, black mantilla. Here is another—An Indian, all covered with yellow and green paper, in strips, glued to his clothes. He looked like a wild Indian, or a walking forest of green and yellow, as the papers rustled, and flew up and down in the wind. All was colour, noise, and glitter.

But, to a thoughtful mind and a deeper-gazing eye, there was a sad and earnest background to the music and the paint of the light-hearted Andaluz. In the morning, and at mid-day, and at noon, as I passed through the Plaza, the streets simply swarmed with beggars of every age and sort, men, women, and children, so wretched, so starved-looking, so fittingly dirty. They seized one's coat, if they were grown-up beggars; they showed their half-naked breasts; they thrust a stump of an arm into your face, tearing off the bandages; they showed their scars of scrofula or other affliction; the children seized your hand, kissed it, and would cling on like leeches. From one and all rose up the bitter, abject cry,—"For God's sake, señor, a bit of meat, a tiny bit, and the Virgin give you good health for ever and ever." Poor, unhappy, forlorn crowd—they make one's very heart ache to look at them!

Then, sitting on the pavement all around the Square—I counted one row of sixty—were the labourers waiting to be hired for farm-work. Now and then a maestro would come up, and send off four or five to work; but when I passed at four o'clock there still sat there a crowd of these motley figures, poorly clad, many with naked feet, many with sandals, nearly all having no head-gear but a gaudy handkerchief tied over their crisp black hair. Poor fellows! with their rough vacant faces, and their unkempt dress, they seemed deserving of help; but work was scarce, and, like the labourers of ancient story, they sat there "all the day idle."

Ash-Wednesday dawned, and one or two mascaras, in defiance of authority, still patrolled the half-empty streets; and, I believe, the "sardina" (a species of small, silvery fish, like the anchovy, which forms a staple article of food among the poor of the interior in the winter months) was carried out and buried, a ceremony still performed in some parts of Spain.

A few horns were blown here and there. I know not why, as I wandered home at dusk; and the soldier's bugle from the barracks outside the town, the setting sun, and the warm atmosphere, almost made one fancy that one was listening to the Aldershot bugle winding, on a bright, still summer evening, along the range of the Hog's Back!

Here is the prayer, sold for a farthing, and repeated aloud at the different houses of the town by poor and ragged vendors on Ash-Wednesday:—

"NA. SA. DEL CARMEN.

"ORACION.—Oh Vírgen piadosísima! refugio y esperanza de pecadores, postrados á vuestros piés te suplicamos, por aquella honra que teneis de ser Madre de Dios, Vírgen perpétua, que cuando mi alma pecadora salga de este cuerpo mortal, me la guardes y me la defiendas de los infernales espíritus, y cuando mi lengua no pueda llamaros, venid, Señora Madre mia del Cármen, acompañada de toda la córte celestial, y llevarnos seguros ante el acatamiento de vuestro dulcísimo Hijo Jesús, y para la hora de mi muerte le encomiendas mi alma: Vírgen piadosísima, no nos desampares en aquella grave necesidad de la tremenda hora, y no permitas que por mis culpas se pierda en nosotros la sangre preciosísima que derramó tu dulcísimo Hijo Jesús.

"*Hay concedidas innumerables indulgencias por varios Exemos. é Illmos. Sres. Arzobispos y Obispos por rezar esta oracion y llevar consigo esta milagrosa imágen.*"

CHAPTER X.

LA SEMANA SANTA; OR, HOLY WEEK IN A SPANISH MINING DISTRICT.

To an outsider, dwelling in one of the most primitive old mining townships of Spain, the presence of Lent is marked by little of especial interest to the eye or ear. The "forty days" were ushered in by a Wednesday of glowing and well-nigh scorching heat, the thermometer, towards the end of that season, standing in the shade at 75 and even 78 degrees.

The churches were draped in black; the priests looked wan and worn; every night, at the corner of every street, and even until one and two in the morning, the wild, wailing chant of the Lenten ditty, the words of which tell, in Latin, of the sufferings of the Lord Jesus, were heard, oftentimes breaking one's rest, and suddenly breaking off in a shout of laughter, which was strangely out of place in the mouth of the troop of boys of all ages who were the singers of a theme so solemn.

Twice a week might be seen the strings of donkeys, each bearing on his panniered sides a couple of huge "atun," the sea-fish chiefly sent to the interior during Lent, the long tails of which flipped up the dust as the donkey ambled along. My Manchegan servant-maid and her husband prepared a grand new dress for their patron saint, San Juan,—a dress of crimson silk, with spangles of gold,—to be put on upon Easter Day. This was the gift of one of the parochial clergy.

Holy Week dawned at last upon a land utterly scorched up; upon crops of barley and wheat brown as sienna; upon plains of beans drooping as though they had been scalded with hot water; upon the wild flowers of the Campo, which would have been as a carpet of scarlet, and blue, and yellow, to the rock-strewn earth, all withering and discoloured.

My old Manchegan servant shook his head. "If rain does not fall, señor, in the Holy Week, God will send no rain at all." Bread had gone up two cuartos (farthings) in the one-pound loaf; the beggars added to their usual cry, "Ave Maria purisima, de me una limosnita, por Dios," the words, "Bread is going from the poor." Up to the Wednesday in Holy Week there was not a cloud seen in the sky; the earth was as iron, and the heavens above our head were as brass. Wearily I started for a four-mile walk along the rocky road to one of my most distant mines. The sun beat down fiercely as in summer; the levante (east wind) blew remorselessly along its clouds of dust. My usual companion, a Spanish miner, refused to converse about crops or weather; he was in the bitterest of bitter humours. Suddenly we came upon a Spanish peasant, with his sandals of esparto-grass, trotting behind a donkey laden with a large pigskin of wine. "Caramba," said my companion, "if you are caught about to sell wine in the Campo, you will be fined 55 pesetas. I wish you joy."

The allusion was to the new "Bando" which had just been issued, and in which it was decreed that any person selling wine or spirituous liquors in the country should be mulcted in the sum of 55, and any person committing the same offence in the town in that of 75 pesetas. This proclamation, issued by the Sub-Governor newly appointed under Marshal Serrano's Government, was considered severe; but as its provisions only extended from Holy Wednesday to the evening of Holy Saturday, it was obeyed in silence. It also, to insure the quiet of the town where it was promulgated, forbade, under a heavy fine, that any coach, mule-cart, or public conveyance should enter within the gates during the same period. This proclamation was, of course, a step in favour of the Established Church, whose ordinances, &c., have been set, as much as possible, at nought by the late Republican Governments.

I returned from a scorching, dusty walk in time to see the first procession of the Holy Week, which commenced at about half-past six on Wednesday evening. It was to start from the largest church in the town, and thither I wended my way. Outside the church was collected already, when I reached it at six o'clock, a crowd of 800 or 1,000 persons, chiefly men, the greater number of the mining or artisan class. They were standing in orderly and decent groups around the doors, and on the steps of the church, and far down into the streets, smoking, chatting, and discussing the all-important question, for the time, what sort of procession it would be this year. It should here be noted, that under the late Republican Governments, the shows and processions have deteriorated in character, and, owing to the law not holding its sheltering shield over them, much licence had become common; but now all has been altered.

The crowd had reached to some 2,000 ere the municipal guards, with their officer, came up, parting the quiet but dense mass as they came, and forming in a semicircle in front of the church doors, their glistening swords and red facings contrasting strangely with the peaceable appearance of the crowd.

I asked leave of one of these men to enter the church, and, with true Spanish courtesy, he replied, "It is open to all, strangers included; the religious ceremonies of Spain will bear inspection: enter, señor." A crowd was surging in and out of the church doors. I pushed in, and the sight within was a striking one. The building was naturally very dark, and darker still from the time of evening; the black drapery and the wax candles lighting up one—only one - side altar. All over the rush matting of the church were men kneeling in prayer, or women sitting in the usual posture of Spanish women in church. Every seat was crowded, while up and down the aisles and nave passed a quiet, orderly crowd, not one member of which failed to sprinkle himself, on entering and leaving the church, with "agua bendita," the blessed or holy water. No service was going on, nor were priests or penitents to be seen as I passed up to the side altar, round which, in a semicircle, on frames, just like an English bier, ready to be borne forth, were grouped the images, each one larger than life, of our Saviour, St. John, the Magdalene, St. Luke, the Virgin, and other saints.

Suddenly the crowd rising, surged towards the doors, and as I passed out into the quadrangle, two gentlemen, in plain English frock-coats and high hats, in deep mourning, attended by a single guard in uniform, passed swiftly into the church. As they entered, the brass band, which stood just within the portals of the church, commenced a low, wailing, melancholy air, and every voice was hushed. This announced the advent of the Governor and one of the alcaldes of the town, who, when the Government at Madrid is favourably disposed towards the Established Church, invariably follow, in their official capacity, the processions, and attend the chief misas of their Church.

"When will the procession move forth?" I asked of a Spanish miner, slightly known to me, who played the cornet-à-piston in the band. He waved his hand towards the sun, now (it was nearly seven) sinking to rest, like a small golden ball, and said, "At set of sun." As the sun sank below, or to the level of the horizon, shedding a ray of parting glory over the rocky, purple moorland, and making the distant Sierra look quite blue and sombre, the band struck up the Dead March in "Saul," and eight men, barefooted, in long robes of sackcloth, girdled around the waist with a knotted cord of esparto-grass, in which was stuck a small black cross, each one bearing a huge wax candle in his left hand, staggered down the church steps, bearing on their shoulders the image of the Saviour.

Each one of these men was masked, that is, his head was swathed in the same sackcloth, with two small slits, intended for eye-holes, but which seemed not always to be over the eyes. The image of Christ was slightly above the size of life. He was in a sitting posture, the tears flowing from His eyes. His dress was a simple dark-violet velvet cloak, with girdle. His legs were bare. His head was leaning on His left hand, His right pointing over the crowds. On His feet were sandals of esparto-grass, as they seemed to me. The men bearing their Lord moved forward about fifty yards, and planted Him upon the ground; while a crowd of fifty men, also in sackcloth, walking, taper in hand, two and two, barefooted as the rest, formed behind the image, the band playing, in repetition, stave after stave of the Dead March.

As the image was planted upon the stone-flags, about two hundred of the people—I need hardly add that I was amongst the number—fell down upon their knees in mute adoration. I only caught one whisper behind me, "The German cura (clergyman) goes on his knees too," from a knot of Spanish miners, who, according to their various temperaments, religious ideas, and education, stood, crouched, or knelt just behind me.

A man, barefooted, robed in black calico—such it seemed to me—of the coarsest kind, descended from the church door, and putting to his mouth a long trumpet—also covered with black of the same material—blew three or four steady, prolonged, discordant blasts upon the instrument.

In a moment, the front bearers shouldered the image of Christ, and the long line of "penitentes," or "humildes,"—for so the train of men in sackcloth are called,—marched forward with slow and solemn step. Every voice was hushed, every eye was fixed on the church doors whence the rest of the procession would come.

Although it was only set of sun, every one of the humildes, or penitentes, had lighted his wax or tallow candle, the length of these being, for the most part, about three feet, according to my measurement of one with which I was entrusted.

Then, from the church doors, the procession began to march forth. Next to the image of the Saviour, "the Christ of us all" (for so we call Him here), came a banner of purple velvet, borne by two men (penitentes), with candles, in the midst of which banner hung a really beautifully painted picture of Christ, fainting beneath His Cross, and weeping, His tears bedewing the rough ground.

Then, walking two and two, as usual, barefooted, and masked as the others, came ten or twelve other penitentes, or humildes; then came the Magdalen— "the nearest to her suffering Lord who had done so great things for her," as an artisan remarked to me. The Magdalen also was in a sitting posture, robed in a long drab cloak, her head between her hands, evidently weeping.

I turned round to my left, away from the procession filing out of the church doors, and a more striking sight it has never been my lot to behold. Right down the slanting, unpaved, uneven street, now crammed with thousands, moved the forefront of the long procession, the candles showing quite sickly and wan against the glow of the even yet sinking sun, the dark images standing out in bold relief against the steely-blue sky—the long line of pale sackcloth dividing the orderly but eager crowd.

Then came the image of the Virgin, robed in black velvet, bordered with spangles of gold, the costly garment she wore being new, and valued at £130 of English money. At sight of the Virgin, the patroness of the town from which I write, every knee was upon the earth—every eye, to my view, was hidden between the hands.

Then came, walking two abreast, some ten or twelve more penitentes, in the same coarse attire, of drab colour; then came St. John, partly robed in scarlet—

I know not why; and then, St. Luke. A long train of penitentes followed, all carrying lighted candles; then came the brass band, playing a mournful and stately refrain; then the priests, robed in black and white, one only being robed in dark purple; more penitentes; and then, with uncovered and bended head, dressed in decent black, the four chief officers of the town, walking abreast, and one more smaller image.

So they moved on, in a long, winding procession, down the narrow street of the Carneceria (flesh market), and right across the market square, or plaza, from which every tent, every mark of those that bought and sold, had been removed, leaving a bare, dusty quadrangle.

Every shop was shut, every window was crowded with ladies and gentlemen viewing the procession, all of whom were bareheaded. I followed in the wake of the long, sickly train of torches amid hundreds of others. Up one rough street and down another, for two weary hours, we wended our way; everywhere the procession was received with respect; everywhere the way was cleared for its approach.

At nine the procession, still attended by hundreds, returned to the dark and silent church; the images were disposed around the one dimly-lit altar; the crowds dispersed, each one, reverently and orderly, going to his own home.

In Spain, I have ever been struck and deeply impressed with the orderly conduct, the courteous bearing, of all those who attend any religious ceremony. There is no pushing, no jostling, as in England—all is quiet, sober, decent.

So ended Wednesday in Holy Week—whether religiously observed or no, I am not to say. What I may say is, that it was observed in an orderly, an uncommon, and a striking manner.

And nearly all those composing the crowd were miners, and persons of still lower, even of the lowest, rank.

Let me pause for a moment here, in my description of La Semana Santa in the Black Country of Spain. Not one ribald word, not one profound jest, met my ears; but a friend, who was present, told me that on his pointing to the image of St. John, and saying "Who is that?" a Spanish bystander said, with a ribald laugh, "Juan Ingles," *i. e.*, "John the Englishman"—in other words, "John Bull."

The same observer told me—and he is a man of the highest honour and veracity—that when he remarked to one of the crowd, "This is a beautiful procession," the answer was, "Buena, pero no vale la pene"; *i. e.*, "Good, but not worth the trouble!"

To me, however, the attitude of the crowd seemed the attitude of reverent and attentive worshippers. They surprised me by their orderly demeanour and reverence, rough miners as they were.

The next remark I would make is this. The humildes, or penitentes, as they are called, are of the people—miners, artisans, peasants, and a few gentlemen. They wear this rough sackcloth, they walk barefooted, they buy this dress out of their own earnings, and they pay six reals (1s. 6d. English money) to be allowed to walk in the processions. Is not this a great mark of faith—of a simple and childish faith, if you like, but still of faith?

We are now at the morning of Holy Thursday; the same fierce sun is smiting down, the same rainless wind is blowing. At 6·30, nominally, the procession was to start from the same church, and I went to attend it. The images, the crowds, the dresses of the priests, were the same; but this time all the penitentes were robed in black gaberdines, tied round the waist with coarse knotted ropes of esparto-grass instead of sackcloth. They wore, each one, a high peaked cap, called "caperuza," a word denoting the cowl of a monk with a peak. These caps, the peak of which was in many cases two feet high above the head, were of a coarse black calico, similar to the lining used for coats, &c., in England. Most of these men, who were the same with the sackcloth-clad men of the previous night, were also barefooted; but this night—and to the end of the Semana Santa—no more masks to the faces were worn by them. In much the same order as before the procession moved forth; but the effect of all these penitentes, in their black gaberdines, and lighted candles and bare feet, was most striking. But, above all this, every one of these men, or nearly every one, wore, lightly thrown upon his caperuza, a crown of thorns (on Good Friday no one of these penitentes was without it)—a crown about three inches broad, of what seemed to me wreathed and entwined twigs of the thorny barberry tree. And not only were all these men, who had sinned and come thus to make atonement, clad in this costume, but hundreds upon hundreds of the children of the lower, middle, and upper classes were clad in the same costume, and followed the procession, taper in hand.

One little boy thus clad, the son of a Spanish doctor well known to me, came to me, and said, "My taper is very heavy. Hold it for me, señor."

Clad in black, then, and crowned with thorns, the

procession walked round the town on Thursday night; but, as they started, a novel feature presented itself. I heard the blare of a strange trumpet, the rattle of a muffled kettle-drum; and twelve men, in buskins, short leather tunics of buff colour, and with steel helmets, quietly joined the procession as it started, falling in just behind the image of the Saviour. Each one carried a dagger in his belt, a huge battle-axe he swayed high above his head. "Who are these?" said I to a Spanish pitman, who stood beside me. "The Jewish soldiers, who destroyed our Christ," was his answer, promptly and readily given. He meant the Roman soldiers.

To the rattle of the soldier's kettle-drum, and the same grand music of the Dead March, once more we went around the town,—down steep hill, threading low alleys, up principal streets, returning at nine to the church from which we had started.

One custom of the Holy Week should be here noticed. These humildes, or penitentes, are men who have openly sinned, and desire to join in this procession barefoot as an act of humiliation. As soon as the procession has dispersed, they take handfuls of flowers, and, going to the windows of the houses around, they knock for an audience, of course pulling the black cowl over their faces before so doing. They proffer the flowers to some girl they care for, and, as she cannot see them, Spanish etiquette votes it quite allowable for her to converse with them at the barred window. Then they return, next day, to another procession or no, just as they will. The reason of this proceeding is as follows. Each penitente has been a peccador, a sinner, and, as such, is unworthy of the society of women who are pure and good; but, having walked once barefoot and in sackcloth, and once in mourning gaberdine, he considers that he has, as it were, paid his dues to God and his Church, and is free to love and be loved again.

On Thursday night a Spanish gentleman came in to chat for an hour with me. Our talk was all of "La Semana Santa" and its processions, and I said to him, "Will you not come with me to-morrow to the early service?"—"No, señor," was his answer; "the service is at 5·30, with its sermon, and, as all the penitentes have been sitting up all night, the church will be thronged, and the people, some of them, tipsy, and excited, and noisy." I said no more, but, at five on the morning of Good Friday, I rose, dressed, and, with my trusty Manchegan miner (my servant, who carried a huge iron bar for protection), I hastened to the Church of San Francisco. The morning was bitterly cold, but the clear, steely-blue of the heavens gave no sign of rain; outside the church was a crowd of some two thousand people of the lower class. The most noticeable feature in this crowd was the troops of penitentes, dressed in their high-peaked black caps, gaberdines, and sandaled feet. To-day, each one carried on his shoulder a black-stained cross of wood, about four feet long.

The crowd was surging in and out of the church doors. I pushed my way in. The sermon was being preached, in short but emphatic sentences, to the crowd that came and went up the narrow aisle. No one sat, no one stayed long, for were there not thousands waiting outside? I passed up to the pulpit with the crowd, and what I heard of the sermon was eminently good. It was delivered in short, jerky, emphatic sentences, like proverbs, so that each person might carry away something to profit him. "Your sins have condemned you, have they not? Lay them, with the heavy cross, upon the back of your Jesus."— "Are you so happy that you need no more happiness? Come to Him who takes away the load and gives peace to all." And then, carried by the crowd, I passed out.

At 6·30 the crowd had become dense, the sermon was over. The procession came forth, in the chill early morn, in much the same order as on the preceding days. Just as it started, I heard once more the "rub-a-dub, rub-a-dub," of kettle-drums, and the Roman soldiers hurried up a bye-street and silently joined in the procession.

Too weary to follow the procession in its long and winding march, I went home to breakfast. My servant put on the table a scanty meal, and said,— "Muy mal dia hoy" (a bad day this). I said,— "Yes, a bad day for food, but a good day for us all." —"Si, señor," said she; "Jesus muy hermoso" (Yes, sir; Jesus was very beautiful). She too, then, had seen the procession! A hasty breakfast and I hurried out, for was not the "Crucifixion en el Campo" (Crucifixion in the country) to take place, some half a mile off, at 7·30? To the usual spot I went, a little plain of rocky, dusty, treeless ground, half a mile outside the town. On the ground where, in former years, the Christ had been crucified, stood a crowd of about six to eight hundred persons, of the mining class. All were waiting, like myself, to see, as had been the custom, the Crucifixion acted out. We waited for half-an-hour; at last the cry was raised, "No Crucifixion this year." In a moment the crowd had dispersed, and we were all hurrying to the church of San Francisco, to which the procession would return. I stood, with the alcalde of the town and the governor (thanks to their courtesy to "the stranger"), in a little balcony above the church doors reserved for "officiales," and, headed by the image of the Christ, crowned with thorns and bleeding great drops of blood, the procession came to the doors of the church. I looked down and around, and the sea of eager, anxious, upturned faces, as the Christ was put upon a raised platform just beneath me, was indeed striking. There and then the ceremony of "selling the Lord" was gone through. (Be it remarked, on each day is acted out some one act in the last days of the Saviour.) The money was paid from one hand into another. All eyes—and there were at least four thousand pairs, I shall never forget that sea of faces—were fixed upon Him who was sold. As the last piece was paid, the Saviour's right hand went up slowly above the assembled crowd, as though in mute appeal against the treachery, and then, from the lips of four thousand of that assembled multitude, went up to Heaven and to God the fierce, earnest, faithful cry, "Agua, agua!" (water, water!) This was the miners' united prayer for rain! Once more, the Saviour raised His hand—once more went up to the steely sky, now growing blue and hot, the impassioned cry, "Agua, agua!"

All was over for the present. The man-servant (a miner) of an Englishman resident here said,—"I saw the clouds begin to gather the moment Jesus put up His hand." And so it was! Ere five o'clock on Friday night a slight shower had fallen, with the wind; the clouds had gathered, and hung, as a cloud of mist, upon the clear horizon.

One more procession moved out ere the rain commenced that evening, and from one and all there went up to heaven, as they threaded the thronging streets, the "sacta" (Latin, *sagitta*), or ejaculatory prayer, like an arrow—shorter even than the ejaculatory prayer of the Gospel, "Agua, agua!"

The body of Christ—the dead Christ—under a glass case, was carried then. It was taken to the church, and reared up aloft, guarded by two angels. No man, even a dying man, I was told, could receive the Holy Sacrament from that hour until the Resurrection morn.

On Friday night late, I strolled down with a friend to the church to see the Roman soldiers keeping vigil and guard over the body of their Lord. We were a few minutes too late. The doors were closed; but, within the church, shrilly as the wind whistled around its antique buttresses, we could hear the measured tramp of the Roman soldiers keeping watch over the body of their Lord. To my mind recurred, as I stood at the chill corner of the street, the words, "Ye have a watch; make it as sure as ye can." So ended the "Watch-night" in my mining town.

Saturday morning dawned. Thank God it dawned as a day of clouds and of thick darkness! The rain poured down in tropical torrents, and each uneducated Spaniard said, "The Lord brought it when He moved His hand."

A few guns were fired off, a few explosions of dynamite took place in the public streets,—evidences of a ceremony which is called here "shooting Judas," akin to that of the Mexicans and other nations, who, even from their ships in the docks of the Thames, flog and drown the traitor Judas. Hundreds of lambs, to be killed for the Easter feast, passed my door, the rain the while falling fast. One and all, we thanked God for that rain.

One word, and I have done. It is often objected to these processions that they give rise to a scene of lawlessness and disorder. True, they have done so in past years, of late time especially. Until a few years since, in this very town, each one of the penitentes used to carry a skull. Many used to join the procession tipsy, and, at the end, they would fight with the very skulls they carried. This, to my knowledge, has been. But it need not be. And, with a population so ignorant, so wholly uneducated as that of the Spanish interior, is not the procession and the acting a good way—nay, under present circumstances, is it not the only way—of bringing before vine-dresser, and water-carrier, and miner the great truths of Jesus Christ and Him crucified? At any rate, I saw many eyes, and those not women's eyes, wet with tears.

CHAPTER XI.

GOOD FRIDAY AT BAEZA.

BAEZA is a cathedral town of the Spanish interior, with a population of some fifteen thousand souls. It is situated just outside the confines of the great lead mining district which has Linares for its centre, and untouched by the wave of commerce and busy modern life which breaks upon the latter. It keeps up its old traditions, its strict Catholic observances, its isolation, and tranquillity, and preserves still its ancient jealousy of the bustling town of Linares.

Linares is the seat of commerce for this part of the Spanish interior, Baeza of tranquillity and refined Spanish ease.

"Baeza quiere pares,
Y no quiere Linares."

So runs the ancient refrain.

Above all things, in its services, and other religious rites and ceremonies, Baeza maintains a proud superiority over other towns of its size. So magnificent are its processions, that they take rank in Spain well-nigh beside those of Seville.

Perhaps the jealousy above referred to should hardly have been mentioned, so slight is it, more especially in the presence of the great doings of La Semana Santa—Holy Week: a kindly and unobtrusive jealousy, which time and increased intercourse between the two towns are yearly softening,—a jealousy now no greater than that existing between "county families" and "business men" in England, of which populations these two towns, Baeza and Linares, are respectively the types.

Good Friday dawned upon the barren Campo with a chill east wind and a cloudless sky. Early in the morning, we, who were bent upon seeing the processions of Good Friday in Baeza, were in the saddle, for the ride from our humble cottage to that town was thirteen miles at least.

At 8·30, as we toiled up hill along the white, dusty road, the sun was beating down with almost tropical force. With head down and dripping flanks, our mules ambled along through a dry, scorching heat, with blinding clouds of granite dust, quite unknown at this season in the moist climate of England. But little did the two horsemen, who looked around from time to time upon the truly magnificent prospect, think of or care for dust and heat.

Below us, its naked banks showing all jagged and irregular against the morning sky, flowed the rapid, winding, yellow Guadalquivir, the tender green foliage of the oleanders which clothe its banks being hardly visible. Beyond it, across its winding valley, like wave upon wave, rose countless hills clothed with the stunted vine and the dusky olive, carrying one's gaze up to the sharp, blue, jagged outline of the Sierra Morena.

To our left, a dim yielding line, on the clear horizon, rose the snow-clad mountains of the Sierra Nevada. To our right, rose one huge pile of mountains, streaked with silver lines of snow, and apparently, seen through the clear atmosphere of this part of the Peninsula, so near, that one could hardly realize the fact that the foot of them was at least twenty miles away.

Here and there, as we mounted some hill or turned some curve, lay, in its sheltered hollow, a little town, stone built, the home of the farmer or the olive-dresser, and so much the colour of the surrounding country, that the eye at first sight failed to distinguish it. Gradually surveying the whole horizon, the view died away, bluer, and yet bluer, until it was lost in the shade of the great mountains.

Such was our ride. Yet here and there closer objects claimed our attention for a moment. At many a corner, propped up against loose stone wall, or nailed against olive tree or ilex, was a little wooden cross, sometimes painted black, and adorned with letters or initial, or with a half-faded wreath. The crosses are put up to mark the spot where a man has died a violent death. If each of these mute memorials could tell its own dark story, it would be the olden story; of the passionate word, the deathly blow, followed by years of bitter and, it may be, agonizing repentance.

Higher and higher we mounted, when, just as we were getting tired, our mules pricked up their ears, and shook themselves together for a trot. They knew more than we did, for a few moments brought us to a wayside fountain, well supplied with drinking utensils for man and beast, of the purest, clearest, coldest water—a spring so celebrated, that Spaniards, who are more particular about the quality of their water than about any other article of food or drink, send their aguaderos (water-carriers) to fill the canteros (earthern pitchers, carried two on each side in panniers on mule or donkey back) to this especial spring from distances of three, four, or even eight and nine miles. Lad and lassie, men and women, in holiday costume, streamed up to the fountain; many of them chanting that wild, primitive, monotonous ditty peculiar to the Andaluz, the words of which are almost invariably impromptu, and the tone of which may be thus correctly described: five or six words are said rapidly upon one note, somewhat high; the voice is then, with the most peculiar and difficult runs, lowered several notes; it is then lowered and raised again, according to the pleasure of the singer.

Hundreds of men and women, chiefly of the lower class, were streaming along the road towards Baeza, as we started onwards. Many women, their right arm clasping tightly the waist of their companion, were "riding pilion" behind husband, brother, or father, on mules or donkeys. All were in holiday attire; and the bright handkerchiefs, tied gracefully enough over the ebon locks of the women, and their gaudy dresses, together with the bright-coloured head-gear of donkey or mule, and the invariable halter twisted neatly around the head-straps of the bridle, made a picturesque and pretty stream, lively enough, too, as they passed us, or we them, all speculating on the one subject that then occupied their minds—" What sort of procession will it be under this Government?"

Happy, laughing faces, picturesque dresses, and ringing, joyous carols of laughter, or of song, or gay banter, are not disagreeable companions at the end of a dusty and somewhat monotonous ride; and certainly a better-behaved crowd I have never seen. They came from mine, from olive-lodge, from the "lodge in the garden of melons," from the vineyard, from the counter, yet there was no indecent jest, no

coarse expression, no oath heard—and such has been
my constant experience of a Spanish crowd. True,
they are ignorant, and cannot read or write, whereas
an English crowd of the same character could probably do either; but the Spaniards of the lower class
(as well as the higher) have one Christian grace unknown to Englishmen, the grace of natural courtesy.

At last we rode into the entrance of the town.
Nothing very striking there. Old and rambling stone
houses, with many of the windows without glass, but
all with a strong cage of iron bars for protection;
streets simply strewed with huge loose boulders of
granite or other stone; crowds streaming with us
towards the large "posada," or inn, at the outskirts of
the township. The posada merits a moment's notice.
It was once a (Franciscan, I believe) convent of considerable size, but now *tempora mutantur*, and the
spacious "patio" (courtyard) stands thick with mule-
carts, and all through the grey stone cloisters, vener-
able and inspiring respect even now, are beasts of
burden, from the lowly donkey up to the fiery little
Andalucian charger, slaking their thirst at the stone
drinking-troughs with which they are fitted up.

Our mules safely tethered, we hastened to the Plaza,
or market-square, an institution common to most
townships of the Spanish interior, wherein the representation of the Lord's last suffering was to take place.
This Plaza is a very large square, the four sides of
which are composed of white-washed stone houses, the
upper stories of which project (as in many old English
towns—Chester, I believe, for one) over the lower, and
are propped up with pillars of wood, which seemed,
in many cases, quite weak and crumbling. Around
this covered walk—for such it is—facing the Plaza, are

many little shops, where are sold various articles, but chiefly the aguardiente,—a strong spirit, distilled from wine and flavoured with aniseed,—in which the Spanish peasant's heart delights at early morn.

Every street is now discharging its hundreds into the Plaza; the crowd is orderly and quiet, if eager; for every eye will soon be gazing upon the likeness of its Lord and of His sainted mother. Wonderful sight, I thought, for the pencil of a Phillip, an O'Neil, or a Frith, is this crowd, as I gazed down from our balcony upon the moving mass beneath me. The coloured head-handkerchiefs of the women; the scarlet and crimson fajas (sashes) of the men,—some standing in the full, rich sunlight, some, more fortunate, in the blue shadow (for in Spain the shadow really is blue!); the ricketty-looking, nearly flat-roofed houses, and far away the snow-capped ridge of the distant mountains, —all these were matter for the artist's hand, and, with the aid of the strains of solemn Passion music, which soon sounded above the hum of human voices, brought over me that strange feeling of wishfulness for something eternally good and of pensive sadness which ever comes from the contemplation of a spectacle more than usually solemn and beautiful.

Suddenly there was a movement in the crowd beneath me—a crowd now numbering several thousands—as the music drew gradually nearer and nearer; but there was no noise nor disorder; and silently a row of men, two deep, dressed in long, flowing robes, with hoods turned over their heads, and each man bearing a huge lighted candle, came silently round the corner of the Plaza, and easily made a broad road through the ranks of the now silent and bare-headed crowd. These were the "penitentes," and their immediate office was to keep a clear pathway for the procession of images soon to follow. And then, as I gazed, it came.

First, borne by four penitentes, our Saviour Himself, clad in a flowing robe of rich claret colour, gorgeously embroidered with gold; firmly around His sacred temples the crown of cruel thorns is pressed, and twined among His hair (real human hair), which, dabbled in blood, falls down over His shoulders. A more awfully natural picture of human agony I never saw. He has fallen upon one hand from exhaustion, and that shows a jagged and soil-stained wound; His head droops a little; His nostrils are slightly widened, as of one who pants for breath. But, oh! the terribly weary, and yet uncomplaining, suffering expressed in the Divine face! Oh! the exhaustion, the mute reproof, the look of utter weariness depicted in it!

As that figure passed slowly up the square, severing, with its quiet, mute, onward march, the thronging populace, every hand crossed its breast, every knee went low in mute adoration.

But He has gone!

In flashing steel helmets, buff coats, and steel breast-plates, behind Him march, two and two, one hundred Roman soldiers, the "Centurion's Guard." Some are riding on fiery Andalucian chargers, which fret and curvet through the crowd,—horses lent by some of the richest men of the town,—some march on foot.

Suddenly the band stepped to one side; the Roman soldiery, four deep, formed up around, above, and below the suffering Christ. The penitentes once more cleared a way through the thronging crowd. Another figure, which we all took for that of Mary the mother of Jesus, came slowly along between the line of bare-footed penitentes. It was La Santa Veronica (Saint Veronica). She bore, holding it by the corners, a white handkerchief in her hands. As she is borne near to the image of Jesus Christ, she courtesies, as it were, being lowered by her bearers to the very earth. Once, twice, thrice, amid a dead hush, this ceremony of her performing her obeisance is gone through; and then she approaches, handkerchief in hand, her suffering Lord. She stoops down, she wipes the sweat, and blood, and dirt from the Saviour's bleeding brow and travel-stained face, and just as she does so, the handkerchief is swiftly rolled up by means of a spring, and another appears in her hands, with the image of Jesus upon it.

The legend of Saint Veronica is well known. She wiped the blood and sweat from the Saviour's face on the last journey to Calvary, and the handkerchief being folded three deep, she bore away upon it three images, as it were, of the Divino Rostro. One—so says the Spanish legend—was lost; one is in St. Peter's, at Rome; one in the Cathedral at Jaën, in this province, the capital town. And now the Virgin herself comes. As she too, in her turn, came round the corner of the street, the whole crowd in that teeming plaza sank simultaneously to its knees upon the dusty, rock-strewn square. I knelt, in company with some thirty Spaniards, in our balcony; and on looking around and about, up at the windows, into the balconies, and below upon the seething, crushed-up crowd, the eye could not discern one head covered or one single standing figure. In her turn, Santa Maria drew near to her Lord and her God, and (as did Santa Veronica) made obeisance to him several times. Her arms move, she wipes her eyes, her pale face is expressive of simple, sheer, approachable grief; her eyes are red and swollen with weeping. Beautifully, as she wipes her tear-streaming, bloodshot eyes, the bands (for they are many) play some of the most plaintive strains of Bach's Passion music, and at the saddest, most wailing note, the Virgin mother draws near and puts her arms around the neck and across the breast of her fallen, fainting, and bleeding son. Many an eye long a stranger to tears is wet with them now. Many a heart, doubtless—though we cannot say—is throbbing with the first pulsation it has felt for good since last Passion Week.

The procession vanished, and a slight, a very slight, indecency took place. As the people, rising from their knees, press too hardly upon the penitentes, these latter, with their heavy candles, beat them back. A blow from one of these candles, or tapers, as they are called, is no laughing matter: they average three or four feet in length, and are one and a half inch in diameter.

And so went out of sight, amid an orderly and gentle, but eager crowd, the first procession of Holy Friday. Well, people, especially Englishmen, who know nothing of Spanish character, and of the ignorance, the exceeding ignorance, of the masses here, often affect contempt, or indulge in ridicule, at the idea of these processions being productive of any good. Yet, when one considers that thousands in Spain know but little of God's great act of love but what they learn, and are yearly reminded of, through them, and when one sees the rough miner, the gay woman, the rude olive-dresser, on their knees, with streaming eyes, at this exhibition, one must surely make a very solemn pause before uttering any word of disparagement or condemnation. True, I have heard the indecent jest and the ribald sneer, but it has been beautifully said that, even of those whose lips utter such language, it may be that " coming to scoff, they stay to hear."

After the procession, we breakfasted in the Casa de Huespedes, or lodging-house for strangers. Opposite to us sat a Spanish gentleman, who, over his sixth egg and third piece of bacalao (salt cod), glared angrily at the strangers who ventured to eat a modest slice of meat. Then to the churches of the town. In each one the images stood, on their framework, ready for the evening procession. The side altars were lighted; the incense smelt fragrant in the dark aisles. The pictures seemed to me poor; but in Spanish churches the light is so bad, and the pictures are hung with such utter disregard to light, that one could form, in so hurried a moment, no fair or trustworthy judgment upon their respective merits.

From the churches, of which we made quite a tour, we passed into the streets; and here we were surprised at meeting two men, heavily manacled around the ankle, bound together. They were, we found upon inquiry, prisoners (condemned felons, in fact), but men who, being "well-behaved," were allowed on Good Friday to parade the streets and solicit alms. I asked one of them what was his offence. " Manslaughter with the knife," he said; " but it was entirely an act of self-defence; and if I had sufficient funds I should be released." At the corner of a side street, a table in front of her hiding her manacles, sat a sweetly-pretty Spanish girl; into a little tray before her every now and again a passer-by threw a few coppers. She, too, was a prisoner, on a "Good Friday ticket-of-leave." We forbore to ask her the nature of her crime.

The last procession was after nightfall. The crowds, the music, and the images, in great measure, were the same. The image of Jesus Christ came up, and, in the dim grey evening light, by the many lit candles, we saw that he was washing Peter's feet. A silver basin full of water was on the ground: Jesus knelt at the disciple's feet, a silver jug in his hand. His attitude was that of earnest admonition, beautifully conveyed, the disciple's that of deprecation; and, as the solemn Passion music broke once more in the dusky evening over that bending crowd, one could almost hear the words,—"Dost Thou wash my feet?" and the solemn answer,—"What I do thou knowest not now, but thou shalt know." In this scene, I should say, the letter of the Holy Gospel is ignored, for our Lord was represented in a long, claret-coloured robe! Then was put forth before the crowd Jesus praying in the Garden of Gethsemane. He knelt, the sweat dripping down amongst real evergreens lit up with candles. Most awful of all was the next. The Christ was bound, bound with thongs of esparto-grass, to flogging-post. His holy back was scored with the marks of the lashes, from which blood seemed oozing out; there was around one of His arms a great black-and-blue and livid wale, evidently the result of a foul blow. Then came many figures of Christ bearing His cross, in each one of which I noticed that His hand and knee were represented as fearfully lacerated and blood-stained. Then night fell all around. The crowds were dense. The Plaza was one mass of darkness, moving forms, and lighted candles. All was hushed and still. You could even hear the night-wind blowing in fitful gusts (had we not all day been praying for rain?) from the mountains to the southward. The end was at hand.

The Crucifixion came at last before our bewildered eyes, and, in its severity, it was truly awful—it was almost too life-like. Night had thrown its shades of gloominess all around. The Christ was raised up aloft in that dim, silent, but teeming Plaza, nailed upon His cross of agony and shame,—a public spectacle, His dying figure barely lit up by torch of penitent or ruthless soldier. Little thin red streams of blood flowed down from His nail-pierced hands, crossing each other at the wrist, and passing to the armpit, and thence trickling down the sides, and soaking in gore the linen cloth at the waist.

I turned away sick and faint; it was all too frightfully real. The blood seemed clotted with sweat, dust, and dirt; the jagged edge of the foot-wounds was terrible to gaze upon. The two thieves, one on either side, had great ugly gashes through their shin-bones. On either side stood the long line of penitentes, whose lighted candles shed a fitful ray over the whole. And then even that great act in man's redemption was finished.

Next came some sweetly-pretty little girls, each one with a pair of silver wings, carrying in their hands tiny banners, inscribed (in Latin) with the words, "For our salvation He hath died." Then passed upward the Roman soldiers, and the Virgin, with the dead body of her Lord in her arms.

One more spectacle later on, and all was over. A glass coffin, at ten at night, was borne past us. It was beautifully illuminated, and in it lay a quiet body, with pale features, peaceful enough, swathed in a linen cloth. Mary Magdalene first, then St. John, then St. Veronica, followed the transparent coffin.

And then all was over. But I went home with altered feelings as to the use of all these externals; for I had been witness to a most impressive, a most solemn sight.

CHAPTER XII.

SPANISH SERVANTS IN A MINING DISTRICT—MARIA, ISIDRA.

So much has lately been written on the subject of servants, that, were it not that the Spanish servants in the mining districts, and other parts of Spain where the wave of progress and change as yet has hardly been heard, preserve, in a striking degree, their originality and individuality, one would hardly be justified in making them the theme of a separate chapter.

When we speak of servants (criadas or criados), male or female, we may do so without going into any specific differences. There is no broad line drawn between nurse and housemaid, butler and groom, inasmuch as the Spanish servant has no training for accepting any particular kind of place, and is ready to turn her hand to anything, making up, by willingness, sweetness of temper, easiness or indifference, for her lack of special knowledge.

Thus, a young woman will be nurse for a year, then take a fancy to cooking, and offer herself as cook, thinking herself fully competent for such simple cooking as she is called upon to do if she can stew, boil, and fry in oil, make a salad or a gazpacho, and boil goat's meat and flour into sopa de macho (goat's soup).

The man-servant, too, turns his hand to anything. Goes errands, opens the door, cigarillo in mouth, or rides on donkey-back behind his master to the mine, the olive-grove, or the shooting-ground. He never wears livery, but adopts his national or provincial costume, and is more of a free lance than a regular servant.

The man-servant is generally a young unmarried man; the maid-servant generally a widow, who, if she have children, must have them in the house with her; or a woman of mature age, say forty years, the younger unmarried women being jealously guarded at home by mother or aunt.

Those who expect in this chapter a reproduction of the several well-defined types of English servants,— the spruce footman, the man-of-all-work, the housemaid, or the trained nursery-maid,—will be much disappointed: for, instead of them, I shall present the hoyden, under the care of her mother, assisting her in her duties as servant, but not allowed to "go out" on her own account; the young widow, who turns to service for a living until she captivate some swain again; and the respectable married couple, who choose to subject themselves to the little trials of service, in order to save house-rent, the woman acting as cook, or nurse, or maid-of-all-work, the man working all day in the mine or the garden.

To state briefly, on the threshold of our subject, the leading differences between the condition of the Spanish and English servant, this may be said,—that the Spanish generally has wages and not food provided, the English both; the Spanish has ample liberty, may dress as she pleases, go where she pleases, and have relations, friends, and followers in the kitchen with her at all hours, whereas to the English servant no such liberty is accorded; the Spanish brings her furniture, bedstead, images, pots and pans, and pitchers, with her into her master's house, thus setting up quite a little establishment within an establishment; the Spanish servant is contented with the roughest, darkest sleeping quarters, not turning up her nose at its roughness and even unhealthiness. This seems hard; but it must be remembered that the homes of the Spanish poor are dark, windowless, one-storied shanties, a rug spread upon the stones being often their only bed; and also, that the dryness of the climate, and the very short hours of rest in the bed-room itself, in part act as a makeweight to these discomforts.

The wages of the Spanish servant are low; but it must be remembered that the rate of living in Spain is much cheaper than in England, the constitution not needing so much solid support beneath the Andalucian ever-shining sun as beneath the frowning skies and chilly rains of England.

The general scale of wages among the Spanish poor would be much as follows, varying, of course, from time to time:—A Spanish maid-servant would receive one peseta (tenpence) per day, without food, or fivepence with food—food merely meaning bread, soup, and vegetables or fruit; a man-servant two pesetas per diem, without food; a ploughman, during the ploughing season, would receive two pesetas per diem, with one meal of gazpacho; a vineyard-man, during the forty days of the vintage, would receive as much as five pesetas per diem. And these wages seem good; but it must be remembered that they are wages for these special seasons; that there is, owing to the drought, no possibility of men being employed on the land all the year round, as in England; and so the labourer, his harvest or vintage finished, goes back to his donkey and his water-carrying until ploughing-time or harvest bids him return to sow or reap.

The usual wages of the Spanish private soldier would be one penny or twopence per day to spend, the rest of his pay being stopped for expenses of dress, &c. His fare is not meat, but soup, and bread, and vegetables. Since the Republican Government, however, the soldier has received, nominally, at least, much more money.

The sailor on board the Spanish man-of-war receives from five to six dollars per month and his food, or, if a preferente (first class), as much as ten dollars. The merchant sailor is more liberally paid, however, receiving from twelve to sixteen dollars per month with his food.

	£.	s.	d.
The Spanish Real (by which all accounts are reckoned) =	0	0	2½
The Spanish Peseta	0	0	10
The Spanish Dollar	0	4	2
The Spanish Pound	1	0	10

The *modus operandi*, when you need a servant, is as follows. You give notice to any one and every one you meet, servants at other houses included, that you need a servant; and the news of your need will quickly spread. Every morning, before the heat of the day, one servant after another will present himself or herself at your door, even as early as five or six o'clock. They never have any character, by word of mouth or by letter; and to ask a Spanish servant to bring you a character would bring an angry flush to her cheek and a strange fire to her eye, and she would turn away at once, saying, "Well, I can go elsewhere. Good-bye."

There are generally drawbacks to each one of these poor creatures, especially in the mining districts, where all is of the roughest; where they are frequently called upon to serve very graceless masters, oftentimes English, French, or German. And you will find much difficulty in getting a suitable servant. One middle-aged, decent-looking widow will promise well, but you will find that her drawback, poor thing, consists of two utterly unmanageable lads, whose vagaries have driven her from place to place. Another, with a kind, dirty, honest face peeping out of her rags, quite alarms you, much as you like her appearance, when she tells you that all her traps, bedstead or cuatro included, are gone to the agencia de prestamos (pawn-shop). Much as your heart yearns to help her, you dare not engage her.

At last, there will come one, whose appearance you like. She has only one drawback in the shape of a daughter, of mature or marriageable age; still, Isidra —for such was the name of one who lived in our house—will help her madré in the house-work, and be useful. At any rate, her bright, black, bead-like eyes and racy smile promise a little amusement. So Isidra and her mother Isabel were reckoned among the tenants of our house. Good-hearted, willing girl as she was, she certainly was a drawback. A more mischievous, hot-tempered, reckless little hoyden I seldom met with. Utterly uneducated, a regular child of nature, with an exuberance of animal spirits seldom seen, she, to use a common but expressive phrase, "led her mother such a dance," that, at last, good and honest as was the old mother, we were fain to part with her. She would have a fit of the sulks, and refuse to work for hours; at last, her mother's patience would tire, and the old lady would beat and kick her daughter with her thick boot until, with loud screams, the daughter would turn upon her mother, and a regular wrestling-match between the two would ensue. At last, the daughter got the worst of it; and the mother, grieved at her tears, would leave the dinner to spoil, hurry down to the trinket-stalls in the market-square, and come home with a pair of brass ear-rings or a tinsel ring, and the two would kiss and hug one another for the rest of the day. Sometimes Isidra would make her escape, and, looking back in fits of laughter at her old mother, would climb and run along the flat roofs of the houses like a cat, the mother wringing her wrinkled hands, and shouting to her worthy daughter to return to her maternal embrace.

The girl was full of natural wit, and loved a joke, as do all the Spaniards, at their masters' expense, and their sayings, which in England would be called impertinent, and resented accordingly, are here so common, and spoken so courteously, that you cannot be angry with them. Indeed, the familiarity of the Spanish servants with their employers strikes me as more natural and far better than the constrained manner and ostentatious distance preserved between English servants and their employers.

As an instance of Isidra's ready wit, I may mention the following. Some members of my household complained of the mosquito-bites at night, and one of the male members thereof said, "But they never bite me." Isidra immediately said, *sotto voce*, "No, nor should I, were I a mosquito."

On another occasion, when I asked my servant to wake me early, her husband, a miner, who stood by, seeing some prickly plants and thistles which I had just gathered in the Campo lying on my table, said to his wife, " No need to wake the Señor. Put a few of his own thistles in his bed,"—and off he went to bed, shaking his sturdy sides with laughter.

The most curious study of Spanish character was when the lover of Isidra came nightly, his mine-labour ended, to make love to her. The strictness with which the old mother watched every movement of her daughter, the jealous care with which she prevented them from ever speaking a word in private, or being alone for ten minutes together, formed a sadly curious spectacle; for it showed, what is only too true, that the lower class of Spaniard does not seek to implant any moral self-control in her daughter's heart, but merely to fence about her purity with external precautions. The rein is held too tightly, hence the licence when a girl is married, and, therefore, as she says, free.

Poor Isidra! Her Novio's name was drawn in the Quinta for a conscript; and the last time I saw her, she said, with streaming eyes, "He has gone to the North; but I have a letter."

Maria, a somewhat fast young widow, shall form our next short study. She came one morning, a bright, smiling, cleanly-looking little woman, with her only child, Manuéla, and, struck with her nice address and appearance, we engaged her.

Maria certainly boasted the nicest disposition and the most unsatisfactory conduct possible! She was willing and obliging, but always out late at night. If she was in the house at evening, she always had two or three very gitano-looking men sitting smoking around her. I expostulated mildly. "They are my brothers," or "cousins," she would say. I spoke more severely one afternoon, then repaired to my sofa and darkened room for the siesta; presently, I was awakened by Maria's voice. In her softest accents, she said, "Señor, you had but a poor dinner; I have the best melon in the town; take it, and render thanks to God, as I do."

This affability disarmed me completely; and we decided to give poor Maria a longer chance, as, indeed, we are all bound to do to one another. If we hope for mercy ourselves, why should we be "extreme to mark what is done amiss"?

One day we returned from a long journey, and went to bed tired and exhausted; the heat had been tropical. At one o'clock in the morning my door was fiercely assailed; I sprang up, lit a match, opened the window, and told the assailant, in no gentle language, to be gone. The only answer was a curse and an oath, with fresh blows at the door, and the shouting of our servant's name,—"Maria, Maria! come quickly, come quickly!" Suddenly, to my joy, I heard, at the end of the dimly-lit street, the watchman's cry, "It has struck one-and-a-half—Viva la Republica Democratica Federal." Away, at the sound, went my assailants. Weary and sick I got out my revolver, and laid it ready on the couch beside me, then lit my cigarillo, and waited to see if the ruffian would return. The sereno (night-watchman) passed under the window, and looked at the tiny oil-lamp; then passed along, singing his monotonous song, "Viva la Republica Democratica Federal." I did not stop him: to do so is a serious matter, and lays one open to a charge of timidity or suspicion—the two qualities never to be shown to a Spaniard. Once let a Spaniard of the lower orders know that you disbelieve his word, or are afraid, or suspect wrong where you are not certain of it, and he will despise you for life.

I sat upon my tiny couch, with candles lit: the sereno's musical cry had died away in the distance—all was still as death. Suddenly, two footsteps came up hastily to my door, and, in one moment, with a heavy block of wood or a hammer, commenced smashing in the lock, cursing poor Maria, who, seeing, I was on the *qui vive*, took good care to be fast asleep.

There was only one thing to be done. Here was I in a strange country, the language of which I could barely speak or understand, in a rough street, with a not very particular population around me. I opened the window, crouched down on the balcony, and gave fair warning—"I have a revolver; I'll fire." The only reply was a curse. I sent one bullet just over the men's heads, with a tremendous shout of "Cometh another." In one minute, before the flattening bullet rang, the two worshippers of Maria rattled, with hasty footsteps, down the street.

On the following night the summons at the door was, to my great surprise, repeated; Maria, too, appeared in "undress uniform" in my bed-room, demanding the key of the front-door to let in the intruder. "Señor, at your peril you refuse; it is the officer of justice come to challenge your shot of last night." I steadfastly refused, and told the officer of justice, if such he was, to come at a respectable hour, and not at midnight. Knowing the unsettled state of the country, I dared not open my doors to a stranger, and, in the morning, the hero appeared. His dignity —and the Spanish official lives for his office—was offended at the idea of any one firing a pistol on his beat.

Burglary in Spain is almost unknown; of robbery on a small scale there is but little; but seizing and carrying off a man and keeping him until a ransom is paid, or stopping an unguarded train to rob it of the little square deal boxes of dollars, which are on their way to Madrid from the tradesmen and merchants at the different stations on its line of road, are not at all uncommon occurrences. Indeed, the crimes that follow in the wake of high civilization, such as skilful swindling, adroit burglary, robbery, and pocket-picking, are almost unheard of in the interior, as also are the crimes so common in England—such as arson, drunkenness, brutal assaults, and the like.

Purloining a little from the provisions of the master, the swift deed of blood with the knife, accepting a bribe, child-desertion,—but not child-murder, for a casa de espositos is always at hand to receive the foundling,—these are the common stamp of crime here existing.

After this last escapade, Maria and her little girl Manuéla, who pleaded hard to stay, were, of course, necessarily to be got rid of. I gave Maria six hours' notice, and told her she must be gone. I wished her well, but said, "Though I shall say nothing about it, I fear your companions are not a very creditable set." This insinuation her proud Spanish blood resented, and she pleaded so hard, that at last I withdrew the words, and the little couple bundled up their cuatres and their few clothes, and said a courteous Adios.

Of course the above, although a true, is an exceptional case; but it serves to show the freedom, almost amounting to licence, allowed to the servant; and also brings out another point in the Spanish character in these semi-civilized districts, namely, the Spanish official's overweening pride of his office.

In the interior of Spain, the best servants are the Manchegans, or people of the province of La Mancha. One rarely does wrong in employing a man or woman of this province. The men wear, in winter, a fur cap, something like the old poacher's cap of England, with lappets over the ears; in summer, a coloured handkerchief, tied in knots at the back of the head, dark serge or leather trousers; and a heavy, shapeless coat in winter; in summer, a calico or coarse canvas shirt. The women wear as head-dress a dark silk handkerchief, pinned under the chin, a short, dark-coloured skirt of serge, and a little silk shawl on gala-days, trimmed with bright-coloured embroidery.

The Spanish servants carry a purse. That of the man is a long, narrow purse, of coarse knitting, with one hole; it is wound and tied round the waist within the faja or belt. To get money out of it necessitates the undoing of the faja, which is quite a serious matter. The woman's purse, oftentimes containing the savings of years, is a bag of coarse calico, strapped under her skirt to her waist. The chief store of money, however, is in a purse under the bedclothes. Sometimes it is deposited in a hole in the garden.

Let me tell you a little of the fare of the Spanish servant. In truth, it is very simple. Like their pleasure, so is their fare. As regards drink, water is the staple; but it must be water from the purest, freshest, oftentimes most distant well. This is brought to the door twice a day, and is sold for two farthings the pitcher. Now and then the friend or brother brings a skin of wine, black wine of Cataluña, or Val-de-Peñas, from the vineyards of La Mancha; but it is little wine that the poor Spanish criada drinks,—she, at least, is quite contented with her everlasting "agua fresca," and she asks no more.

But the wine is cheap enough. If bought wholesale, that is, in a skin or barrel, it would come to little more than twopence-halfpenny per quart; it is, in fact, much like the English beer, and, like it, strengthening. It is greatly used by the wet-nurses in the foundling hospitals, who find that they can suckle upon it without suffering. In fact, the Val-de-Peñas, which is much of the same body as Burgundy, almost takes rank beside the English stout for the support it affords to nursing mothers. The only other drink which the Spanish servant affects is the aguardiente (literally, "burning water"). This is a spirit distilled from these cheap wines, and strongly impregnated with aniseed, which makes it a good pectorate. Every man-servant drinks his copa of this (*i. e.*, wine-glassful) every morning ere his work commences.

As to food, the Spanish servant eats dry bread, with onions or fruit, and every sort of light, savoury fry and soup. To sit down to a good joint is a thing unheard of with them; and certainly they thrive upon their simple fare, and are stronger servants, and harder, more willing workers, than are their fellows in England. The standard dishes are, among the servants, the following:—Gazpacho, that is, lettuce, cucumber, onion, and bread chopped up together, and soaked in a basin of vinegar, oil, and water. Berengenas and beans, that is, the berengena, or egg-plant (*Solanum melongena* of the botanist), a pulpy, oval fruit, of purple colour, fried in oil, with dried beans.

Cocida, mutton or goat's flesh boiled to rags, and served up with garbanzos or peas. Tomates and pimientos fried in oil, with slices of bread. The pimientos are of two kinds, pimiento dulce, or mild capsicum; and pimiento picante, or peppery capsicum. And, as regards soups, there are the sopa de arroz, or rice soup; sopa de tomates, sopa de fideos, or vermicelli soup; and sopa de jamon, or soup of bacon. Very simple, then, is the poor Spanish servant's fare, always eaten out of one dish, the spoons of man or maid servant dipping into it quite mechanically. As to simples, wonderful—and oftentimes not misplaced—is the poor Spanish servant's faith in the herbs that grow around her. For fever, they will give the juice of the orange, with a few grains of magnesia. For the stilling of a crying baby they will not give the poppy-tree, which maddens the brain of the English peasant-child of the Midland Counties, but the berries of the arbutus-tree, if in season, here called "madronios," which have, beyond doubt, a certain soporific power. For colic, or griping, they give rue or a decoction of red sage; for a cut finger they use the barcamina, a sort of ice-plant, to lay upon the wound; for biliousness, a cup of strong coffee, with the juice of two lemons squeezed into it.

The Spaniard of the lower orders has faith enough to believe in this fact, namely, that in every locality, in every climate and land, the Almighty has planted the very herbs which are adapted to cure the special diseases of that locality, or climate, or land. The Spanish Government, to a certain extent recognizing this truth, pays a certain number of herbalists to experimentalize, and collect herbs by flood and field. 'Dioscorides' Herbal' is the text-book of these collectors.

Simple, then, indeed, are the dress, the food, the drink, and the medicines of the Spanish servants. With them, simple as they are, they are most contented, even happy, thriving, and joyous.

And, lastly, in our general picture, let us take a glance at the character of the Spanish servant. Not always quite honest, not always quite truthful, she is yet full of good-nature, and uncomplaining, sympathizing, and gentle. The Spanish servant, male or female, thinks of her master or mistress as a friend, and treats them accordingly, and is ready at all times to do anything for them. The Spanish servant is never tired of getting up from his or her scanty meal to serve you. Give him or her a fair share of freedom, of kindness and courtesy, and they will repay you with all the fervour and affectionateness of their nature.

I shall leave the reader to draw his own contrast between the condition and character of the Spanish and English servant, merely premising that in many points I think we might learn of them. And having presented to you an Isidra and a Maria, I will next offer you the portraiture of an ignorant and superstitious, but most faithful and noble-hearted Manchegan servant, Isabel.

CHAPTER XIII.

A STUDY OF A MANCHEGAN SERVANT—ISABEL.

A SERVANT's life and character are not usually very full of romance, and Isabel's life and character were very simple. Indeed, their very simplicity, the simplicity of her life, the transparency of her very beautiful character,—a transparency so rarely met with in our world of attrition, and intercourse of bad and good,— chiefly warrant me in making Isabel the study of a separate chapter.

Isabel was an orphan. She dwelt with her widowed mother in Infantes, a small town of La Mancha, perhaps the dullest and most despoblado province in the Peninsula. Its 7,500 square miles contain little more than 220,000 or 230,000 inhabitants. The land, as a rule, consists of dreary steppes, where one windswept, arid plain, whose dust is impregnated with saltpetre, succeeds to another. In the summer there is fierce, blazing heat, and scarcely a tree or wood to break off the blazing rays; in the winter the levante, dry and piercing cold, sweeps over the plains. The Manchegan peasantry, however, living in their humble huts of earth or rudely thrown together stones, are among the most affectionate, temperate, honest, and, above all, witty of the Spaniards of the interior. And is not La Mancha the land of Don Quixote and Sancho Panza?

A STUDY OF A MANCHEGAN SERVANT. 273

There are bright green tracts, however, as there are in everything that is dreary, even in the steppes of La Mancha. There, are some of the fine olive-groves; there, are the slopes crowned with vines of Burgundy; and every poor peasant, every Manchegan housewife, has, in autumn, her "cueros" (the skins of pig or goat dressed entire, and looking, when filled with wine, very much like the carcase of the animal itself, bloated and shorn of hair) of the Val-de-Peñas, or rough red wine, which maketh glad the heart of the weary. His crisp, salt, sparkling jest—a little rough sometimes, perhaps, a little spice even of the indecent in it, though he does not deem it so—and his glass of rough red wine are the Manchegan peasant's delight. The women are most homely in their habits, most neat in their dress, most thrifty in their house-keeping,—first-rate "hands" at knitting and needle-work of every simple kind.

I saw Isabel first bending over the couch of a dying woman, and was struck with the tenderness of expression on her pale, kind, homely face, and the plaintive tones in which she kept on repeating the usual term of pitying affection among the peasantry of the interior, "Pobre! pobre!"

A little instance of this poor servant's homely ideas shall here be given. The dying person, of whom I went to take leave, had just been prematurely confined, in a high fever, of a still-born child. As I left the house, poor Isabel brushed quietly past me, and, to my astonishment, brought the little dead body for me to look at, with the simple words, "She dies; but she must be proud of giving birth to so fine a child: she will be proud, and it will arouse her a minute, to know that the Englishman has admired it!" Such an

VOL. II. T

incident, of course, is, in all its surroundings, exceedingly painful. Some may say it is "out of place" here; but as this record professes to be a simple, modest, and truthful rendering of Spanish life and character, without any gloss, I think I may be pardoned for inserting this, may I not? Anecdotes such as these seem to me to give a vivid picture of the Spanish poor in all their want of civilization, of polish, and yet in their natural goodness, in the naturalness of their feelings, oftentimes overflowing. Truly, if the Spanish poor have not the blessings, they certainly escape many of the curses of civilization and polish; if they have not the polish of "good manners," they often have the polish that comes from a naturally sweet disposition; if they do offend by their rough, uncultivated ways, they yet possess the interest that attaches to originality of thought, expression, and action. There is no stereotyped "gentleman's servant" in the interior of Spain.

Her poor young mistress died, and Isabel came into our service. In another chapter, the installation of Isabel and her Manuel (she was a married woman) in our casa has been noticed, and the ground need not be again trodden. The pair came, with their rude Manchegan furniture, their alforjas (provision bags), their jarros of Andujar ware, and last, but not least, their image of San Juan—a little dressed-up doll, with outstretched wooden arms, bright rosy cheeks, and dark streaks of paint for his hair, the simple Penates of the Manchegan peasant and his wife.

If countenance be an index of character, as all Spaniards firmly believe is the case, Isabel certainly would be, I thought, a treasure. Her pale, pensive face brightened up whenever Manuel came home, or any good fortune befell ourselves, with a singularly sweet, gentle smile. Her quiet, plaintive voice, and her neat dress, certainly were better than any written character or testimonial, of which the criada of the interior knows absolutely nothing. Indeed, had we asked for a character, the usual "Bueno, then I go elsewhere," would most probably have been the abrupt end of the matter.

Affection takes the place of calm reason with the peasantry of La Mancha. Isabel soon became, with her rough, witty, stalwart husband, truly attached to us and our lowly home; and no offer of higher wages or a better home would tempt her for a moment to think of leaving us. "No," was her invariable reply; "you have trusted Manuel and me, and been kind to us; where you go, we shall go with you." In sickness and in health, Isabel was like a kind, simple-hearted elder sister more than like a servant. She knew nothing save what her natural goodness of heart taught her—the breathings of that Good Spirit, we are sure, that "bloweth where it listeth"—of the command, "Honour thy father and thy mother," with the promise attached to its performance; yet no one ever treated a mother more loyally, tenderly, and devotedly than Isabel. Whenever Isabel received her wages, it was "one-third for herself, one-third for Manuel, and one-third for 'mi madre' (my mother)." The pair were truly attached to one another, and poor Manuel's sad face, when his wife had the least "angustias," *i. e.*, sickness, was painful to behold. "Tengo muncho sentimiento que Isabel tiene las angustias" (I am deeply affected at Isabel's sufferings). Rough miner of La Mancha, he had the heart of an affectionate child!

She had only been married a few years—she is now thirty-six, and Manuel ten years older—when she came to us, because, though Manuel had long been an admirer and an accepted one, she did not think it right, just after her father's death, to leave the madre in her lone and desolate home. Time, however, softened the madre's, as time alone softens all, sorrow, and Isabel and Manuel became one, settling in our town, near his mining work, some twenty miles from Infantes.

Shortly after she came to us, a black-edged letter came from La Mancha. It was an ill-written scrawl, merely to say that her mother's only sister had just died. Isabel shed a few silent tears, then sat down (for a wonder, she could write a few rude hieroglyphics, a rare accomplishment on the steppes of La Mancha) and wrote a few lines to her aged mother,—not a consolatory epistle, but a few words of helpful assurance; for, as the Spanish and English proverbs both are agreed in, "A little help is worth much pity." This was the substance of the letter, as she herself told us:—" Manuel will be home early to-night. We shall both think of you; but we shall go out and buy you the mourning you will need, so do not be anxious on that score." She came upstairs, and said,—"I am going to take my letter to the correo" (post). Home she came in a few minutes, and first went to San Juan to ask his advice or solicit his prayers; then she went to the "cama," or bed, in the clothes of which lay, carefully secreted, the stocking full of silver, the hoardings of many weary years of work. It was with no niggard hand that her kindly spirit poured out an ample store of dineros, and together, ere supper was tasted, the two went forth into the dimly-lit streets to buy the simple articles for their mother's mourning. With great joy she showed me her wealth of mourning—a plain black serge dress for the madre, with two black silk handkerchiefs for the head,—this last the regular " mourning attire " of the decent Spanish poor. For herself, she had bought nothing save one handkerchief, of homelier stuff than silk. Isabel expressed herself as very pleased with her little purchases, as she spread them on the bed for our inspection. " But," said she, " when I wake at night I shall think of the still lonelier mother at Infantes."

Many were the acts of courtesy, kindness, and even devotion of this humble sister. How often, in mixing with the lowly Spanish " decent poor," rude and uncultured as they are, is one reminded of the Divine Master's words of truth, " There are last that shall be first."

One night my wife was taken seriously ill, and in the poorer suburb of a Spanish town of the interior help is not easily accessible. Isabel and her lord had gone to bed, but I knocked softly at their door, and the cloud of tobacco-smoke showed me that one, at least, of the pair was awake. In less than five minutes Isabel's pale, sweet face and quiet rap were at the bed-room door, and, to my surprise, in fur-cap, heavy boots, and Manchegan manta, behind her was Manuel. " Now," said he, " we both come to pass the night with you and sit up with the señora : Isabel to nurse, you and I, if occasion be, to go for el medico." Quietly and tenderly as a woman, Manuel went to my wife's bed-side, carefully examined the face, pronounced it as his opinion that it was not " calentura," rolled himself up in his manta, and sat down opposite to me, close beside Isabel. He only spoke once or twice, and then it was in whispers; and so they watched with me through a part of the weary night.

A Spanish night-watch is dreary indeed. All around you dogs are howling, shut out into the street; the donkeys bray from the back of every house the livelong night; and, as the Spaniards themselves say, " A donkey's bray by night is a doleful bray." The Government of the country has just changed hands, and instead of " Viva la Republica Democratica Federal," as a prelude to singing the hour, the sereno had changed his watch-word to the customary one, " Ave Maria purisima! Las dos menos un cuarto. El se - - - - reno." After this occurrence, I had occasion, one midnight, to go for some article I had forgotten into the little ante-room adjoining the quarters of Manuel and his spouse. In a moment the quick, watchful, anxious ear of Isabel had heard me, and, thinking illness was come again, she called out, " Don Hugo, es la señora mala?" *i. e.*, Is the señora ill again? I heard Manuel give a grunt and shake himself up, and, dreading another midnight invasion, gave the Spanish assurance, " Muy bien, gracias," — the equivalent to our English " All's well."

Not always does one see such tenderness and watchfulness united with high spirit and high sense of right and wrong; but in Isabel's character the two were united.

A Spanish artisan overcharged me grossly for some work done within earshot of Isabel. She came into the room, her eyes alight with indignation, and swept my friend downstairs. " Go; I will come and settle with you at your master's house." When he had gone, she took the bill and one-third only of the money in question with her, and returned in triumph with the receipted bill.

One more instance of Isabel's affectionate and anxious character, and that side of her character shall be dismissed. One dark night, when the streets were in a disturbed state, I had occasion to go a short distance. Isabel and Manuel were sitting over their fry of garbanzos and lard, each, a huge knife in hand, slicing and eating their cake of coarse bread; by their side stood, or rather lay on the table, a small pigskin bottle —the Scriptural bottle—of Val-de-Peñas, a Christmas present from the widowed mother at Infantes. As I put my hand on the door (I should say, that, in some of the poorer sort of houses in the interior, you must pass through the kitchen to get to the street-door), Isabel jumped up, and, one hand on the lock, the other on my arm, said, "Do not, I beg, go out to-night. We shall not enjoy our supper if you do." Was there not real, deep, unaffected feeling for a fellow-creature's welfare in those simple words of a poor Manchegan peasant?

Isabel was strictly truthful in all her dealings with and words to her employers; but her truthfulness seemed to spring rather from the devotion to kind employers—a trait so constantly illustrated in semi-civilized life—than from high principle. And do we not see, in the devotion of the semi-civilized person to one who is kind, and whom he feels to be his superior in many ways, the germ of a possible devotion to a higher and better Maestro than earth can offer? Indeed, are we not all led up, from devotion to earthly duty to devotion to a duty higher than that laid on us by daily life? Do we not learn what Divine love is, first, by realizing the depth and intenseness of an earthly love, and are we not in the way to know more of God's nature when we receive and give a pure earthly affection, than many creeds could teach us? Truly, it seems to me, we all, civilized or uncivilized, need these stepping-stones. Poor Isabel! She would have cut off her right hand sooner than have told me an untruth or deceived me, I verily believe; yet she thought nothing of swerving from the truth for her employer's good, as she expressed it.

Many of the sayings of this couple were at least pretty, if not beautiful. Thus, of one who had wasted good health and fine opportunities, poor Isabel only said, "Pobre! a broken life!"—an expression that struck me at the time as exceedingly beautiful in its simplicity and truthfulness.

Again, when I noticed to Manuel that he did not sing his Andaluz ditties one day, he pointed to the sun, overcast with storm,—"Sun and song go together, like a pair of mules, señor." Like many of these homely sayings of the Spanish poor, there was truth at the bottom of it; for who does not feel more ready to sing or whistle on a bright and sunny than on a cloudy day? But whistling is unknown in the Spanish interior,—at least, I have never heard it.

One other trifling instance of Manuel's wit. The Spaniard of the interior holds the quality of uncomplainingness in high esteem. One of his words of high praise is to say of a man, "He never complains." Poorly or strong, I always answered the morning inquiry of my servants by saying, "Muy bien, gracias!" *i. e.*, "Thank you, I am very well." At last, Manuel said to his wife, "We must call the Englishman 'Siempre Bien!'" (Always Well!)

The last thing each night, before they retired to rest, the two always came into our room—even into our bed-room—to say their "Que pass' usted buena noche," the Spanish "Good-night." And certainly they were a quaint spectacle: Isabel, in her neat evening toilet, with her kind, pale, homely face and bright smile, and Manuel, in fur-cap, faja with huge knife, and heavy boots, with his wooden, weather-worn, mahogany-coloured face, always giving his partner a sly nudge as they entered the door, and always making some little sally of wit. His weather-beaten, whimsical face was quite a study for a painter, and the colour of his face reminded me of some of Murillo's darker subjects.

Once Manuel, whose work lay at some mines a few miles off, and who, when necessarily absent at night, always returned for food and rest the following morning, punctually as clockwork, at eight, had been absent all night, and in the morning came not. Ten, eleven, twelve struck, and the ingredients for the breakfast-fry, in which his rude taste delighted, still stood in the pan uncooked. Noon came and waned into evening, still he came not. Poor Isabel! her face pale as ashes, a tear slowly trickling down either cheek, sat by the dying embers, helpless, and well-nigh hopeless. The country roads were not very safe, Manuel's work was dangerous, and, had all been well, he might, she thought, have sent a message.

Seeing how weak and faint the poor woman was from taking no food, I said, "Isabel, Manuel will be here all safe and sound speedily; eat something, and brighten up for his coming."—"I cannot eat bread or drink water until Manuel comes," was her sad, quiet, and strikingly Scriptural reply.

Poor thing! only on those mornings (about four in the course of the week) on which her Manuel came home did she enjoy the savoury and scalding fry in which the Manchegan peasantry delight. On other days (No-Manuel days, as she called them), her breakfast was simply a piece of dry bread and some celery, and a cup of water. That, varied with a little garlic (I always dreaded garlic days), was all she allowed herself; " for," said she, " when Manuel is at work, why should his Isabel feast?"

Night drew on, and no Manuel. Poor, pale-faced woman! I shall never forget her anxiety, as she sat rocking herself backwards and forwards that night beside the dying embers of the ornilla. The night before, ere retiring to rest, she had prepared a little surprise for Manuel, when, at eight o'clock, she should hear his ambitious double-rap. She had placed two pieces of my half-smoked cigars in the mis-shapen wooden hands of her patron saint, San Juan, who stood (as I have elsewhere said is often the case) at the foot of their bed, as the guardian of their life and slumbers,— a strange wooden image, looking stranger still with two cigars in hand. These cigars were to greet Manuel, and to appear as though they were a present from San Juan. Thus, in this poor creature's simple, homely ideas, a little religious lesson would be inculcated in her simple and misdirected, but true and loyal faith.

At last, late at night, a tap was heard at the door, —not the usual rat-tat-tat, but a modest, half-ashamed, single knock. It was Manuel. He had been detained, owing to an accident to one of his fellow-workmen, but was safe and sound himself.

I hurried down to offer my congratulations, and poor Isabel's face was a picture,—all sunshine and showers—tears and bright smiles fighting and conquering by turns. She went up to the bed-room, she lifted St. John from his table, with a cigar in each hand the Saint descended, and was carried to the supper-table. Manuel possibly, when he saw the tinsel of the saint's dress appear round the corner of the stairs, had dreaded a little lecture; but when San Juan's outstretched hands offered him two halves of Havana cigars, his soul was at rest again.

"Gracias á Dios, y á San Juan, Manuel," said poor Isabel. Then she carried up San Juan, despoiled of his cigars, kissed him, and placed him in his proper place again.

Duty first—this was a religious duty—then pleasure. Isabel soon had the humble repast, which had waited for her Manuel all day long, frying famously. Garbanzos, a bit of jamon dulce de Estremadura (sweet ham of Estremadura), and garlic, and pimientos. O luxury for a miner of La Mancha!—rich feast to sleep upon! And the two warm-hearted, simple people crouched over the glowing ornillas, and each, wooden spoon in hand, their vows performed, their thanks offered, ate their bread with a cheerful heart.

Well, Isabel was a treasure! But do not let any one who comes to the interior count upon getting one of such transparent simplicity of character, such devotion, such child-like faith. Of a truth, there are more Isidras and Marias than Isabels among the servants of the interior, although, doubtless, many and many an Isabel might be found frying her garbanzos, or knitting gracefully, with her small, well-shapen hand, in her little stone cottage among the barren steppes of La Mancha. Well has an English poet sung :—

> " Full many a gem of purest ray serene,
> The dark, unfathomed caves of ocean bear ;
> Full many a flower is born to blush unseen,
> And waste its sweetness on the desert air."

But one never sees a Manchegan servant-maid without a hiccough.

CHAPTER XIV.

THE SPANISH MINERS' UNITED PRAYER MEETING.

A POEM.

How long, O Lord, the Holy and the True,
   How long, dear Lord, wilt Thou withhold Thy hand?
Lo, for these many months nor rain nor dew
   Have visited and blessed our thirsty land!

The green grass withereth and the floweret dies;
   Sweet carol to the Spring no bird hath sung;
The earth is iron, brazen are the skies,
   Long hath the blight on vine and olive hung.

Sure 'twere enough, Lord, Merciful and Good,
   That on our plains long since the sword began;
Wilt Thou withhold the green herb giving food,
   Thy wrath fore-adding to the sin of man?

Yet, why reproach we? Soon shall come the Tide
   Of Passion, and that Friday, blest of all,
When He who pleadeth at His Father's side
   Shall walk* among us, and the rain shall fall?

But, no; with scorching wind and molten sky,
   Friday's dim dawn grew into dazzling day;
'Mid teeming crowds we watched, with wistful eye,
   Its sad procession thread the narrow way.

What men are these in sable dress who come,†
   Thorn-crowned each brow, and in each eye a tear?
Bare are their feet, and muffled is their drum,
   Seeming as men who mourn, what do they here?

---

* In the common parlance of the Spanish miners, it is said, "Jesus leaves His Father's side on Good Friday, to bring a blessing to men."

† The "penitentes," or "humildes," men who have sinned, and pay for the privilege of helping to carry Christ, and the Virgin, and Saints, thus doing penance during the Holy Week.

Whom bear they on, in robe of royal hue?
  Death's Conqueror say ye? But His eye is dim!
Bid ye in that bowed form the sinner view
  The God who made, the Man who died for him?

Yet bear Him on, and let His gaze of love
  Melt each hard heart and smooth each suffering brow,
While His long train of faithful saints on-move,
  Who suffered once, who walk in glory now.

Yea, bear Him on, and let His falling tear
  Bless our parched earth. But see, He faints, He dies;
With wan, sweet face, a woman* draweth near,
  Kisses His pale brow, wipes His weary eyes.

"And wilt Thou leave me, dearest Lord, for ever,
  No more with gentle voice to succour me?
Lord, of my love, my hope, my life the giver,
  I weep for ever if I weep for Thee!" †

So, following on through many a dusty street,
  Came we to where a church door opened wide,
Beneath whose crumbling stones, where four ways meet,‡
  Poured and stood still the mute but living tide.

All bruised His knee, His holy Form down-bowed,
  Scarce grasped His cross with bloodless, quivering hand;
His gaze reproachful melting all that crowd,—
  See in the midst the suffering Saviour stand!

Oh, weary brow! Oh, agony too vast,
  Too real, for these lewd eyes to look upon!
Oh, gaze of wonder, waking all the past,
  My black, black past—Lord, do not me disown!

But, by Thine agony and sweat of gore,
  But, by Thy broken, bruiséd, bleeding knee,
But, by Thy great deep love in days of yore,
  And by Thy Mother's love, remember me.

* Saint Veronica, who, when Jesus falls beneath His cross, is carried to His feet, and wipes His face, the handkerchief retaining the impression of the sacred face.

† Saint Veronica's passionate prayer as she wipes the holy brow.

‡ Many of the Spanish churches open into a plaza, or square, as was the case in the processions here referred to.

The unheeding billow, or the hill-side lone,
  Full many a time hath listened to a prayer
True as hath e'er been wafted to the Throne
  From dim-lit aisle on incense-laden air.

And shall no God the rugged miner hear?
  And shall no seraph bear, on wingèd feet,
An answer swift to them that worship here,
  God's air their incense, and their church the street?

He said, who ask shall have, shall find who seek;
  He said, in sorrow we should come to Him.
And hath his ear grown deaf, His arm grown weak,
  His heart grown flinty, or His eye grown dim?

Then thrice to Heaven the wan, white hand was raised,*
  As though in mute entreaty. Thrice the prayer,
"Give us the rain, Lord, and Thy name be praised,"
  From thrice a thousand voices rent the air!

And, lo! scarce larger than the hand of man,
  Such cloud as erst gladdened the prophet's view
(How swift from lip to lip the tidings ran),
  Floats into sight athwart the cloudless blue.

Full many a prayer for blessings of the earth
  Meets its best answer in the spirit's gain.
But we the Saviour, in our day of dearth,
  Sought, and at eve it fell, the blessèd rain!

---

* By means of a spring the image of Jesus raises its hand three times towards Heaven to implore rain, the assembled crowd crying " Agua, agua, agua," thrice, i. e., " Water, water, water."

CHAPTER XV.

LITERATURE OF THE SPANISH MINER.

THE title of this chapter would seem almost one given for the sake of mockery to any one at all conversant with the lower classes in Spain, for the genius of the Spaniards of all classes certainly is not literature of any sort worthy of the name; and, of the mining class, it is doubtful whether one in every eight, were the test applied, would be found able to read. The education of the young, compulsory in theory, is not carried out in practice, although slightly on the increase at the present time. The Spanish miner, then, seldom can read; and, if he can, his tastes do not lead him to it; and again, if he desires to spend some of his time in reading, the books within his command are always, or nearly always, trashy. They may be divided into the following classes, of each of which a specimen shall be offered in these pages. The religious, or superstitious; the fiercely political; the witty and coarse; the semi-obscene. And when I say books, I mean small pamphlets or broad-sheets, sold in the streets and squares for two or four farthings a-piece, with grotesque frontispieces, generally, and flaming titles.

There are no books, properly so called, in the Spanish mining towns — certainly, no book-shops; and, in the cases of the rich and well-educated, it is a very rare thing, in the interior of Spain, to find a book-shelf! And so, with nothing but an incredible miracle (which, by-the-bye, he does not now believe), told in rude, doggerel verse, the semi-obscene or blasphemous tale, and the pamphlet of some political partisan within reach, the poor Spaniard betakes himself and his surplus cash to the bull-ring, the cock-pit, the gambling-saloon; he throws the iron bar for money; he rolls the bola, or iron ball, for money; he plays "trugé," the usual game of cards among the miners, throughout the evening; or rattles the dominoes at the coffee-room, for money, too!

You will say, then, why write about his literature? I answer, because the nature of what there is in circulation among the reading miners is of a type almost passed by in England; and because, in these pages, my object has been to compare the state of the Spanish with that of the English miner in all particulars.

The pamphlets in which the Spanish miner indulges are generally of four pages in length, and chiefly consist of verse, the rudest doggerel. They are wretchedly printed, in the lowest Spanish patois or slang, according to the province in which they are designed for sale; and so bad is the grammar, and so impure the Spanish, that no one merely conversant with pure Castilian could understand them without trouble. Out of every ten words one would be a slang or patois term, not to be found in any dictionary!

These little pamphlets, costing, as a rule, one cuarto, or farthing, per page, generally consist of two, four, or eight pages, and are sold at every street-corner. Sometimes, on the road to a mine, the vendor will take his stand with a "new and curious recital." Miner

after miner will produce his penny for it, and the long
stream of fluttering papers, as the purchasers hasten
onward, will present quite a curious, but, indeed, a
sad, a very sad, spectacle. For are they not, these
books, oftentimes poison to the mind? Can a mind
be built up sound and strong upon superstition,
obscenity, the scurrilous joke, or the political propa-
ganda? It would be contrary to all precedent were
such the case.

I will offer you now, kindly reader, a type or
specimen of the various kinds of pamphlets to which
allusion has been made; and you shall form from them,
unaided by any criticisms on my part, your own
estimate of the influence for good likely to be exercised
on the character of the poor Spanish miner by the
cheap press of Spain.

Here is a specimen of the best class, the religious or
superstitious. Do not be surprised at the wonders it
recounts—at the improbabilities, I should say, impossi-
bilities, of which it is full. Were it a sober tale, believe
me, the Spaniard, who lives upon excitement, would
not buy, much less would he read it. The subjoined
poem, translated by me with the greatest difficulty
from a two-farthing broadsheet into the same rude
doggerel in which it is written, was a short time since
quite "the rage" out here. The miner read it out,
with many a sneer, to his group of fellow-workers
when the long Andalucian day was drawing to a close;
the monthly nurse pondered it well, and read and
re-read it, *sotto voce*, counting her beads and saying
her "aves" in the still watches of the night, as I
myself can testify.

Here, then, it is, translated word for word, without
any attempt at embellishment on my part:—

New and Curious Paper, setting forth the miracle which the most holy Christ of the Wood and the Virgin of the Guide did in a Farmhouse near Ronda in the present year.

(Let me add here, a miner, reading the title, said, "In the present year? Why, it has no date, so we can't tell when it was done!" He was right. The "new and curious paper" bears no date!)

<pre>
    Queen of Heaven, grant thine aid,
    While it is by me essayed
    In this history short to tell
    All the wonders that befell
 5 A poor Christian labourer
    In our Spain, this very year ;
    Who in Ronda his bread won,
    With his wife and infant son,
    And his daughter, fair and dear,
10 Entering on her twentieth year!
    To this poor man's house there came
    Bandits seven, men of fame.
    As they bound wife, son, and man,
    To her room the fair girl ran,
15 And, to keep her body chaste,
    She its portal locked in haste.
    At her door each robber banged,—
    "Thy three dear ones shall be hanged,
    If thou dost not instantly
20 Yield thy person up to me."
    And her mother, crying, said,—
    "I and father will be dead,
    If thou dost not instantly
    To the robbers give the key."
25 Not one thought of honour lost
    Brave Rosaria's full heart crossed ;
    But, with courage pure inspired,
    Quick she took a gun, and fired
    Through the door. The thieves then slew
30 Father, mother, baby too ;
    While at them Rosaria sent
    Shot upon shot, till off they went.
    Ere their footsteps on the moor
    Ceased to sound, she oped the door.
</pre>

35 Lo! the robber chief there lay,
   His life-blood ebbing fast away;
   Other twain lay him beside,
   One was dying, one had died!

The valiant maiden then takes up the two dead men, the one wounded, and sets off with them, strapped on a mule by her own hands, to the office of the judge at Ronda. Arrived there:—

   Admiration and surprise
40 Kindled in that good man's eyes,
   As he listened to the tale
   Of Rosaria, calm and pale,
   As he looked upon the dead,
   Hearing how their blood she shed.
45 "Yes," said he, "'tis true the twain
   Robbers here by thee are slain.
   But, señora, tell to me
   Who, in slaying them, helped thee?"
   "Holy Christus of the Wood,"
50 Said she, "in my peril stood
   With His succour at my side,
   And the Virgin of the Guide."

The judge then offers her a guard of men to pursue the remaining four robbers, but she refuses any aid save that of "the Virgin and her father's horse":—

   To the temple then she went,
   Fair Rosaria, and she bent
55 To the nailèd Christ her knee,
   And, in anguish, thus spoke she,—
   "Sinful, at Thy feet I lie,
   Thanking Thee, O God, most high,
   For that Thou, the succour sure,
60 Hast vouchsafed to keep me pure.
   Now, dear Christ, lend me Thy skill,
   These four robbers left to kill;
   And, if so, I vow it Thee,
   In a convent soon I'll be.

65 O, dear Lord, give me Thy power,
   Vengeance on these brutes to shower!"

She sallies forth, with her gun, on horseback, meets the four remaining bandits, shoots three dead, and one delivers himself up to her in a dead swoon. She thanks God, and carries the four bodies (one alive, but fainting), on her one horse, back to the judge; he compliments her on her heroism:—

   Then, Rosaria, unto thee,
   Alms were given right speedily,
   And in Ronda's town hast thou
70 Many a good work wrought ere now.

Some account here follows of the Feast to the Virgin and Christ, instituted by the maiden, and then comes the moral:—

   "Christian" reader, here discern
   God's own truth, and deign to learn
   How a girl of twenty years
   All unaided, without fears,
75 How to use her gun unskilled,
   Put to flight, or maimed, or killed,
   Seven robbers, who had been
   Long the terror of the scene.
   Ask ye why her hand was strong
80 To repress this crying wrong?
   She had asked her Lord for aid;
   From her youth up, she had prayed
   To that God of whom we pray,
   That, at our last earthly day,
85 Unto us it may be given
   With His Christ to dwell in Heaven.—AMEN.

Note.—Two hundred days of indulgence from Purgatory are given by certain bishops to all who will say a Creed and an Ave to the Christ of the Wood and the Virgin of the Guide represented at the head of these pages.

Gross exaggeration as the above narrative must necessarily be, it is a fair type of the religious element in the Spanish miner's literature. Another favourite topic, although less so than the miracles, is the Passion of Jesus Christ.

The chief and most noticeable feature in the treatment of Scriptural subjects is the way in which every fact recorded in the Holy Gospels is so overlaid and entwined with legendary lore, that one hardly knows where truth ends and fiction begins. Thus, in the most popular recital of the betrayal of Christ for thirty pieces of silver, the following, among other pieces of mythic lore, occurs. The paper is called "Mystic and Contemplative Narrative of the Passion of our beloved Redeemer":—

> Judas, having betrayed his Lord,
> Went to where the Virgin sat,
> And, with a false smile, he said,—
> "Why, Holy Mother, grievest thou!
> If I had my will, and were able,
> Thy Son should soon be free."
>
> For joy at his tidings, the Virgin
> Gave him a very rich supper,
> A supper so complete and rare,
> That no delicacy was wanting
> Oh, Judas! false traitor! thou shalt pay
> For thy great deceit.

Some of these religious pamphlets are exceedingly quaint. One, called "The Spiritual Numerator," with a clock for frontispiece, offers a thought, or rather contemplation, for each hour. Thus:—

> Two o'clock striketh:
> At two consider
> That thou hast two eyes

To see good things with;
Also two ears hath God given thee
That thou shouldest hear two good things,
The preacher's voice, and thy confessor's sentence.
Also thou hast two nostrils,
That thou mayest smell two things—
The fragrance of glory
And the stench of the pit.
Also two hands to work with,
And keep hunger away, &c.
These are the lessons of two o'clock.

But it is time to turn to the consideration of the moral element, as it is found sparsely, and very feebly, represented in the miner's literature. Here is one of the few specimens of moral tales. It is called—

The Life of the Man who does Well, compared with that of Him who does Ill.

Of Him who does Well.	*Of Him who does Ill.*
Being industrious at school, All respect him.	He begins to rebel against his mother, And will not go to school.
In his earliest years He makes true friendships.	He plays tricks on his mother; He goes out throwing stones.
In his hours of solitude He learns to paint.	He robs his parents' purse, And runs away from home.
He pities deeply, and helps The sick and suffering.	At billiards he loses every pen, And is punished as a vagrant.
In the army he fights well, And drills his men gently	Then he forges a bill, But Justice overtakes him.
At last—	Thrown into prison, he hears With indifference his sentence.
In a severe action wounded, The doctor comes to see him.	He escapes; and murders a man To obtain his money.
At once, with holy unction, He receives the last Communion.	Sleeping in the Campo, The guards seize him.

He makes his will fairly ;	He is condemned to death ;
Dies : and his parents long weep	In chapel he confesses his guilt.
for him.	
" Beneath this simple stone,	By the halter he dies ;
Rests at peace a holy man."	He has no tomb : and none are
	found to pity him.

Grotesque and rugged as is the above, it is certainly good in tendency. But the specimens of this sort are few and far between indeed. Turning from the religious and the moral to the comic and the obscene, we shall be surprised and shocked by the scurrility, the coarseness, and the indecency of much of the cheap literature in the market.

Here is a pattern or type of the scurrilous—a narrative said to be based upon fact. Two priests, or curas, in charge of parishes, each have a querida, or mistress. They find it needful to effect an exchange of parishes, and, to save expense and trouble, they change their queridas also. This incident, embellished and intertwined with the coarsest and most scurrilous jokes at the expense of the clergy, formed a great amusement for some in the Spanish mining districts. But it is a subject at once too sacred and too coarsely treated to be entered upon more at length in these pages. And, besides, one shrinks at the present moment from dwelling at all on the faults and vices of the Spanish priesthood. Like all other classes and professions, it certainly, and undoubtedly, has its faults; but where is there a profession—especially if it be one kept up in defiance of nature, as is the case with a celibate priesthood—which has not its faults ? And, when to their enforced celibacy is added the fact that the priests, who in other days had, in many cases, only £20 to £50 per annum from Government, trusting to their parishioners (in many cases very poor) for any addition to their salary, have now had even that wretched grant refused them for years since the accession of the Republic, and have to live upon alms, or by their wits, can one wonder that in some, if not in many, cases they become debased and reckless?

Surely nothing alters a man's character so much for the worse as a soul-eating poverty. True, it may make a sinner a saint, but, inasmuch as it takes away from a man those opportunities of doing good to others which open his heart and soul, and denies to him all ennobling and elevating pleasures and pursuits of science or art, it is far more likely to make a saint a sinner. But the poor country clergy—who often now have to turn their hand to mending watches, making beehives, hen-coops, and the like, and who certainly do it with true Spanish cheerfulness and goodwill—are fiercely satirised, and too often obscenely so, in the cheap literature of the Spanish miner.

From the scurrilous and semi-blasphemous, the transition to the coarse joke and the obscene story is not very great. Here is a specimen of the coarse printed couplets, read and sung to an attentive group by the Spanish miner:—

> You were in the train upset by bandits,
> So I was, in truth;
> Gladly would I be again upset,
> Never more to see my wife.
>
> Oh! ye poor men who lecture,
> Thinking to gain a living,
> When you ask for money,
> All will rush to the door.
>
> *Moral.* Stick to the wine and cigarillo!

> If a wife takes to becoming intellectual,
> Her husband must make baby's pap!

This last sentence would not, from all I hear, find much favour with a certain advanced party in England now.

> Glorious are the laurels
> That a poet wins.
> What is the good to him?
> He never has a peseta in his pocket.

This is a true remark enough; for, of all persons in Spain, literary men, even of talent, are perhaps the least appreciated.

> I love to quaff the wine, and say,
> Life is bitter, but it is only one swallow.

This last a most thoroughly characteristic *refran*.

> Mountebanks and rascals hate politics;
> And why? Because a lover of politics is sure to be an honest man!

All these quotations are from one broadsheet—a popular one, the couplets of which are often sung out by the miners. These couplets are, indeed, low, and coarse enough. In them there is evident a certain crude materialism of the worst and most sensual kind,—an utter absence of admiration for what is good because it is good, whether it profits or no.

Let us turn now to a still sadder page—the simply ribald and indecent. Alas! although I have said but little of it, the indecent element enters into nearly all the secular cheap literature of the Spanish poor.

Here is a specimen, and by no means one of the worst. It is called 'Juan Lanas: a very Racy Narrative.' And racy it certainly is. Would that it stopped at raciness. Let me premise, ere presenting 'Juan

Lanas' to the reader, that the history here referred to was sung in front of the writer's house, and other respectable houses, by a blind man, night after night, crowds of women, young and old, admiring and applauding.

Juan Lanas : Verses referring to a Poor Peasant, and the Bad Night he passed, when, returning home, he found his Wife about to be Delivered, and his House dark, and his Dinner uncooked.

On a dark and rainy night
Came John Lanas from his work,
Found his house without a light,
And his wife bedewed in tears.
  Oh ! but what a night to rest !

Said he, " Leave your grief at once,
Make my supper, light the fire."
Little thought he she was suffering
For the love of the past year.
  Oh ! but what a night to rest !

Said his wife, " Leave everything,
Run for oil, and kill some fowls ;
Tell my mother, bring the nurse,
And a bottle of rich wine."
  What a night for John to rest !

" Get me meat and bacon too,
Get me peas and chocolate,
Candied biscuits, rose liqueur ;
I am in a dreadful way."
  What a chance for John to rest !

Reeling, tumbling, stopping, falling,
Poor John to the town went on ;
Got the goods, and, home returning,
Put rich soup upon the fire.
  Not a wink of sleep for John !

Said the midwife, "Come you here, John,
Soon your wife will have a son;
Hold her up." And then his wife said,
"This is not your fault, dear John."
    Oh, he had no rest at all!

" Light the candle, bring the relic;
Virgin, of deliverance good,
Come and help thy suffering sister;
Yes, we 'll say a Litany."
    Oh, but what a night for John!

"Well? and, after all, a daughter;
What a pity; chew some hair,
Then be sick. Now, bring me scissors,
Thread, and clothes, and sash, and broth."
    Oh, but what a night for John!

Poor John went to get his supper,
When he heard the midwife scream,—
" John, go get of peony syrup,
And some fern of maiden's hair."
    Not a wink of sleep for John!

"Yes, and viper's root, and white lead,
And some sprigs of fever-fue,
And some vessels, and some treacle."
To the town once more John flew.
    What a sleepless night for John!

Tired, returned he; then the midwife
Put the child into his arms,
Saying,—"Nurse your precious daughter,
She is worth a lump of gold."
    Not a wink of sleep for John!

To her home the midwife hieth;
John begins to think of rest,
When his wife's dear mother crieth,
"I've a bad pain in my breast!"
    When will come some sleep for John?

> Reader, John Lanas speaks to you,
> Saying,—" Now that once you know
> All a woman's evil customs,
> All the misery they bring."
> (Never sleep hath come to John !)
>
> "Do not trust in them, as I did,
> But into your pocket put
> Your right hand, for two brown farthings,
> And just buy, and read, my book."
> For John had no sleep that night!

In the above thoroughly Spanish ditty, I have suppressed all that could offend an English reader. Certainly, it is an indecent and coarse song; but it is one of thousands, and is sold and sung without reserve to admiring crowds of the lower, respectable orders. But it is a sad witness to the depth to which a naturally high-minded population, such as the Spanish mining population, has been suffered to fall, simply from the want of " true religion and useful learning," that such themes as these, over which a veil should be ever drawn, should form the staple of their songs, and really rejoice their hearts.

There is but one more element—the political—to be noticed here; and of that, time and space forewarn me to abstain from quoting a specimen at any length. Is it not enough to say, that, as a rule, the political pamphlet is read by very few, and understood by still fewer, and that, generally, its aim is to spread broadcast the seeds of dissatisfaction with any Government—save that of the Democratic Federal Republic; that is, the division of the country into small cantones, each with its separate Government? The most popular pamphlet on this subject, perhaps, is that called 'All or Nothing,' with an inflammatory prologue, by Roqué Barcia, a pamphlet written not without real talent and insight into national characteristics. But to go into details would be to impose too great a task on the already wearied reader. Let me only now ask the reader to follow me from sunny, semi-tropical, uneducated Spain to two other climes.

The Spanish miner has no genius for mining—to him it is simply a means of winning bread—and so he has no distinctive literature. But turn, for one moment, to the German miner; he, at any rate, has his love of mining and his *esprit de corps*. He has his regular mining ballads, sung from the mine-owner to the pitman, all of which (and they have lately been published in a collected form in Leipzig) have a hearty, genial, moral tone, free from superstition and ribaldry, I believe, yet full of nature and of true religion. Here is the favourite song of the German miner, and many of my readers, doubtless, will be familiar with it; it is called "Ein Bergmannslied," but is better known by the name of the chorus to each stanza, "Glückauf,"—*i. e.*, "God-speed."

I.

The merry bell, from yonder steep,
  Hath pealed its matin lay;
To where the shaft looms, dark and deep,
  Come, comrades, let's away!
Yet give your loves a parting kiss,
A hearty kiss, then good-bye bliss,
  For such the life we lead;
    And now
God speed our work! God speed!

II.

With fearless heart, and nimble tread,
Each lad the shaft descends,

And at his post, for daily bread,
  With sturdy stroke contends.
The waggons rattle ; all around
  Of pick and axe is heard the sound ;
  But of the blast take heed.
    And now
  God speed our work ! God speed !

III.

And, oh, if in the darksome mine,
  Death's hand on me be laid,
He who hath willed it is divine,
  And, well I know, can aid.
So, farewell, loves, dry up your tears,
It is not death the miner fears,
  For Heaven is free from need
    And cares.
  God speed our work ! God speed !

How unstrained, how hearty, how natural, is the tone of this last!—above all, how healthy! To pass to it from the ephemeral themes that we have dwelt upon, necessarily, is like passing from the stagnant and relaxing river into the restless, bracing sea. And compare the literature of the poor Spaniard with that of his English brother, and see how few, in comparison, are his advantages. Take only one Society, that for Promoting Christian Knowledge, in England, and think of the blessings it puts within the reach of thousands, and then despise not the poor Spanish miner.

CHAPTER XVI.

A SUNDAY'S WALK AMONG THE SPANISH MINERS.

So far as scenery is concerned, this part of the Black Country has nothing of grace or beauty to recommend it. Charles Kingsley has beautifully said that the Fen Country of Lincolnshire has a certain wild beauty, as of the sea, to charm the traveller. Waste after waste, field after field, hedgeless, treeless, but still with a certain amount of verdure, there meet the eye. But here the case is different. Here nothing but rolling plains, sometimes bearing crops of stunted corn, sometimes studded with that ugliest of stunted trees, the olive, are to be seen; and, when once the harvest is reaped, which is in May and June, the fierce sun soon turns what was green into wastes of withered stubble, and dry, arid dust.

It is not, then, natural beauty which will make our Sunday's walk interesting or picturesque. But the old tale of "eyes and no eyes" is true as ever, and a keen observer will find many things to interest him in our Sunday's walk.

On the Friday previous to the Sunday here described, one of the best-hearted, most popular, and richest men of the town had died, and, contrary to that Spanish law which decrees, and rightly enough, that every corpse be interred within twenty-four hours of death, the funeral of this man was delayed until Sunday, at nine o'clock.

On Saturday night, at twelve o'clock, I passed the windows of his ample house. To my surprise, a crowd of some hundreds was thronging around the window of the dead man's bed-room. I elbowed my way in. The windows, almost to the ground, were wide open, and there, lying stiffly upon his iron bedstead, was the dead body of Don Juan, exposed to the public gaze. The room was barren of every sort of furniture, save that at the foot of the bed was placed the gorgeous white-and-gold coffin, in readiness for the morrow's ceremony.

Two Spanish servants were watching, sadly enough, beside the corpse of him who had once been a generous master and a genial friend. A huge wax-candle burnt at each corner of the bed. The arms of the dead man were crossed, or rather folded upon his breast; kid gloves were upon his hands; his dress was the same that he was wont to use for state occasions; his massive gold watch-chain lay loosely on his breast; a few flowers were spread around his head.

"He sleeps calm enough now, anyhow," said a Spanish miner, who was looking on. "Will he meet Christ at the Judgment Day with those white-kid gloves on?"

We shuddered, and I passed on, at the ribald remark.

On Sunday morning, when I went out to get a breath of the balmy air before the heat of day, the poor decked-out body was borne forth to its last long home. But first it went to the church, where it was deposited, its coffin covered with passion-flowers and orange-blossoms, amid a whole circle of pig-skins full of wine, sacks of peas, and of wheat, upon the floor of the church. These last were the offerings to the priests of the church, who, for the space of half-an-hour, said the solemn Spanish service for the burial of the dead.

Then, followed by over 2,000 people, the long train moved forth, headed by eight priests, to the rough and rocky and unkempt cemetery, where the genial comrade, the warm, kind, honest heart was to find its last earthly resting-place.

My walk lay onwards to the distant mines, and I determined, as the day had dawned so full of interest, to jot down all that interested me.

First, then, came a Spanish herdsman carrying a tiny lamb, literally "in his bosom," and, behind him, a boy, whose burden should have been the lightest, bearing on his shoulders, by its two fore-legs, the lame mother; and I could not help remarking how vividly the words of the Holy Scripture were thus illustrated, "The little ewe lamb, which lay in the poor man's bosom, and was unto him as a daughter," and "The shepherd who beareth home his lost sheep on his shoulders rejoicing." And rejoicing these men surely were, for gayer prattle I never heard.

The most painful part of the walks in the Spanish interior, is that you hear on every side, from mule-driver, donkey-driver, and—when you pass a washing-ground—washerwomen, the coarsest and vilest language imaginable,—language so coarse, so obscene, that one can hardly persuade oneself that one is walking in a civilized and in a (so-called) Christian country. The muleteer or donkey-driver calls his donkey by an obscene and vile name. If enraged, he will say to his companions, "I spit upon ten," pronouncing the word diez (the Spanish for ten) as though it were Dios (God), as I have before observed, and so conveying the worst and rankest form of blasphemy against the Creator's name. While the mildest form of vituperation among the washerwomen will be, "Your mother was a w——; go you and wallow in the water-closet."

Indeed, low-sunken, degraded, and utterly ignorant as are the masses in Spain, any one who judged of them by their language would form an estimate of their moral state even lower than would be correct.

Just before we left the dreary, dusty outskirts of the town, we came upon a litter resting in the middle of the rock-strewn road, the four bearers standing by smoking and wiping the perspiration from their foreheads and bare chests. The litter was covered with black canvas, and was curtained round with the same, to keep off the fierce glare of the sun. In the litter lay a fine young fellow, who had just broken his arm in two places by a fall from a ladder in a distant mine. He had been carried thus for five weary miles! Of course, owing to the rocky and uneven nature of the roads, the only means of transit for a wounded man from the mine to the hospital is the litter.

I said to one of the bearers,—"Is he badly hurt?"

"Bastante malo" (Badly enough) was the heartless answer.

Amid the stunted growth of wheat and barley I noticed a number of dark purple flowers, and, casting my eye over the fields, which were of sandy soil, running down to the water's edge, I noticed that they lent quite a purple hue to the corn, much as the "red poppy" tinges the English corn-fields with its pervading scarlet. On plucking one, I found it to be a sort of purple iris, with four or five flowers on each stem, and sword-like leaves. I asked my guard the Spanish name for it, and he said at once, "Lirio del campo" (the lily of the field); and, looking at its exceedingly delicate petals, which wither almost as soon as plucked, and its beautiful hues, varying from deep crimson to the darkest purple, I could not help thinking that this, if, as I believe, it ranks among the Flora of Palestine and be found on those slopes of corn-fields that run down to the shores of the Lake of Galilee, might be the "lily of the field" to which "even Solomon, in all his glory, was not arrayed" in equal beauty!

The botanical knowledge of the Spaniards, high and low, is something pitiable. Indeed, of the natural history of their country they know absolutely nothing, and one name serves for twenty different flowers. Every bird is a "pajaro" (or "bird")! Every insect or reptile is a "becho" (or "beast")! Indeed, the only real botanical knowledge in the interior is confined to the "Government herbalists." These are a kind of what, in England, would be called "quack doctors," who go forth from the large towns in the spring months—February, March, April, and the earlier part of May—and, rambling over mountain, meadow, field, and more, collect specimens of the various herbs and plants mentioned in their text-book.

These men are licensed and paid by Government for their labours, and are thorough believers in the fact (noticed in my sketch of a Spanish winter garden) that each locality bears among its flowers and herbs the very cure appointed by Providence for the diseases of that special district.

Their recognized text-book, which they carry with them on their rambles, is 'The Herbal of Dioscorides,' translated from the Greek into Spanish, and "conforme el Catalogo Nuevo del Santo Oficio de la Inquisicion." The book is profusely illustrated, and bears date, "Valencia, 1695."

There are, however, several sacred flowers, every feature of each one of which is dear to the heart of the poor Spanish miner; and, chiefly, he reveres with a superstitious reverence the passion-flower. Pluck a sprig of it from some rude road-side hut, and he will delight in dissecting it, and explaining its history, "Here," he will say, "are the seven petals: these are the disciplina of the Christ; here are the three Marias; here, in this twisting tendril, see the cordon of the Christ; here are the three clavos (nails) with heads; here is the bitter cup, or caliz; here are the five fajas, or swathing bands for burial; here (in a little space beneath the crown of the flower) is a drop of honey: taste how sweet it is: yes, indeed, for it is the blood shed for us; and, lastly, here is the corona! Is it not all perfect, señor? Gracias á Dios!"

As you pass on your way, and it begins to grow toward evening, you will meet little knots of picturesquely dressed campo-men, or labourers; they are all hurrying to the town to get there by half-past four or five o'clock. Arrived there, they sit in a wide semicircle on the paving-stones around the Plaza, or market-place,—a motley crowd they are, too,—and there they wait until the steward, or farmer, comes to hire them. I have often counted 200 waiting, at early morn, or at eve, to be hired; seen many fulfilling the words of the Scripture, by "standing there all the day idle," and, if you ask one of them why he is not at work, his answer will be given in the words, "Because no man hath hired me!"

So strikingly, in this primitive land, with its many Oriental elements, are the very words of Holy Writ illustrated.

Passing through the olive-groves, where the lumps and cairns of granite, half-covered in wiry creepers, offer shelter to innumerable reptiles, the only sound you will hear is the shrill silvery note of myriads upon myriads of cicadas—a silvery tinkle that absolutely fills the air. The only sign of life will be the numberless brown and green lizards, darting across your path with the speed of lightning, to hide themselves in the crevices of the stones.

The mining population have a curious superstition regarding the green lizard, which sometimes is as much as a foot-and-a-half in length.

The superstition is as follows:—Occasionally, whether naturally or by accident, the tail of this reptile is divided into three points of equal length, or nearly so, in which case it is called by the ignorant Spaniard "the three-tailed lizard." If you can catch one of these, and place it in a box, with a quantity of small bits of paper, each bearing one number of the coming lottery, from which you have to make your choice of a number, the three-tailed lizard will always eat up the ticket which bears the winning number. That this belief has been constantly acted upon, in implicit faith in the wisdom of the lizard, I can myself testify; indeed, no earthly argument would persuade the miner that his theory about the three-tailed lizard is an incorrect one.

Should the lizard refuse to eat any one of the squares of paper, he will dip its three tails into black ink; and as the poor wretch crawls away, and crosses and re-crosses its proper prison-floor, the number of the successful ticket will be easily (so the gambler says) deciphered from the trail! No doubt a lizard with three tails would make a hieroglyphic which might be turned into a numeral, far more easily than the ordinary one-tailed reptile, as Mother Nature has fashioned it, not for making numerals on paper, but for steering and aiding its lightning-like flight.

So, through the olive-grove and over the crumbling stone wall, and through the "patio" of the olive-guard's comfortless lodge, we pass on toward the mine. The tender green tendril of the vine is already hanging gracefully over the rude framework put for its support in front of the dark stone shanty. Already the kindly, rough hostess has espied your advent, and is awaiting you with a stirrup-cup of Val-de-Peñas blanco (white wine of La Mancha), which she presses on you, and you must not refuse; and she bids you depart with the Spanish religious woman's benison, "Vaya usted con Dio y con la Virgen!" (Depart you with God and the Virgin!) And now we are at the mines.

On the day on which I write, two deeds of blood occurred. I had not been there ten minutes, and was sitting in the tiny house of a stalwart Welsh miner, when a pistol-shot rang out from the neighbouring venta—a house of bad repute, on the outskirts of a mine. Two men had quarrelled, and one passed by, escorted by his friends, a pistol-bullet in his bandaged arm, from which the blood was slowly oozing out. Sickened at the sight, I returned home somewhat early, and while on the road my companion, a Spanish miner, said, "Do you know the postman of this mine has been stabbed, and is nearly dead? There he goes." I looked, and half-a-mile in front, sure enough, was the litter, followed by a crowd of miners, which contained the body of the poor lad who had fallen a victim to a quarrelsome drunkard's knife—a knife that had, ere now, taken one human life. Just ahead of the litter was a cloud of dust, slowly receding. It was the body of Municipal Guards, escorting the murderer to the prison, there to lie, perhaps, for months or even years, awaiting the doom of human law in Spain—not death, but imprisonment. Slowly I dragged my sickening heart and weary footsteps toward home. The shades of evening were falling, and I had yet a mile of lonely road to travel with my one companion. Suddenly, rising up silently from behind a block of granite, two men, the brass plates upon their breasts and leather shoulder-belt proclaiming them Guards of the Campo, drew near me, and, gun in hand, one on either side, began to accompany me. I asked what it meant, and the chief answered, quietly, " It is a bad time of day, and a bad day for crime; we will see you to the outskirts of your pueblo." This they did, and departed as silently as they had joined me.

As I neared the washing-grounds and watering-troughs, a couple of troops of Hussars, in stable-dress, were riding down to water their horses from the posadas and private houses where they were billeted, mingling with the crowd of water-carriers, male and female (these latter in their yellow serge petticoats, brown, plump feet, and rich black hair framing a mahogany face), who were filling the pitchers on their donkeys for their last evening round. The Hussars, with bare or sandalled feet, tight-fitting blue-jackets, and trousers of any colour and shape, sitting bare-backed on their spirited Andalucian steeds, and curbing them without bridle, by the steel nose-band, formed a group for a painter. All was noise, oaths, strange language, and confusion.

At the hospital a crowd was collected to know the result of the doctor's examination of the poor lad who had been cut down in the prime of life by a felon-stroke. It was all over: life's brief drama, for him, was ended; the alcalde of the town, followed by two guards, pushed his way through the crowd to perform his office.

Just then the poor father of the lad rode up on his donkey to ask what was the matter. "A man stabbed," said the rough but tender-hearted crowd; "but we don't know who it is." And, little dreaming that he was turning his back on the still warm body of his only son, within those mouldering hospital walls, the father, humming his Andalucian ditty of love or war, rode slowly on to his night work at the mine! "Telle est la vie"—in Spain!

CHAPTER XVII.

LIFE AND CHARACTER OF GERMAN AND SPANISH MINERS CONTRASTED.

Having drawn out in detail the prominent points of contrast between the life and character of the English and Spanish miners, it may be interesting to some still following the fortunes of the miners of Europe, and sharing with them their sorrow and their joy, to transport ourselves to that triangular district of ground pregnant with mineral, which is bounded on one side by the fine, rugged range of the Erz-Gebirge, and on another by the rolling waters of the Elbe.

The contrast between the life and character of the English and Spanish miner has been seen to be great; that between the Spanish and German will prove to be greater still.

The following are stray notes and reminiscences of the mines and miners of the Erz-Gebirge, a district, the central town of which is Freiberg.

The mines of the Erz-Gebirge are chiefly of lead, silver, and galena ore, and, some years since, were exceedingly rich in metal, but have now been worked to an enormous depth, and are found to be daily becoming poorer. Most of these mines are the property of the Saxon Government, which, like that of Spain, has been wise enough to monopolize the best mines in its wild country, and thus secure a considerable income in addition to its revenues. Each mine is managed by one or more German engineers, who are very able and capable men. Indeed, as in Spain, the profession of the mining engineer is considered one of the gentle professions, and men of good family and position enter upon it. The engineers of this district have first to pass through a severe course of study at the Mining Academy of Freiberg, and then to serve an apprenticeship to practical mining engineering, the Saxon Government thus securing efficient and tried managers of the mines.

In Spain, the official working staff of a mine is cut down to the lowest dimensions compatible with some amount of safety; and the machinery is often old-fashioned and defective, whereas in Germany the number of paid officials constantly exceeds the real demands of the work, and the machinery is of the best and newest construction. In fact, roughly stated, it may be said that practical mining is really the genius of the German mind, as of the English, whereas the Spaniard too often only lends himself to it as a necessity.

Stand with me, as the sun is just reddening the crest of the wild hills of the Erz-Gebirge, and see the German miners pass to their weary round of dark and unhealthy and ill-requited work. Here they come, in their long blouses, wearily plodding their way along the stony paths. They look worn, sad, and somewhat stupid men, their air far different from that of the jaunty, careless, ephemeral Andaluz. And why so? Simply because their wages, poor fellows! are on a scale probably lower than that of any body of men in the world, and poverty and poor, hard fare make a man's step weary and his face sad. Yet, ere the bell has sent forth its summons over hill and dale, every man is here, in his place, ready to descend the shaft. And well for him that he is ready, for few laws are stricter, and none are more severely insisted upon, than the Mining Code of Saxony.

True, the Spanish code of mining laws is strict enough; but then, although first-rate in theory, in Spain we never think of enforcing our laws!

Every German miner is subject to imprisonment for any neglect of duty; and whereas his Spanish or English brother (although the English has no special mining code) would hardly bear a reprimand for absenting himself from work without a fair cause, the poor German actually hardly complains if he be marched off to prison for his slight omission. The Englishman's love of money, high wages, and sterling common-sense, lead him to work regularly; the German works regularly because he is punished in default of doing so; the Spaniard neither takes thought for the morrow, nor will submit to the slightest restraint; he is a caballero (gentleman), and will do as he pleases.

Here, then, around the dressing-houses, waiting to put on their dark calico blouses for the pit-work, are the underground men. There is no cigarette in mouth, but each has just put out his clumsy pipe of crockeryware. They stand, a group of broad-shouldered, short, silent, impassionless men.

And now, listen to the roll-call! There are no absentees from duty. The manager then, in dead silence, takes out a form of prayer from his pocket; every head is bared. How exquisite is the spirit, how simply beautiful and touching are the words of the prayer that now wells forth from his lips, praying the Almighty God to protect them throughout their dangerous work, and to keep wife, sweetheart, children, safe against their return home. The prayer ended, the response, "So be it," is murmured from the lips of the assembled crowd, who now press into the undressing sheds.

Germany is the land of law and order; and although the Cornishman would object to this "prayer by law established" (in the district of which I write), because he prefers extempore, and the Spaniard would wholly disregard it, yet the Saxon miner loves, and feels a comfort in, the petition offered for and with him, and is thankful to accept and join in it; and although one half of his number is Roman Catholic, and one half Lutheran, yet all join in prayer on the brink of the pit to "the one Lord and Father of us all."

I should say that the moment the prayer is concluded a hundred stentorian voices join, with bare heads and uplifted voices, and eyes upturned to the clouded skies, in a hymn, much, in character and feeling, like the English Morning Hymn at the end of the Prayer-Book.

Then the poor fellows descend, as the bell chimes out once more from the stone turret, to seek their work and their labour until the evening.

But how does the German miner descend, and what words are on his lips as he leaves the daylight, perhaps never, in this world, to return to it alive?

He is sent down in the *Fahr-kunst*, or "man-engine," which is worked by the pumping-engine, and consists of a number of stages, attached to the rods, the miner stepping from one to the other until he reaches the particular level where lies his work.

The mines are so deep, that to descend by ladders would tire the poor fellow out before his day's work was begun.

And what words are on his lips as he descends? No ribald jest, such as the Spanish miner loves, is heard; no grumbling nor silence, in which the Cornishman indulges. No; he is singing the beautiful song, the miner's song of Germany, "Glück-auf" (God-speed), of which I have elsewhere given a translation, or one of the touching, spirited, and beautiful songs of the Fatherland.

And what of his work below ground? Well, he is most industrious, most faithful; he is not so smart as the Spaniard; he is not so sturdy as the Cornishman; he is slow certainly, but very sure in his work, thinking a long while before he acts, but when his mind is made up as to the right course, plodding on unceasingly and faithfully.

At last the "shift" is over, and the miner comes to the surface. He dresses, walks homewards, his huge German pipe (filled, by-the-bye, with most abominable tobacco, as we ourselves can testify) in the corner of his mouth, musing as he goes.

And then he gets home to his homely, nay, his coarse fare. Black bread and potatoes form the staple; meat is a luxury hardly known to the poor Saxon miner. The Spaniard has his savoury stew; the Cornishman, his solid meat-pie; the Saxon has neither.

One of the chief luxuries of the miner of the Erz-Gebirge is a well-fatted dog. Some short time since, the landlady of a well-known beer-garden on the outskirts of Freiberg, much frequented by the miners, was obliged to have an old favourite, in the shape of a poodle dog, destroyed, owing to his dirty habits, enormous obesity, and asthma. The miners heard of the death of their old pet, and instantly a dozen applications for the carcase were made to the landlady. She graciously delivered the dog, for a certain sum, into their hands. He was boiled at once, and many a hearty supper was made on that night of dog's flesh, "and," said one of the miners, " first-rate flesh it was, too."

The miner's drink is Läger-beer, much like the English table or small beer, coffee (which he drinks twice a day), and water. He hardly ever drinks spirits, and very little wine. So soon as his meal is concluded, he lights his large china pipe, and " blows a cloud."

The cottage in which the Saxon miner lives is very poor. His family, too, live in a state of great poverty. He, unlike the Spanish miner, ever puts his pride (if he has any) in his pocket, and consents to earn a thaler or two by being the servant of one of the students at Freiberg, that is, he will clean their boots and walk upon errands for them. Fancy the pride of a Spanish, or the well-filled pocket of a Cornish, miner consenting to perform acts so menial!

Strangely do the Saxon contrast with the Spanish miners on the point of education. The law of Government schools for the poor and compulsory education is almost identical in both countries; and yet, whereas not one in eight of the Spanish miners can read or write, there is scarcely a single Saxon miner who cannot do both! The Saxon miner, to all appearance, has more stamina, if less flesh, than the Spanish. Indeed, his climate is very cold and dry in winter, and not too hot in summer, and so his fare is more substantial. He is, in appearance, a short, broad-shouldered man, with long, muscular arms, and little flesh.

When sick the Saxon goes to the Government hospital, where he is (unlike the Spaniard) really well cared for, and has good, if not first-rate, medical treatment.

In one point the Spanish and Saxon miners present a feature of great similarity. Neither is given to strikes. But the reasons which induce either class to be quiet are very dissimilar. The Spaniard does not strike because he is lazy and contented; the Saxon because he is, and feels himself to be, in the very land of law. Indeed, the Saxon's conduct is ever that of a steady, industrious, obedient man.

On one occasion only, in the whole of my experience, did I witness a case of general insubordination on his part. It happened on this wise. The centenary anniversary of the founding of the Freiberg Academy was to be celebrated in great style. There was to be a banquet, a procession, in which all the societies, Freemasons, friendly, &c., were to join, with all the tradesmen of the township, and the professors and students of the Academy.

The poor Saxon miners thought, naturally enough, that they also ought to have the privilege of joining in the procession, and, as miners, to aid in the festivities of a mining academy, and the professors and students urged for them their claims to the Administrator of the Province. With true German stubbornness, he steadily refused to give these poor fellows a holiday, in order that they might join in the general demonstration.

"Any one," said he, "who stays away from work

on that day shall be imprisoned according to the Code of Laws."

For once the Saxon blood resented the indignity, and, *en masse*, the miners struck work. In a body, with bands playing, the miners promenaded the town, and going to the Town Hall, where the students, professors, &c., were banqueting, they gave them a serenade.

After this, the students (English and American chiefly) invited these poor fellows to partake of six barrels of beer, with hams, and bread and cheese, in some gardens hard by. They enjoyed their holiday and treat greatly, and expressed their gratitude. Quietly they repaired to their homes that night, and, at the usual hour next morning, went to the mine. Here, however, the police arrested six or eight who had headed the procession, and they were forthwith subjected to a week's imprisonment!

You will ask naturally, what then are the amusements of the Saxon miner compared with those of the English and Spanish miners? Oftentimes, his homely meal finished, he repairs to the " Turn-Halle," or Gymnasium, to practice gymnastics; on other occasions he goes to sing the ringing songs of the Fatherland at the saloon of the especial Musical Society to which he belongs; or, if ambitious, or obliged so to do, he will go for instruction to the Mining Schools.

Unlike the easy-going Spaniard, who thinks nothing of Sunday, working on that as on any other day, the Saxon hails Sunday as (excepting Easter and Christmas Days) his real day of rest,—rest in its truest sense, religious worship and moderate recreation. As a rule, whether Lutheran or Roman Catholic, the Saxon miner goes to church on Sunday morning. At one o'clock the German Sunday is considered, so far as the strictly religious observance is concerned, at an end; and at two o'clock the amusements or recreations of the day commence.

These recreations consist of concerts in the restaurants or beer-gardens of the town. He cannot, so poorly is he paid, afford to go to the garden where the military band plays, and where the fee for admission is three groschen (*i.e.* threepence), so he goes to hear one of his own bands play. In the garden he meets his sweetheart, who comes attended by her mother and others of the family, and, when once the nervous eye of love has espied its object, he gets a seat at the same table, and soon gets into conversation with the fair-haired girl of his choice.

Soon, after a few interviews of this kind, the couple become engaged, and then the lady is supposed to be his property, and he has the privilege of always paying for her share of refreshments, but never for that of her mother!

Then evening draws on and dancing commences, the officer in plain clothes not thinking it beneath him to stand as *vis-à-vis* to the homely miner and his girl.

Quarrels are very rare; and if, now and then, the Saxon blood is roused, the quarrel is settled, not with the fists of the Cornishman or the deadly knife of the Spaniard, but with a good stout cudgel, with which the combatants belabour one another's heads and shoulders most mercilessly.

The Saxon miner does not, as a rule, marry young, since, as in Prussia, every man is supposed to serve for three years in the army. There is, therefore, a certain amount of immorality. By an account lately taken, the proportion of births of illegitimate children per week was eight to every seven legitimate!

The appended estimate of the character of the German and Spanish miner is from the pen of an agent who had served both in the Spanish and Saxon mines.

"The Saxon miner," he writes, "is a slow, serious, obedient, careful, truthful man; the Spanish, a lively, reckless, deceitful, sharp, careless fellow.

"The Saxon seeks his work singing some beautiful or even religious song of the Fatherland; the Spaniard, too often with ribald jest and profane song on his lips.

"The Saxon is educated; the Spaniard not.

"The Saxon loves home and home pleasures: he shares his joys with his family. Not so the Spaniard, who frequents the *café*, or smokes his cigarette among a host of his brethren in the street.

"The Saxon is harmless and quiet; the Spaniard, treacherous and noisy: the one never raises hand against his master; the other, in a burst of ungoverned rage, will even draw his knife, and then lament for hours, or even weeks, the work of one rash moment."

ENGLISH CEMETERIES IN SPAIN.

CHAPTER I.

CADIZ.

In the course of my wanderings in Spain, I have ever made it a matter of duty to visit and take notice of the last earthly resting-places of my countrymen who have died thus far from their native land. And I have thought that a short account of some of the principal English cemeteries in this country might prove interesting to many who read these pages. Some, at least, of them must have a relation, or friend, or acquaintance, whom the short, rapid, fatal diseases of this country and the swiftly-following funeral (for interment in Spain follows on the very heels of death) have consigned to a Spanish grave; and all Englishmen take, I venture to think, sufficient interest in their countrymen abroad to welcome any intelligence of those plots of ground where they find their last long home. Many, too, who come to Spain to end their days in a climate purer and less trying than that of England, may like to know that they may, at last, peaceably " dwell among their own people," for we all, more or less, share the feeling of Shakspeare's dying queen,—

> "When I am dead, good wench,
> Let me be used with honour."

At Madrid, Cadiz, Seville, Malaga, Linares (this last the great centre of English mining works), Barcelona, and, I believe, Bilboa, those who are taken away may rest amid their own people. In other words, at each of these places there is a burial-ground reserved for Protestants of all nations.

A few remarks on the subject of Protestant burial-grounds in Spain may not be out of place here. Inch by inch, as it were, those burial-grounds have been won from the ignorant Roman Catholic Government of the country, and only won by hard fighting. But with a liberal Republican Government, an English community would only have to ask, and a burial-ground would be at once acceded to it. Here, then (gathered from various authorities), is a brief *résumé* of the history of Protestant Cemeteries in Spain.

In the reign of Philip the Second of Spain, all who were Protestants were, at their death, exposed as malefactors. Their dead bodies were offered—to use the graphic words of the Philistine of Holy Writ—as meat "unto the fowls of the air and to the beasts of the field." But not much stress need be laid upon this part of the treatment of Protestants. In death, the poor lifeless body could not suffer; in life, they did suffer, and had suffered.

Another stage of the fate of the dead Protestants in Spain (so I find in 'Murray's Handbook,' Part II.) was in the year 1622, when the Secretary of the

English Ambassador died suddenly at Santander. Funeral rites were refused to the corpse of this heretic, and it was thrown into the sea. The poor, ignorant, and misled fishermen recovered the corpse, fearing that its presence would drive away all the shoals from their waters, and threw it up high and dry. Some time passed on. Protestants in Spain were few, and those few did not care to avow themselves as such. They knew what was reserved for the Protestant dead too well. "English bodies must be left above ground, to the end that the dogs may eat them."

Another stage then succeeded this. To the honour of Cromwell, it must be said, that his ministers negotiated a treaty with the Spanish Government for the decent burial of Englishmen—a treaty which, about the years 1666-1668, was finally ratified and approved—if my remembrance of dates serves me rightly—to the ministry of Charles the Second.

The first English burial-ground was purchased somewhere about the year 1796, by Lord Bute. It was, however, unenclosed, and a simple field—a word which, to Spanish ears, implies barrenness and openness. This was at Madrid.

The next stage at which the Protestant burial-grounds in Spain arrived was in the reign of Ferdinand the Seventh, who granted permission (unwillingly and ungraciously) for an enclosure of land for a Protestant burial-ground in towns where the English were represented by a consul.

'Murray's Handbook' informs me that the first enclosed cemetery for Protestants was founded at Malaga, by the British Consul, Mr. John Mark.

I have gone briefly through what may be called several

of the stages of Protestant burial, or rather non-burial, in Spain. Let me now tell you, as we enter the enclosed Protestant Cemetery of Cadiz, what is the last stage.

I took for my guide a rough, uneducated peasant,— I always select a peasant or boatman for my travelling companion in Spain, their remarks are so *naïve*, so homely, and often so true,—and with him I journeyed to the Protestant Cemetery of Cadiz. We passed down the self-same avenue described to you in a former chapter. I should have said, that it is formed of silver poplars and acacias; many of the latter are being now daily removed.

On our right lay the Spanish Cemeterio; down towards the sea, on the left, lay the British. We passed down the narrow, sandy road (though it was nearly Christmas, it was ankle-deep in sand and dust), and, just as I heard the sea moaning against the wharf, we were at the unpretending green gates of the Protestant Cemetery of Cadiz.

As, in answer to our ring, the keeper of the cemetery admitted us into his little garden of the dead, I said to my rude companion, "Are there many sleeping here?"—"Very few, señor; and those mostly English, Germans, and Norwegians; but after you get the Church separated from the State, you'll have lots of Protestants lying here; there are plenty now in Spain, and we'll soon have it full." This, then, was the last stage. It had been reserved for a simple peasant to settle, in his homely way, a matter which the bigotry of priests and the philosophy of kings and statesmen had for centuries kept in abeyance.

There is a little avenue of trees running up into the heart of the cemetery, which gives it a pretty and refined appearance. It is, in fact, a little strip of garden, sheltered by an avenue; there is a decent little lodge at the gates, and the whole is thus kept under lock and key.

The little avenue of trees on either side the path is of cypresses and feathery pines, rather stunted and young, but ever green and pretty. The garden at their feet had very little the appearance of a winter garden; it was one mass of bright colours,—quite like an English garden in June or July. Most noticeable were the clumps of the red geranium, or "flor del principe," which grows to a shrub in Spain, sometimes eight and nine feet in height, and is a universal favourite. Other geraniums, white, pink, and red, of smaller dimensions, were there in abundance; while a row of rosemary and lavender shrubs fringed each side of the walk. I noticed also a few straggling rose-trees, and that English winter favourite, the chrysanthemum, called very aptly by the Spaniards "flor del hiberno" (winter-flower). A few straggling trees of the bastard tobacco did not add much to the beauty of the garden.

The plot of burial-ground itself is not very well kept. The surface is uneven, and, as usual in Spain, one misses the green grass and the shapely little mounds of an English churchyard. Here, the loose sandy soil was but thinly sprinkled with grass, and looked neglected and dry. The most noticeable feature, however, were the clumps of the scarlet and scented geranium, which grew all over the cemetery. At the foot of every tree, and in masses around every stone, they clustered; and the effect of the dark green foliage and bright scarlet flowers against the dusky stones was exceedingly pretty. The ground is very thinly sprinkled with gravestones or monuments of any kind, and those that there are, though in some cases very costly and well kept, are not graceful or in good taste. The most prominent of these is a marble obelisk, some sixteen feet in height, but without any adornment. It is to the memory of Richard Davies, of the island of Madeira and of Jerez : died October 2nd, 1870, aged 61. At the foot is written, " God is Love." " Thy will be done." It is enclosed in railings, half-hidden by malvarosas and flor del principe.

Whenever one enters an English cemetery, one's eye lights upon texts of Scripture breathing of resignation and hope, or quaint verses expressive of the especial feeling of the mourner whose loved one is laid there. In Spain, in those cemeteries of the country which I have visited, I have hardly observed anything of the sort.

There is another marble obelisk, much like the one just described, but of more modest height, and girt with more modest flowers. It is to the memory of Emily Adelaide Hughes, died January 10th, 1864, aged 25. Close to it is by far the most graceful monument in the whole cemetery—a plain stone cross, well proportioned. It is to the memory of a Swedish merchant, and I subjoin the simple inscription, as I noticed that it was the usual form of inscription on the monuments of the several Swedes and Norwegians who rest here. The favourite with these seemed the simple cross of stone or iron, about four feet in height, which I have always considered the most suitable of all memorial stones. The invariable inscription on these stones smacked, I thought, as did the neat iron or stone cross, without any adornment save the flowers that clustered at its base, of the simplicity of character of these Northern folk. Here is the typical one:—

"Mauritz Levin, Född i Stockholm, den 14 April, 1844; Dod i Cadiz, den 6 Februar i 1865." I think these few words need no translation. I conceive them to mean simply—"Born at Stockholm; died at Cadiz."

Protestants of all nations have laid aside their differences, and sleep together here peacefully enough —English, French, Germans, Norwegians, Swedes, Spaniards. I noticed also memorials over the graves of English and American sailors, and one in memory of an English Marine Light Infantry man, who had met here with a violent death. Some of these graves are merely marked by a ring of scarlet geraniums, many have a plain iron cross, with a few bricks at the base. On one of these I noticed a Latin inscription, but it was so battered and weather-worn as to be hardly intelligible. The oldest form of memorial seemed to be this cross of iron, and another, which I have not noticed elsewhere, and will here describe. Four or five of them stand just at the entrance to the cemetery. It consists of a simple square block of stone, or bricks faced with cement, and with a sloping roof (I know not how else to describe it); it stands about $5\frac{1}{2}$ feet high; in the front is a small square indentation, on which the inscription is written. These appeared to be the oldest, and on one of them I found, so far as I could decipher it, the date 1844. But of this I am not positive. Several stones had been placed there in 1853.

The old stereotyped tombstone of the English churchyard, with its usual quaint verses, was represented, and, as it always brings back to an Englishman's heart and mind many recollections of peaceful days gone by, I copied the stanza on one of these.

It was on the Welsh master of a trading vessel, who had died, I presume, in the harbour:—

> "Alas! my son, and didst thou die,
> Without a friend or parent nigh,
> No hand to wipe thy fainting brow,
> To raise thee up, or lay thee low?
> Thy Father's God did there (*sic*) sustain,
> A Saviour's love did soothe thy pain;
> And we'll adore His holy name,
> Who in all climes is found the same."

One always reads these verses with regret, yet in England the humbler classes seem to like nothing so well. A few words of Holy Writ, one would think, would be far preferable; but I have often argued with the country poor in England on this point, and they have invariably clung tenaciously to their doggerel rhymes: and over a new-made grave one's words must be few and very tender.

Scripture, simply and judiciously used, seems to me to contain the proper expression of every sort of human feeling—regret, intense affection, sense of bereavement, bright hope, or lowly faith. What can be more touching—to pass for a moment to the green lanes of the Weald of Sussex, where the writer spent his happiest days—than this, on one who had prayed that her life might be spared,—"She asked life of Thee, and Thou gavest her a long life, even for ever and ever"? Is not the play upon the word "life" here simply exquisite?

I should have said before that the iron crosses and inscriptions over the Swedish or Norwegian dead sometimes have a more severe simplicity than those described above. Here is one:—

> "G. STROMSTEN, Sverige."

Nothing but that! Well, after all, as my weather-beaten companion remarked, "It's all the poor fellow needs!"

In shape this cemetery is a long strip of ground. It is enclosed on three sides by a substantial stone wall, about eight feet high, over a part of which hang the walls of a small bull-ring, giving it a thoroughly Spanish appearance. It is dotted all over with little clumps of trees, many of which are hazels, and, I believe, almond trees, though these latter were leafless, and I could not be sure what they were. The fourth side of the cemetery is enclosed by a high iron railing. At the farther end, as I strolled up, I saw that there were no grave-stones at all—nothing but a clump of hazels, which were fast shedding their leaves. The ground at this end seemed quite shifting sand, but all over it were scattered groups of red and scented geraniums.

I thought that there was nothing more to see, and was turning away, when a tiny little cross, half-smothered by the rustling fallen leaves and the geraniums, attracted my attention. It was evidently the last resting-place of some tiny child, probably of some poor parents. It consisted of four bricks and a tiny iron cross, without any inscription, fixed between them. As I have described the most prominent, so it is but fair that I should thus mention the least pretentious of them all. This little grave was under the shade of the nut-trees: on one side, the withered leaves, heaped up, almost hid it; on the other, pious hands (doubtless a mother's hands) had planted a geranium shrub—not the scarlet, but the modest scented geranium, the "malvaroso" of the Spanish garden.

At this end of the little enclosure I noticed a dozen

little rush-baskets, showing their heads out of the sandy soil. I inquired of my companion what on earth they were. With true Spanish caution he devoutly crossed himself, and refused to approach them. I went up to them, and pulled aside the little covering, and behold, it was the little nursery of tomato plants of the poor porter of the cemetery. He had scooped a dozen little holes, and set in each a little tomato plant, and put these rush-baskets, half-covered with earth, as a sort of cowl to protect them from frost or wind. He soon appeared in person—(when you least think it, a Spaniard will be watching all your movements, from behind a tree, or some other vantage ground: the other day I was looking for a particular flower in some public gardens, when I suddenly saw the black, piercing eyes and the muzzle of the gun of the guard of the gardens, peering at me over a wall hard by!)—this gatekeeper, and evidently thought it quite justifiable to raise his little crop here, and pointed to a few little trenches in the sand hard by, "and here I shall grow just a few potatoes." My guide entirely sympathized with him, and the two men shook hands heartily over the political economy here displayed: "It is best to utilize the ground."

Certainly, the little plot of potatoes and the tomato nursery took up but a modest space, and were out of sight, and he kept the little garden and avenue of his cemetery in beautiful order.

On the whole, the Protestant burial-ground of Cadiz, though not particularly well situated, is really neatly kept, and always looks bright and pretty, with its modest avenue of feathery pines, and its green geranium clumps, with their gaudy flowers straggling all over the shifting soil.

As I passed out the train from Seville thundered by, just outside the railings—a strange contrast, with its haste, and rattle, and eager faces, all telling of life, and bustle, and work, to the scene I was leaving, the quiet home of the dead, with no sound but the rustling of the withered nut-leaves and the sea breaking on the shore.

CHAPTER II.

CORDOBA.

It was a great privilege to spend even a few hours of these short winter days in Cordoba under the very shadow of the stately walls of the Mosque, which once was reckoned the third only in the whole world, those of Jerusalem and Mecca alone being esteemed by the Moors superior in sanctity to the Mosque of Cordoba.

Cordoba, once the "important city" (as the name implies), now is important only from its natural beauty and its antiquity. Its narrow winding streets— so narrow that, summer and winter, the sun never scorches them, a provision due to Moorish skill and forethought—are now almost deserted. Its bridge of sixteen or seventeen arches, spanning the far-spreading waters of the Guadalquivir, scarcely echoes with a single footfall. Around the cistern, with its gurgling fountain, in the patio, or courtyard of the Mosque, where once unnumbered ablutions were performed ere entering the holy inner courts, only two or three beggars cluster, with their never-ending whine, "Una limosna, por Dios!"—"An alms, for God's sake, give me!"—and a few children.

How constantly in Spain—let me pause a moment —are the words of Scripture brought home to one and verified. The beggar's cry at the door of every sacred court, "Una limosna, por Dios!" how forcibly does it recall the words of the Bible descriptive of him who, "Seeing Peter and John, asked an alms." Never, again, until the other day, did I fully realize the force of the expression in the Gospel, "The night cometh, when no man can work." I was walking home, about the time of set of sun. Suddenly—it was an autumn evening—the golden ball sank below the horizon, and, in one short quarter of an hour, all was dark, and hard work it was to pick one's way over the broken rocky path. No man could work then.

The walk around the lonely city-walls of Cordoba is the most striking feature about that city. The old, grey Moorish wall, now crumbling in places, with its constant turrets, and its orange-trees clustering under its shade, and showing their rich dark fruit aloft here and there; the quiet deserted convents; the quaint antique bridge, with Moorish water-mills still at work under its arches; the seminary, a long stone building of great antiquity, now used for the training of candidates for the priesthood, towering up above the river, and half-hidden by its grove of orange-trees; these, with the crisp, springy English turf, gnawed down by droves of goats, along the river banks, if seen on a bright day, when the sun smiles upon every tower, form a scene of unrivalled antiquity, beauty, and peacefulness.

One looks up from the low-lying banks of the sleeping river at the turrets, and walls, and pinnacles, and gateways of the city, and thinks of it as it was. Little more than eight hundred years ago it was a kind of second Jerusalem,—a joy of the whole earth, so they said. Its population, I believe, exceeded one million; its mosques were numbered by hundreds; and the glory of days still more ancient than the Moorish shed an everlasting halo over its head. Here Seneca and Lucan were born; here Averroes, too, in later days, lived, and Cespedes painted. This was the birthplace of Sanchez, of Meria, and Morales.

I wandered into the courtyard of the Mosque at eve. One religion had given place to another, and devout Christians were hurrying along, under the dusky rows of orange-trees, to their evening service. I walked then, in the grey eve, outside the lonely city-walls, and was astonished at the wild, lonely, grey beauty of the scene. One or two dogs were prowling about under the shade of the silver poplar-grove; a goatherd was driving home his herd, its leader, with its tinkling bell, proudly leading the way; a solitary fisherman was tying up his tackle; and I followed—not knowing how far it might be safe to loiter outside the walls at evening — a string of muleteers and mules, who went tinkling along the dusty road to get within the gates ere night,—the stately, but now crumbling Moorish gateway opening on to the river, now called the Puerta del Rio, or river-gate.

I rose early next morn — it was bitterly cold; though we have no snow and scarce any rain in Andalucia, we get bitter dry east winds, and ice at night, though rarely of the thickness of half-a-crown —and set forth for a tramp to the English cemetery.

The walk was full of interest,—full of quaint and picturesque details. Although it was nearly Christmas-time, the dust was blowing in clouds. First we passed (I say we, for, as is my custom, I took with me a poor Spanish workman) the Socorro Hospicio, where some three or four hundred poor find a home. This institution numbers among its inmates the widow, the aged of both sexes, the orphan, and the foundling, and is an old Moorish castle in part. Then we crossed a broad dusty Plaza, or square, at the corner of which, around a small movable wine-shop, stood eight or nine muleteers, in quaint gitano dress, *i. e.*, huge blue-and-white rugs wrapped round the upper man, white stockings to the knee (at least they were meant to be white), and loose knee-breeches, with brass buttons; women with yellow serge dresses, and green or red kerchiefs on their heads. To the right, just across the square, rose the ancient and most picturesque crowd of turrets and campanile of the Convent of San Cajetano, now only used as a church, the oranges hanging in yellow clusters over the grey walls that encircle it. Then we struck into a dusty ancient road, with crumbling walls of tapia, that is, lime, mud, and stone, alternated with hedges of the sword-like pita, or sharp aloe, and prickly-pear, or chumba, a diminutive sort of prickly-pear One feature here, and elsewhere in Cordoba, surprised me exceedingly. At every cross-road of these walls stands a huge stone cross, rising out of the walls. Yet the walls are said to be Moorish.

Again, you see the cross on the old Moorish door of the Mosque, amid all the Arabic characters. Why and how is this?

Among the many noticeable features on the road to the cemetery, there is one which must not be passed by without a word—I mean the "huertas," or market-gardens,—in England not very picturesque, but in

Spain exceedingly so. These gardens are enclosed in an old grey wall of tapia, over which hang the fruit and foliage of the orange-tree and lime: they are kept fruitful by irrigation, for which purpose an old Moorish "noria," or well, with its quaint water-wheel turned by an infirm mule, stands at the end of the garden, under the shade of a huge spreading fig-tree. You see the silver stream flowing into the trenches that intersect the "huerta," and notice the bright, rich green of the garden in marked contrast with the sandy barrenness of the surrounding country. In the midst of the garden stands an old stone house, half-hidden by orange-trees, to which, in the heats of summer, the family to whom the garden belongs come for a three-months' cooling and escape from the dust of the town.

Our road led on over slopes of olives, sandy, and covered with withered bents. One barren hill after another rose in front, and, nestling in the hollow of one of these, lay the smelting-works of a large English lead-mining company, the tall brick chimney of which was giving forth volumes of smoke. Within these works, I had been informed, lay the English cemetery —certainly not a very picturesque site, so far as the immediate surroundings were concerned.

The director of the "fabrica" courteously, on my presenting my card, conducted me to the spot. We went through the busy works, with their fierce furnaces, and streams of molten lead being carefully refined, and walked up the rocky incline, on whose slope lay the little spot I had come to see. All around told of activity and life; the little cementerio was, like the surrounding and distant hills, peaceful and quiet enough. It is a very tiny enclosure, set aside by the piety of the Consular Agent at Cordoba, an Englishman, Mr. Duncan Shaw. It stands on the slope of the hill, within its four substantial walls of stone, or tapia, and is kept under lock and key. I suppose, although I did not measure it, it would be about twelve yards square. It was consecrated, about eleven years ago, by the then Bishop of Gibraltar, whose two daughters accompanied him to the spot.

Inside there is no beauty; but the rough bent grass is cleared away every month, and the few tombstones are kept clean. Owing to the drought, it is a very hard thing to keep a Spanish cemetery in really good order, unless there be a well within its walls; the long, straggling bents and thistles will spring up in tangled luxuriance, and, no sooner have they sprung up, than they are withered, and form a brown tangled mass of withered herbage. Nowhere as in this arid climate does one see fulfilment of the primeval curse—"Thorns also, and thistles, shall it bring forth."

People of all nations, as usual, sleep in the "Protestant" cemetery. Swiss, English, Spanish, French, are here represented.

The most beautiful, because the most simple, perhaps, of the ten or fifteen tombstones found here is one over a French child of a year old:—" Ici repose Rose Virginie Campiche. L'Éternel l'avait donnée: L'Éternel l'a otée: Que le nom de L'Éternel soit beni." A block of chiselled stone, with a plain cross at its head, forms the tombstone.

Here is a Swiss inscription, like those of the simple Northern folk which I noticed in my chapter on Cadiz, without any adornment:—" Ursula Putzi y Klas: Nacio en Luzein (Suiza): 3 de Setiembre, 1820 Falleció el 7 de Junio, 1864 : En Cordoba."

Two little crosses mark the grave of the child of the Consular Agent and that of his nephew. In Spanish is written the text commencing, "Whosoever shall not receive the kingdom of God as a little child," &c. One little tomb had been covered with white pearly shells, which the avarice of some dishonest hand had stripped off, leaving only one or two to show what it had been. In one corner of the cemetery stood an old and shattered, but still fruitful, olive-tree —its only ornament.

When one of the first interments took place at this spot, a crowd of Spaniards, attracted by the novelty, pressed in to witness the ceremony, the grand Burial Service of our Church being always read in Spanish here. Some disaffected person from the midst of the crowd called out, "The body moves," upon which the minister quietly sent to the town authorities for their doctor to give his certification that life had fled long since: this obtained, the funeral service was quietly concluded.

I have, myself, in conducting funerals, always found the Spaniards who come to see an English funeral most reverent, kindly, and orderly; but what I have related above took place some eleven years ago.

The view from the top of the rocky hill in whose side the cemetery nestles is exceedingly grand. At our feet, in the hollow, lay the Moorish turrets, and crumbling walls, and orange-groves of Cordoba. Just across the valley on the right, where runs the line to the rich coal-fields of Belmez, rose up the long, barren range of the Sierra Morena, with Las Hermitas, as it is now called,—one of the few monasteries left in this part of Spain,—half-hidden in one of its huge clefts. Generally, the Bishop gives freely to travellers an order to see over this monastery, with its thirty inmates living on herbs, and praying all day for the welfare of Cordoba; but just now they were preparing for the Pascua, and I was refused an order.

On the left, with my glass, I could just discern the outline of the snow-capped mountains of Granada; on every nearer range of hills one's eye could see the old watch-towers, at regular intervals, once used for purposes of rude telegraphy.

CHAPTER III.

SEVILLA.

TIME flies quickly enough anywhere; but in Seville more quickly than elsewhere. At least it seems so to one who has but a day and and half to see the chief sights in that magnificent city. It is a saying often quoted by English tourists, " Seville can be seen in a week"; but the cathedral alone would well repay a week's careful study. Then there is the Picture Gallery, where every picture of Murillo's would tempt one—and there are twenty-four—to sit before it in pensive study; to say nothing of the pictures of Zurbaran and Cespedes. There is the Alcazar; the house of Murillo; the large hospital; the almost larger Fabrica de Tabaco; the Palace of San Telmo; to say nothing of the scattered piles of antique architecture, and, (wondrous sight!) only three and a half miles off, the Roman Amphitheatre, still showing, below ground, its tiers of crumbling seats and its mosaic pavement, only lately re-discovered, the famous Italica, now called Santi Ponce.

However, faithful to my determination, I tore myself away from these entrancing prospects, and trudged off, with a Spanish guide, to visit the last resting-place of my countrymen who die at Seville. Noon was almost passing into evening as we traversed the narrow Spanish streets on our road to the cemetery, some two miles outside the town. We went across the Plaza de Fruta, as gorgeous and luscious a sight as Spanish fruit-markets ever are; then into the suburbs. The houses so poor, the clouds of dust so irritating, the dresses of the people so gaudy, the noise—tinkling of mule-bells and shouts of drivers—so truly Spanish! At last we struck into the open country, following a long, white, dusty road, hedged in with white stone walls and prickly-pear, or "chumba,"— the two are hardly distinguishable to an English eye.

Out in one of the field of habas (beans) I saw several lonely forms wandering about—men and women; all had a handkerchief bound over their face. I was puzzled to understand it; but in a few moments we came in front of the portals of a large stone building abutting upon the road, with the dreary words written over it, "Home for those suffering from Elephantiasis." This is a species of leprosy, which eats away the face of those whom it attacks. I said to my guide, "Are they ever cured?"—"No, señor," he said, "never never, never." I could not help thinking of the well-known lines, "All hope abandon, ye who enter here." The Hermana de Caridad, in her white cowl, rosary, and sable dress, stood at the door, and I asked her leave to walk round the hospital. It was very bare but beautifully clean and comfortable. There was evidently every accommodation for the separation of those suffering from the various degrees of this fearful malady. The kind Sister took me from room to room. "Thank God," she said, "we have only about eighteen in now; indeed, our home is empty." She might well say so; for I fancy there were beds for a couple of hundred. She took me to the "comedor," or dining-room, and offered me a taste of the savoury dinner preparing. She told me, in contradiction to my guide, who would not even approach the door, but sat, smoking furiously, on the stone wall across the road, that some of these poor sufferers did recover, and leave their shelter. I asked to be allowed to make a small offering for these poor creatures, and she gracefully accepted my offer. Looking at the few pieces of silver I put into her thin white hand, she called out to some of the inmates, " There, I am so glad; there is enough for a Government ajar a piece for you, and more." The poor fellows' half-muffled faces seemed to light up with a smile, I thought. It was little luxury enough; and one could only wish to have been able to do something to soften their exceeding bitter lot!

Soon we came to the large, well-enclosed, but not yet laid out or finished Cemeterio of Sevilla—I mean the Roman Catholic Cemetery. A coffin, on an open hearse, drawn by four horses, with black and yellow trappings, was just entering the gates, with the usual long string of followers, robed in their dark winter capas, or capes. The coffin was covered with black velvet and gold stripes; upon it lay two crowns of immortelles.

About a quarter of a mile to the left lay the English Cemetery, under the shadow of the crumbling and broken, but still stately walls of the Convent of S. Hieronymo; thither, walking across a rough cornfield to save time, we bent our steps.

This little cemetery, enclosed in four high stone walls, the wall of the ruined convent forming one side of the square, is most picturesquely situated. On one side, completely shadowing it, stands up the ruined pile of the old convent; far away to the left, yet seeming, in the setting sunlight, quite near, ran the blue ridge of Castiljeha, many villages nestling in its clefts, on one side running down to the ruins of Italica, on the other, melting into, and lost in, the purple of the setting sun.

The little cemetery of our countrymen is forty-five yards long by forty broad. It is much like an English garden in winter, and is beautifully kept, with its regular flower-borders and sandy walks, now strewn with autumn leaves. Here I noticed the English chrysanthemum, dewy, but bright as ever, called so aptly by the Spaniards "flor del hiberno" (winter-blossom); here were monthly rose-trees, in full blossom, cypresses, almond-trees, one or two hazels, clumps of "dama de noche" (dame of the night-hours), a plant which only gives out its fragrance after sundown,—no unfitting type possibly, thought I, of some who rest here, yea, of many who lie down to rest hampered and crippled by a thousand trials, yet who, after all, may have been faithful to their God, and may prove chief among His jewels after the night has fallen upon them. These, with geraniums, lemon-verbenas, acacias, a Judas-tree, and rose-trees trained all round the white walls, were the flowers and shrubs that caught my eye at first. I should mention also, trim borders of an ever-green like our English box-tree. Out of one flower-bed stuck a few stumps; here the poor grave-digger and porter had, he assured me, raised a helpful little crop of Indian maize!

In one corner of this little cemetery were four or five bricked mounds, overgrown with plants, with little, if any, inscription. This, I was told, was the Jews' burial-ground.

In the centre of this little winter garden, for such it may be called, the most prominent object of all, stands a tall white marble cross. It is the tomb of Mr. Cunningham, the American Consul, I was told. "A good man, a good man," said my guide. "In the troubles of the cholera he gave a thousand dollars for the sick, and much more privately. Well, the good God will give him harvest for the seed he sowed!"

The dead, as usual in the Protestant cemeterios in Spain, of all nations lay here. Here was the tomb of a German, with the simple words at the foot, "St. John iii. 16"; here was a French tombstone, wreathed with black and yellow immortelles, no text upon it, but at the foot of the inscription the touching words, "Cher père adoré!" A mother and her son, named Barlow, occupied another prominent place. Several Protestant Spaniards, too, were resting here.

In the centre of this little cemetery is a stone tank or well, over which twines a little arbour of rose-trees. Unobtrusive as it is, it is the cause of this little spot being so fertile, and, like so many in the world who do the most good, it is hardly seen. Be it remembered, a Spanish garden without a well ceases to be a garden at all.

Then I went outside to see the little home, adjoining the cemetery, of the gardener. As we passed out through the narrow door, he plucked and gave me a beautiful and fragrant rose-pink carnation. "And now," said he, "I will introduce you to my house." Poor fellow! a chapel and a new house for him and his señora are soon to be built, but at present his "house" is a dark, reed-thatched, windowless hut. I saw nothing in it but the earthen floor, a poor half-starved cat (who, by the way, had accompanied us all round the cemetery), and a string of tomatoes adorning the walls. Well might he say,—"The English have a good name, but they will have a better when they build me a house."

A few steps from his home brought us into the dusty

patio of the grey, ruined convent walls of San Hieronymo, which overshadow the cemetery.

The pile, even in death, is stately and magnificent; it is lofty and wide-spreading, but a ruin. Under its groined roof a herd of pigs were squeaking and quarrelling over their Indian corn; above them rose the chief tower of the convent, inlaid in places with blue encaustic tiles. At the top of the tower stood a delicate stone cross, showing snowy white against the clear blue evening sky. I could not help thinking, here is a true type of human nature. First, like the swine, eating and quarrelling in the dust; then, one step above him, some sort of visible church to guide him; lastly, the sharp, true cross to be reached, and, that once borne and overcome, the blue sky and peace of heaven, the "mas puro lumbre" of the Spanish poets.

The garden of the convent was full of herbs, evergreen trees, and avenues of oranges. The old stone gateway was guarded by four or five savage-looking hounds, so I did not enter. The walk home, by a different road, was interesting—the huge hedges of sword-like aloes, the groves of pomegranate trees, the constantly recurring huertas, or market gardens, each with its antique Moorish noria, or well, and its mule slowly turning the dripping-wheel to irrigate the garden.

Flocks of goats and donkeys, each herd having its leader, with its tinkling bells; women, in strange bright dresses, riding, pillion fashion, with their señores; droves of turkeys, some numbering over one hundred birds, driven along by gitanos, with long tapering wands like our fishing-rods, enlivened the dull and dusty road; but I was not sorry, after a weary day of tramping from morn till eve, to find myself once more in the narrow streets of the Juderia of Seville.

CHAPTER IV.

LINARES.

ONE of the most beautiful little English cemeteries in Spain is that of Linares, a town devoted chiefly to the mining interests, and numbering now upwards of 30,000 Spanish inhabitants, situated in the heart of Andalucia.

Linares, although its name and position are probably unknown to most Englishmen, is now an important town, owing to its situation in the very heart of the lead-mines district, at the foot of the Sierra de Jaën. It is in the province of Jaën, from which town it is distant some twenty miles. The country around is wild and rocky; the heat, in summer, tropical; olive-groves and barley are, next to lead, its natural products. Here, about twenty years ago, some enterprising English, French, and German mine-owners obtained concessions of land from the Spanish Government, and still carry on their work cordially side by side with the Spanish mine-owners. The little English colony numbers about seventy all told, of whom some forty live in the town of Linares, and the remainder, chiefly mining captains, upon the mines, three and a half miles from the town itself. The great proportion of the English mining agents are Cornishmen; some few are Welsh, and others North countrymen.

Little as the name of Linares is known, it may yet interest some in England to know that the high feeling and spirit of the mine-owners has obtained a beautiful little spot for the burying-place of their dead; and that in the spring of 1873 they formed a committee, and subscribed funds, to endow a chaplaincy temporarily, the late Bishop of Gibraltar cordially supporting and aiding the plan pecuniarily; and that now an English chaplain to the mine-owners and mining-agents, many of whom have wives and children with them, has been residing at Linares since the summer of 1873.

The cemetery lies a mile outside the town, and is reached by a rough and, sometimes, almost impassable road. The environs of a rough Spanish mining town are always unattractive, and the surrounding country, as you pass out of the dirty, unpaved streets, is bare and devoid of beauty. Spreading fields of barley or waste land are first passed; then you come to a roadside cross or massive stone, about sixteen feet high: its proportions are graceful, but the inscription on it is now illegible—it probably, with others along the same road, marks the scene of some horrid murder in days gone by.

On one side of the road to the cemetery are the tall, smoking chimneys of the mines, and the few white-washed houses along their edge, backed by the great piles of granite blasted out of the mines. On the other lies the purple ridge of the Sierra de Jaën, a red, rocky, but in places wooded, line of hill. You pass men and women, donkeys and mules, the former in every sort of strange costume; the women with yellow, short gowns, and red kerchiefs bound over their heads; the men (each with cigarillo in mouth), driving their donkeys, with panniers and tinkling bell, before them, wear chiefly huge woollen rugs, sometimes bound with cord around the waist, but oftener not; trousers open below the knee, studded with brass buttons; and either thick waterproof hats, or red or blue handkerchiefs tied over their heads. Sometimes, but rarely— for the road is all but impassable for such—a springless mule-cart will come jolting and jumbling along.

On the slope of a hill, with stunted olives all around, lie, side by side, the Spanish and English cemeteries, their white stones looking bright and showy in the evening sun. The space is not large, but amply so for the size of the English and German colony. It is a plot of gently sloping ground, enclosed in high stone walls. The gate is locked, but a gardener is always at work within, and, when called, admits us at once. There are but few tombstones, and they are half-hidden in rose-trees, prickly-pear, or ivy, so that the place looks exactly like an ordinary English garden in winter. The flower-beds, in which stand the simple tombstones, are beautifully kept, an abundant supply of water being at hand from the old stone well in the corner. Three narrow walks, neatly gravelled, run up the cemetery. In the flower-beds, along the walls on either side, and at the ends, stand the few (some twenty or five-and-twenty, there are not more) memorials of those who rest here, so that the borders in the middle are entirely devoted to gardens. Rose-trees are in profusion, and even now are bearing a few sickly blossoms. Geraniums (*Pimiento Indico*), a pretty little shrub, with bright orange-coloured fruit; prickly-pear in clumps; tiny pimiento, or pepper-trees, the most graceful tree of Spain, with its thin, drooping foliage, and graceful clusters of pepper-berries; small acacias and cypresses are here in abundance; and in the centre stands a fine Piña de Cyprés, now laden with cones. Three or four tombstones stand out prominently, but all are of modest dimensions here.

Two of these are to the memory of two fine young men who came out from England to help to work one of the mines: the one died aged twenty-one, the other, thirty-three. Another is to the wife of a gentleman still living here. Close by is a tiny wooden and stone cross, to the memory of the little child of a German gentleman, still living at Linares.

Most of them have a text of Scripture as part of their inscription: on one I noticed, "As in Adam all die, so in Christ shall all be made alive;" on another, "Whosoever believeth that Jesus is the Christ, is born of God."

Tastefully let into the wall are one or two slabs of stone, with a simple cross upon them.

There are three graves—the three latest—that bear no stone at all, the loose sand of which the soil is composed being simply heaped above, in the shape, as far as possible, of an English grave: one full-sized, the others small. They tell, silently, a sad tale— a poor mother lies there, with her two infant children! In the fierce summer of 1873, she and her children fell victims to the swift illness of the climate, and, immediately the funeral was over, the unhappy husband left for his native land and his father's house in Cornwall. So, at present, no tomb has been raised above them.

In this cemetery is a tiny room for the gardener, where he rears his plants for the "garden," as he calls it, and keeps a nursery of singing birds in cages.

Adjoining is a tiny arbour, wreathed over with the genuine old English ivy, where the officiating minister robes, and waits to see the funeral procession winding slowly and wearily up the ankle-deep, sandy, scorching hill.

A funeral at this cemetery is a touching sight. It is celebrated in the evening, in order that all the English may attend. On the afternoon when there is to be one, along the rough road from the mines will be seen, without exception, every one of the "mining captains," as they are here called, chiefly rugged, strong Cornishmen, galloping into the town on their fiery little Andalucian horses, in clouds of dust, to be in time to take part in the procession.

Every one comes: partly, perhaps, because it is natural that the several members of a small foreign colony, in a strange land and a wild district, should, to use a common phrase, "hang together"; partly, perhaps, because the Spanish custom is that all who had even a slight acquaintance with the dead should follow him to his last earthly resting-place. Be this as it may, all the English attend the funeral of one of their number; all gather silently around the minister, and join fervently in the responses; and, when the ceremony is concluded, stroll slowly homeward, in sable groups, each to return to the clank of machinery, and the under-ground "work and labour" of his mine, until his night also, when he can no longer work, cometh.

THE AUTHOR'S ADIOS.

EVEN in a Spanish mining town life has its quiet resting-places, and the quaint, walled gardens, with their creaking ever-turning norias, still hang undisturbed and unbuilt upon on the outskirts. I know of no more quiet, more beautiful scene, and of no greater repose to the busy, active, over-wrought mind, than to leave the confinement of the sala, the dirty streets, the oaths and cries, and wander out into one of these gardens at early morn or dewy eve. There, at least, everything is suggestive of repose and peace—everything is fresh from the Creator's hand.

The Andalucian early morn is exceedingly beautiful. At seven o'clock the sun is warm, but not unbearably hot; the air has a keen, cold, crispness about it, which exhilarates one's frame, and braces it for the heat and burden of the day. Wander, at that hour, into the huerta, or market-garden; look up, as you walk around its narrow paths, into the sky, which is bluest of the blue—of a clear, rich, deep transparent blue, unknown in the hazy heat of midday. The washerwomen at the tanks are just—in their gaudy yellow petticoats and gay head-gear—finishing their early work; the fig-tree, hanging over them, lends its deep dark shade and damp aromatic scent. Seated beneath it, you hear the early chirp of the sparrow or bee-eater just

being concluded before the heat of day. The old
mule slowly is turning the dripping-wheel of the
Moorish noria, or well; the distant sounds of labour
and unrest hardly reach hither; the irrigation is well-
nigh finished, and the tomato and pimiento plants are
holding up their heads amid the rich steam that goes
up from the grateful earth. Here, too, if it be in the
month of May or June, may be seen the straggling
avenues of pomegranate-trees, showing all their wealth
of scarlet blossom, which contrasts grandly with the
rich dark green of the foliage. The dahlia and the
hollyhock are in profuse abundance; but, if it be June,
the harvest on the surrounding slopes has long since
been gathered into the floors. The rose, the geranium,
the cineraria, have fallen to the earth long since; for
the Andalucian summer has gone, and autumn is upon
us, with its brown stubbles and scorching skies.

A walk at early morning brings into a man's heart
many good and pure thoughts. His heart is then at
its freshest and purest, and he goes back in fancy to
the playmates of youth, now scattered far and wide—
in the barrack beneath the scorching suns of India,
in the sweet grey parsonages of the old land, in the
snows of Canada, in the dewy churchyard. He wanders
once more, in fancy, through the green meadows of
his happier days; looks once more into the bright
eyes of the girl he romped with, and meant to have
won; hears the click of the cricket-bat in the playing-
fields of Radley, or Harrow, or classic Eton, and once
more, with heaving chest and bare arms upon the
banks of Isis,—contrast how strange to his present
dirty, teeming town, with its talk of lead, and its
idolatry of dineros, its dust, its noises, its unhallowed
associations!

> "Ah, happy hills! ah, pleasing shade!
>   Ah, fields beloved in vain!
> Where once my careless childhood strayed,
>   A stranger then to pain.
> I feel the gales that from you blow
>   A momentary bliss bestow,
> As waving fresh their gladsome wing,
>   My weary soul they seem to soothe,
> And, redolent of joy and youth,
>   To breathe a second spring."

Night, too, the Andalucian night, has its own peculiar beauty. The clear, blue, star-spangled sky; the sweet, aromatic smell of the herbs; the dead silence around you, save the chirrup of myriads of cicadas, which absolutely fills the air, as with a chorus of ten thousand silvery bells; the wild ditty of the gardener, as he strums his guitar to words of idle love. And all these, when evening has spread her pall over hill and dale, awaken a different train of thought, but one equally pleasing and refreshing, after the busy, weary day is spent. Were it not for night and morning in the gardens, life would have no place for contemplation; a man would know no quiet resting-place in this Spanish mining town. Reader, Vaya usted con Dios y con la Virgen, y con todos los santos (God and the Virgin, and all the saints, go with thee on thy journey), is the writer's parting wish for you. Will you not wish him the same?

THE END.

www.ingramcontent.com/pod-product-compliance
Lightning Source LLC
Chambersburg PA
CBHW020322240426
43673CB00039B/885